Red-Green Revolution

RED-GREEN REVOLUTION

THE POLITICS AND TECHNOLOGY OF ECOSOCIALISM

SECOND EDITION

VICTOR WALLIS

POLITICAL ANIMAL PRESS

TORONTO · CHICAGO

Political Animal Press
www.politicalanimalpress.com
Distributed by the University of Toronto Press

Cataloguing data available from Library and Archives Canada
ISBN: 9781895131574

Cover based on a design by Kevin Cockburn
Printed and bound in Canada

TO INEZ

Contents

Preface to the First Edition

Over the quarter-century of this book's gestation, the alarm signals that struck me as I began working on it have risen to an almost deafening volume. Climate scientists are constantly finding that their dire projections pale in comparison with the actual pace at which life-sustaining natural infrastructures are breaking down.

The disaster that ecological activists of the last half-century have sought to prevent is already vividly present. Its most dramatic expression, apart from the endlessly repeated scenes of fire, flood, parched earth, and emaciated polar bears, is the tens of millions of refugees, desperate for a place to live.[1] Some are fleeing sea-level rise and flooded or storm-battered homes; others are fleeing wars precipitated by sustained, drought-induced collapses of the food supply (as in Syria, Central Africa, and Central America). Still others are fleeing wars and repression that reflect long-standing imperialist projects, but whose initiators have become ever more intransigent as they seek to ward off the prospect of a diminished resource-base.

Increasing percentages of the refugees, if they survive their typically harrowing treks or dangerous sea voyages, come up against vast numbers of agents "trained, armed, and paid to stop them."[2] This drive to "stop them" is promoted by a ruling class which at the same time relentlessly stokes the economic engines of capital that gave rise to the climate crisis in the first place. While the top US mouthpiece of this ruling class, along with his acolytes at the

---

1   See Ai Weiwei's 2017 documentary, *Human Flow*, where the number of refugees is given as 65 million.

2   Todd Miller, *Storming the Wall: Climate Change, Migration, and Homeland Security* (San Francisco: City Lights Books, 2017), 30.

Environmental "Protection" Agency, mocks the reality of climate change, the military leaders who command the system's armed enforcers have had no hesitation (for at least the last fifteen years) in publicly situating what they acknowledge to be the *consequences* of global warming – the droughts, floods, and hurricanes that directly or indirectly have pushed mass migration to its current extreme levels – at the center of their concerns.

The alternatives are sharply etched. The currently dominant forces, rather than join the fight against climate change, erect walls to block out its victims. By militarizing the problem, they not only draw resources away from any possible remedial steps; they also accelerate the spread of devastation.

What other path can be chosen? That is the subject of this book. The short answer is that a radical power-shift is needed. But it's one thing to recognize this and quite another to draw the indispensable majority into the struggle to achieve it. Part of that task consists in relating the overarching ecological goal to popular aspirations at every level. Another part consists in developing a political mechanism – a political force – that can embody and enforce the collective interest. Yet another involves discovering, explaining, advocating, and applying all the measures needed in order to slow down – and, where possible, reverse – the dangerous environmental trends.

Reversing at least some of these trends is indeed still possible. It will certainly require the mix of alternative energies, conservation practices, and social reorganization discussed in this book. The culmination of work along all these dimensions, insofar as it can be achieved, will be the restoration of biodiversity. Restoring biodiversity will entail, among other things, restoring moisture to parched earth and drawing carbon back out of the atmosphere and into the soil, where it can support life rather than endangering it.

The struggle to restore the soil and the struggle to create a just social order have up to now been carried on mostly as parallel political movements, without much mutual awareness, let alone collaboration, at the mass level. Such collaboration, however, or at least the striving to attain it, is the true centerpiece of Red–Green Revolution.

Many people have contributed to this book. My greatest intellectual debts will be apparent in the text and the footnotes. Particular chapters have been improved, vitally in some cases, by comments from readers listed in the Acknowledgments.

I am deeply grateful to Alex Wall and Lewis Slawsky of Political
Animal Press for their encouragement and to Alex especially for his
close reading of the entire text and his many valuable suggestions. I
thank Stefan Schindler for putting us in touch.

For the original development of the essays that make up the core
of the book, I am grateful to the editors and, in the case of *Socialism and Democracy*, editorial board members of all the journals
in which the pieces first appeared. I received especially important
substantive comments on Chapter 1 from the late James O'Connor,
on Chapter 5 from John Bellamy Foster and Fred Magdoff, and on
Chapter 8 and the Introduction from Johanna Fernández.

My life-partner Inez Hedges has been with this project from its
inception. Her moral support and her patience have made my work
possible. She read every chapter in its initial version, always holding me to high standards of communication while setting a distinguished example with her own writings on the political dimensions
of film and literature. We have learned to express gratitude in many
languages; I do so here with my dedication.

Victor Wallis
Somerville, Massachusetts
April 2018

Preface to the Second Edition

I feel at once gratified and humbled that this book is going quickly into a second edition: gratified at the book's reception, yet humbled by the insufficiency of even the most complete awareness – on the part of all who have plumbed the ecological crisis, let alone any single one of us – to propel a social movement of the scope and depth necessary to halt our species' headlong rush to destruction – not only of itself, but of the rest of the living world.

Red-Green Revolution offers an overview of the *range* of considerations on which the necessary social movement must be built. Earlier writing had exposed the immediacy of the danger and also – going back even to Marx and Engels – its links to capitalism; I have sought to build on this by examining the technological debate, the relationship of piecemeal to comprehensive change, and the question of how every popular constituency could come to identify its own interests with the broader struggle to preserve the health of the ecosphere.

A "popular constituency" is any sector of the population that is not wedded by self-interest to the business-as-usual, perpetual growth agenda of the capitalist ruling class. The latter relentlessly accelerates all the destructive trends. As fire, flood, war, plague, and migration spiral out of control, and as capital seeks by the most desperate means to retain its hold on global power, the popular or non-capitalist majority finds itself in a moment of revolutionary potential which is at the same time, paradoxically, a moment of looming disaster.

The original scenario of socialist transformation presupposed a working class that had evolved as an organized entity through various stages of struggle, shaped in tandem with capitalist development but culminating in a revolutionary consciousness. Not only in the United States, but also more generally in the early industrializing countries, this process had advanced significantly by the late 19th century. As of the early 21st century, however, after several advances and retreats, the international working class finds its former power-bases globally dispersed, leaving it fragmented, disoriented, and ill organized on the various home fronts. With the encroaching ecological calamity, it thus faces a political challenge that appears to far overshadow its now limited capacities.

The recent period, as I discuss in Chapter 8, has seen efforts to re-situate popular political agency away from the working class, but the dispersion of energy among various constituent groups has resulted in forfeiting political initiative to a still powerful though increasingly discredited capitalist elite. In the absence of a cohesive challenge to this elite, "morbid symptoms" proliferate. These reach extreme form in the US, with its toxic blend of militarism, racism, imperialism, and climate-denialism, facilitated by an archaic constitutional regime that fosters electoral and judicial roadblocks against even the most limited projects for transcending the hegemonic credo of private interest.

Against this leviathan, and propelled by the sense of emergency, we see expressions of simmering outrage along with embryonic movements of systemic opposition, but we have yet to see a powerful counter-hegemonic force. The basic alternatives have not changed since this book first came out, but they etch themselves more sharply with each passing year.

The text of this book is unchanged except for updated references and minor editorial corrections. I have added an Epilogue to address the most recent developments. These for the most part embody a continuation of established trends, which themselves have taken on increasingly alarming proportions, as signaled by the unprecedented scope of forest fires in Brazil, Siberia, and the Western US. The scenario of environmental collapse has been overlaid, however, by (1) the COVID-19 pandemic, (2) heightened economic and social polarization, and, most recently (3), the outbreak of a war that could itself spark global catastrophe.

The one development for which I would now qualify my argument pertains to China. Where I earlier referred to present-day China exclusively in terms of the productivist priorities that it shares with the US, I would now add that the Chinese government shows a growing awareness of the need to address the climate crisis. How far it will go in scaling back its economic agenda is not yet clear, but the ideological move deserves recognition because of its contrast with the currently dominant US trend and also, especially, because of the increasing demonization of China by US politicians and media outlets, and the dangers that this portends.[1]

My greatest hope is that the issues discussed in this book will move from the margins to the forefront of public attention. Only then will the necessary changes become possible, and only then will we be able to develop the structures needed to keep them on course.

Victor Wallis
Somerville, Massachusetts
March 2022

---

1   See the article by Jeff J. Brown and Jeremy Kuzmarov at https://covertaction-magazine.com/2020/10/25/fools-crusade-why-united-states-provocations-towards-china-will-lead-to-disaster/

INTRODUCTION

WHY ECOSOCIALISM?

It is increasingly apparent that the conditions of life—not only for humanity but for other species as well—are being undermined. Most people, even in the United States (where environmental issues are routinely downplayed by opinion-makers), know that there is a real threat to our collective survival. But the scenario is so vast, the problems so complex, that it's hard for us to feel that we can respond in any clearly definable way. And the demands or seductions of daily life are too compelling—for most of us—to allow us to envisage sustained and effective resistance. Those who are able to face the looming reality can easily feel trapped. Walter Benjamin's prescient metaphor of our being caught in a train without brakes— his image of "progress"[1]—comes easily to mind.

To puncture the resulting sense of helplessness, we need an approach that is at once immediate (short-term) and comprehensive (long-term). A comprehensive approach is a radical one. It embraces every aspect of reality. Without such panoramic sweep, we cannot even begin to counter the multifold scale on which the threats to life present themselves—whether in the form of war, hunger, pollution, illness, repression, insecurity, or insanity. It is hard to think of a social scourge that is not related to one of these. These are in turn related to each other, and all are related, in their present incarnations, to environmental breakdown, which manifests itself

---

1 Michael Löwy, "Marx's Dialectic of Progress: Closed or Open?" trans. Victor Wallis, *Socialism and Democracy*, 14:1 (2000), 42.

not only at a global level, but also in the immediately felt disruption of natural settings and rhythms, in the accelerated pace of human activity, and in the artificial separation of humans—behind a phalanx of walls and machinery—from the rest of the natural world.

Climate change is the most highly publicized environmental threat, but it is not the only one. Others flow from it and/or feed into it—including ocean acidification, depletion of fresh water sources, pollution of air, water, and soil; deforestation; species-loss. Old illnesses revive as rising temperatures lead to the spread of insect-borne diseases; new illnesses appear with the insertion of toxins into our surroundings.

The power-holders who have profited from prior economic development have at least a vague sense that the environmental crisis threatens their continuing operations, but instead of reconsidering their priorities, they double down, as quintessential imperialists, in asserting their entitlement to global control over the resources that remain. The resulting squeeze translates into an ongoing resource-war, which, in the characteristic manner of a feedback loop, only magnifies the scarcities and the antagonisms that sparked the imperial drive in the first place. War not only brings death and destruction to the targeted zones, it also has dramatic effects on the society whose government initiates it. It swallows up a huge share of that society's resources, preempts any capacity within that society to plan for economic/ecological conversion, creates a permanent pretext for political repression, and fosters a self-perpetuating culture of violence, transmitted through flag-waving ideologues, a venal mass media, and an unholy mix of police officers, vigilantes, weapons manufacturers, and mentally unstable individuals (many of them military veterans; some of them in positions of high responsibility).

Merely to list the issues that together define the big picture is at the same time to remind ourselves of the steps that are immediately needed. These may at first be envisaged separately, but an effective response will require a political force that comprehends their interdependence. The effort to constitute such a force is the great political task of our time. The underlying idea of a radical challenge to the existing order is, of course, not new. But what has only become clear within living memory is the awareness that this imagined force—and the new social order that it would create—is a necessary instrument for our collective survival. Tying the venerated idea of revolution to the new condition of having to overcome the environmental threat to our existence is what has given birth to the now widely used concept of ecosocialism.[2]

What Kind of Synthesis?

The appeal of ecology extends, at some level, to the entire population. Socialism, in turn, has become an increasingly attractive concept even in the United States, especially among young people, who on the one hand often face gloomy economic as well as ecological prospects and, on the other, have been less battered than their elders by reminders of the flaws in socialism's earlier incarnations. Ecosocialism—the synthesis of ecology with socialism—thus has enormous potential to inspire a majoritarian political movement. As I argue in Chapter 1, the ecological and the socialist goals could hardly be more compatible in principle.

The precise character of this synthesis, however, has been a matter of controversy, even among those who are thoroughly committed to both of its strands. Although there is broad consensus on the ecosocialist goal, there are at the same time theoretical disagreements that bear on political strategy. When the global environmental crisis first became generally recognized (after 1970), the typical response of socialists, given their already established social/economic critique of capitalism, was to argue that the ecological critique would in effect have to be grafted onto the existing understanding of capitalism's dangers. This approach was articulated in James O'Connor's idea of a "second contradiction" of capitalism (the first contradiction being between capital and workers; the second,

---

2   The wide use of the concept is exemplified in the Final Manifesto of the 3rd International Ecosocialist Conference (2016), alterecosoc.org/wp-content/uploads/2016/10/manifiesto-inglesez.pdf   Although collective survival was already endangered by the Cold War nuclear arms-race, the environmental crisis is more systemic (not subject to the possible rash actions of any single individual), and it accordingly points more directly toward a systemic response.

between capital and nature).[3] The alternative view was that capital, as analyzed by Marx and Engels, had from the beginning subsumed the natural world as well as human labor within the domain of what it sought to control.

In effect, the dispute among ecosocialists revolved around contending views of the Marxian legacy. The initially prevailing tendency, associated with O'Connor's approach, was to highlight the ultimately disappointing ecological record of twentieth-century socialist regimes, to note those regimes' orientation toward surpassing capitalism's industrial achievements, and then to read back into Marx a productivist disposition (i.e., a propensity to uncritically extol economic growth), thereby blaming him in some measure for what they saw as a convergence of socialism—at least in its then-existing form—with capitalism. The alternative approach, signally expressed in the writings of Paul Burkett and John Bellamy Foster,[4] entailed a re-examination of Marx, drawing attention especially to his critique of capitalist agriculture. It was in relation to capitalist agriculture—with its disregard of long-term requirements for a healthy soil—that Marx referred to a "metabolic rift," introduced by capitalism into what has now come to be called the Earth System.[5]

The two approaches—that of treating ecology as an addendum to Marx vs. that of treating it as integral to Marx—have been characterized by Foster and Burkett as reflecting successive stages of

---

3   James O'Connor, "The Second Contradiction of Capitalism" (1988), in idem., *Natural Causes: Essays in Ecological Marxism* (New York: Guilford, 1998), 158-177.

4   Paul Burkett, *Marx and Nature: A Red and Green Perspective* (Chicago: Haymarket Books: 2014 [1999]); John Bellamy Foster, "Marx's Theory of Metabolic Rift," *American Journal of Sociology*, 105:2 (September 1999), and *Marx's Ecology: Materialism and Nature* (New York: Monthly Review Press, 2000). The prevalence of an ecological orientation in Marx, throughout his life, is documented in Kohei Saito, *Karl Marx's Ecosocialism: Capitalism, Nature, and the Unfinished Critique of Political Economy* (New York: Monthly Review Press, 2017).

5   Marx wrote: "Capitalist production...disturbs the metabolic interaction between man and the earth..." *Capital*, vol. 1, trans. Ben Fowkes (New York: Random House, 1976), 637. See John Bellamy Foster, Brett Clark, and Richard York, *The Ecological Rift: Capitalism's War on the Earth* (New York: Monthly Review Press, 2010), 45f. On the grounding of the "Earth System" concept, see Ian Angus, *Facing the Anthropocene: Fossil Capitalism and the Crisis of the Earth System* (New York: Monthly Review Press, 2016), 29ff.

ecosocialist thought.[6] The second stage cannot be said to have fully superseded the first, however, inasmuch as the expanded "ecological" understanding of Marx and Engels has not been fully accepted by those who cling to the productivist characterization of Marxist thinking. Ways to talk "around" a Marxian understanding—not directly rejecting it, but failing to acknowledge its full scope (notably including its ecological dimension)—will continue to flourish for as long as capital permeates the knowledge industry.[7] What interests us here, though, is the political consequences of whether or not one views Marx as being himself, in effect, an ecological thinker.

It is a striking fact that the disaggregation of domination-of-nature from class domination matches a similar disaggregation that became popular in the same post-1970 period with respect to oppression along lines of (especially) race and gender. What we find, along all these dimensions of concern, is an approach to Marxism that tends to pigeonhole it as applying only to a narrowly understood domain of production relations. Advocates for the "new social movements" that arose in the 1960s perceived Marxism through the prism of the Communist project, which, in their view, had failed to acknowledge the importance of power relationships other than those directly defined by class. We explore that response in detail in Chapter 8. But what is significant in terms of the ecosocialism debate is that O'Connor himself saw a connection between his approach to the environment and the then-prevailing approaches of feminist and anti-racist activists (respectively) to the issues of gender and racial oppression. All such movements would, in his view, pursue "different yet *parallel* [his italics] paths to socialism."[8] As I argue in Chapter 8, this whole stance of insisting on the basic separateness of the struggles not only ignores the historical origins of the various forms of oppression, but also—and for that very reason—impedes the process of merging the corresponding resistance movements into a coherent political force.

---

6   John Bellamy Foster and Paul Burkett, *Marx and Nature: An Anti-Critique* (Leiden: Brill, 2016), 2ff.

7   An example of this effect is the academic prestige accorded in the 1980s-90s to postmodernism (see Chapter 8).

8   Victor Wallis, "Ecosocialist Struggles: Reminiscences, Reflections, and Danger Signals," *Capitalism Nature Socialism*, 25:1 (March 2014), 45 (citing O'Connor, "The Second Contradiction," 169).

TOWARD AN ECOSOCIALIST POLITICS

The task of evolving a political force inspired by ecosocialism is what drives all the chapters of this book. Between the defining synthesis of ecology with socialism (Chapter 1) and the culminating discussions focused on how social movements can be unified (Chapters 7 and 8), a number of themes will draw our attention—some of them recurring in more than one chapter.

The issue of technology is present throughout. Likewise, a constant theme is the cultural transformation—more provocatively envisioned as transformation of human nature—which is an indispensable component of the ecosocialist project. There are countless examples of the interpenetration of technological and cultural change. The concept of culture reminds us that the desirable evolution of technology cannot be established on the basis of crude quantitative indicators such as the speed with which a task can be performed, or with which objects or persons can be transported from one location to another. Every such process is embedded in a whole network of relations, not only among people but also involving air, water, and soil, as well as other forms of life.

As explained in Chapter 2, "devices"—whether tools, machines, vehicles, power-generators, weapons, or chemical agents—are only one component of a technology. Nothing about the device itself tells us where or when or how extensively it will be applied, all of which are crucial to defining any particular technology. We live under a socio-economic regime in which large-scale decisions on such matters are made mostly based on profit considerations, ignoring the impact of the resulting choices on nature's life-sustaining infrastructure. The age of capital has been the age of fossil-fuel burning. So tight has been this link that when its potentially disastrous impact became known to the oil companies themselves—by their own research in the 1970s—they could think of no better response than to suppress that awareness, hyping a culture and politics of perpetual expansion.[9] The corresponding technology was one in which, for example, almost everyone became dependent on a per-

---

9   www.theblaze.com/news/2015/09/17/report-exxon-in-the-1970s-pioneered-
    some-climate-research-then-did-an-about-face-on-theissue/

sonal motor vehicle, as they would later come to rely on a personal communication device (see Chapter 4).

The critique of technology is central to the discussion of ecological alternatives. Too often, however, the critique limits itself to discussion of alternative energy-sources—an approach which perpetuates the popular assumption, fostered by capitalist culture, that for every problem of addressing people's material needs, there is a precise technological solution, for which we need only await the latest innovation. What such discussions typically ignore is not only whatever *increase* in energy-consumption the new devices will require, but also the perpetually expanding encroachment on the Earth's finite supply of materials and space. An ever-mounting proliferation of private cars becomes acceptable, on this view, provided only that solar-generated electricity powers them—with ever-more refined guidance systems and congestion-detectors (not to mention robotic drivers) as added benefits.[10] The cultural critique of this scenario leads us back to the question, what is this all for? Further, what are the requirements of a good life? Such questions return us to consideration of our core needs, allowing us to see perpetual growth as an addiction that must be overcome: not only to preserve what's left of the ecosphere, but also as desirable in its own right, giving scope for us to tap into the wealth of human social interaction—in both work and diversion—that has always been potentially available.

Innovation, as discussed in Chapter 3, may or may not be a good thing. But the benefits of any given innovation must be assessed not only in terms of such immediate goals as reducing the amount of labor-time necessary to accomplish a particular task, but also in terms of the total complex of changes that the innovation

10 See Erik Brynjolfsson and Andrew McAfee, *The Second Machine Age: Work, Progress, and Prosperity in a Time of Brilliant Technologies* (New York: Norton, 2016). In their enthusiasm, the authors have written a book from which one could not guess that an ecological crisis exists. Their counterparts among those who do acknowledge the environmental crisis are the advocates of "green capitalism" (see Chapter 6). An extraordinary aspect of high tech is the vulnerabilities it creates. Thus, computerized cars are subject to remote hacking, whereby assassinations can be made to appear as "accidents." See whowhatwhy. org/2015/07/23/newest-remote-car-hacking-raises-more-questions-about-reporters-death/ and the experiment shown at www.wired.com/2015/07/hackers-remotely-kill-jeep-highway/

entails—whether in the form of infrastructure, energy and raw materials requirements, spatial and social impacts, or unpredictable side-effects (including those of a social or psychological nature). The almost cult-like reverence for innovation that permeates US-American culture is a clear expression of capitalist interests, in their constant search for newly marketable commodities. But this is not the only possible goal for innovative thinking. An ecosocialist premise would stimulate innovation in quite different directions, notably toward a rethinking of assumptions about basic human needs and how they can be met. Given the obvious distortions produced by assessing need via market-demand—whereby if you don't have the purchasing power, your need counts for nothing –, what institutional mechanisms can be put in place to accommodate both individual and collective needs? Chapter 4 offers an overview of relevant practices—and alternative possibilities—in every sector of the economy. This is a constantly evolving topic, but what repeatedly emerges is the importance of viewing every imaginable innovation in its widest possible context and, related to this, alertness to the distinction between what is essential to human life—or at least what is universally desirable—and what is wasteful or destructive.

BUILDING THE MOVEMENT

Having established the merits of ecosocialism in relation to the various economic sectors, and having shown the importance of viewing technological questions as only *one aspect* of a much broader agenda of transformation, we next shift our focus toward the more immediate obstacles—and opportunities—associated with building the necessary popular movement.

Among those who recognize the environmental emergency, the most common political posture remains one of calling for specific "green" business practices and for governmental incentives and regulations designed to push these forward. We are still at the early stages of any widespread recognition that the problem lies with capitalism itself, although Naomi Klein's popular book *This*

Changes Everything (2014) took a valuable step in that direction.[11] But in the absence of a systemic alternative,[12] people are tempted to buy into the agenda of so-called "green capitalism." The limits of that approach need to be clearly understood before the more radical demand for ecosocialism can gain traction. The promise and limitations of green capitalism will occupy us in Chapters 5 and 6.

Given the urgency of arresting dangerous trends, it's necessary to support immediate improvements even if these are only partial. What is insufficiently recognized, however, is the degree to which, even when such improvements are made, the dangerous established practices continue mostly unimpeded, while the corporate sponsors of those practices retain political clout which they ultimately use to undo the improvements, as is now being done by the Trump administration with its gutting of federal environmental services and its removal of virtually all federal restrictions on fossil-fuel extraction.

Token green measures may bring some relief, but they fail to challenge the power that keeps the toxic practices going. How can people be persuaded to target that power and build a political force capable of supplanting it? This is a multifaceted challenge that goes beyond just showing the limitations of green capitalism. It entails on the one hand exploring the sometimes indirect arguments whereby the green-capitalist—i.e., market-based—approach is upheld. On the other hand, it requires attention to positive models, both actual and potential, of societies, movements, institutions, or even individuals that embody a cooperative rather than an aggressive/competitive approach to work and life.

The negative dimension of this process involves our unmasking the mode of thought which resists looking at the totality of complex systems, preferring instead to examine their components one by one. With such a reductionist approach, it can appear reasonable to assign prices to natural phenomena or processes, giving rise to contentions that capitalism has imposed its framework on the nat-

---

11 See Naomi Klein, *This Changes Everything: Capitalism vs. the Climate* (New York: Simon & Schuster, 2014), and Suren Moodliar's review essay, "System Change without Class Struggle?" *Socialism and Democracy* 29:1 (March 2015).

12 An important work on the systemic alternative is Fred Magdoff and Chris Williams, *Creating an Ecological Society: Toward a Revolutionary Transformation* (New York: Monthly Review Press, 2017).

ural world (see Chapter 5). Forgotten in such thinking, however, is the multiplicity of roles that a given species or local ecosystem may play. Think, for example, about forests. Not only do they provide wood or block the spread of cropland or settlements—the aspects directly relevant to capital. They also 1) replenish the oxygen supply, 2) keep moisture in the soil, 3) protect against mudslides, 4) offset high air-temperatures, and 5) provide habitat for birds and animals—all functions for which there is no realistic way to attach a price.[13]

The same resistance to conceiving of totality shows up also in the postmodernist tendency to disparage any wide-ranging theoretical framework (using the derisive term "grand narrative"). Each phenomenon or constituency is thereby defined purely in its own terms. Any attempt at an overview is regarded with suspicion. This extends even to the question of ecological crisis itself. While its separate manifestations are noted and denounced, the idea that one should respond with urgency to an underlying systemic drive is seen as unrealistic and is consequently scorned as an expression of "eco-catastrophism."[14]

Contrary to what the anti-"catastrophists" say, however, working for a comprehensive alternative, even if undertaken with urgency, is in no way incompatible with fighting for short-term improvements. On the contrary, it can bring inspiration to short-term struggles and can help orient them. Inversely, long-term struggles draw experience and grounding from their short-term counterparts. This mutual conditioning is similar to what occurs (as we discuss in Chapter 8) in the intersection between the various specific anti-oppression struggles and the larger struggle to dismantle the class rule of capital, which, as it actually operates (through corporate as well as state entities), plays a defining or limiting role in shaping every sphere of life. Inversely, again, only to the degree that all the particular oppressed constituencies come together—in

---

13 See Magdoff and Williams, *Creating an Ecological Society*, Ch. 8.

14 On the reality of the catastrophic danger, see Angus, *Facing the Anthropocene*. I discuss the anti-"catastrophist" perspective in Chapter 7.

a unity grounded in common class interest—can the end of such domination be prepared for.[15]

Positive models appear at a variety of levels. Indigenous societies remind us of how humans lived before the advent of class society. Their egalitarian social relations link up with reverence for the natural world. Although there is a wide gulf between indigenous communities and "modern" society, the disastrous impact of business-as-usual in the latter means that the indigenous perspective will earn increasing consideration. People from the two worlds see the need to join forces, as shown in the broad support generated throughout North America—spreading outward from indigenous groups—for resistance to various oil-pipeline projects.

Beyond the indigenous model, the positive alternative has always evolved along two strands which are partly complementary to each other and partly antagonistic. One is the tradition of workers' self-management, associated with cooperatives, direct action, anarchism, and movements from the bottom up. The other is the tradition of socialist revolution, entailing party organization and a focus on attaining and exercising state power. The latter tradition has been in disfavor with much of the Left in recent years, but this does not mean that it can be dispensed with. The challenge is to build on what was positive in its earlier expressions, while at the same time drawing on the bottom-up approach and integrating it into a new model of socialist democracy. Those who look to any single national case to exemplify this will be frustrated, because the transformative impulse is in every instance beset by hostile class forces—if not internal, then external. But within the succession of attempts, one nonetheless can find partial successes that give grounds for hope, be it health services or urban gardens in Cuba, or community kitchens and clinics in Venezuela. Most impressive, as new models of social commitment at the level of the individual, have been Cuba's international volunteers, whether in healthcare, education, or disaster-relief. Such examples may sometimes arise in countries where (as in Cuba) they are promoted by the government,

---

15 On the links between particular and general struggles, see Victor Wallis, "Richard Levins and Dialectical Thinking," in Joseph G. Ramsey, ed., *Scholactivism: Reflections on Transforming Praxis in and beyond the Classroom*, in *Works and Days*, vols. 33/34 (2016/2017), 465-469.

but they also can be found anywhere that people, on their own initiative, form cooperative institutions—a process that can also be
seen in the United States.[16]

THE PRESENT MOMENT

The dialectic of oppression and resistance is age-old. Marxian
thought has disclosed its historical dynamic under the regime of
capital, as the critique of capital leads to the idea of the "society
of associated producers" (Marx's own term). At first, this idea
appears only as a theoretical alternative, although the deficiencies
of capitalist rule are already evident. But the longer capital remains
entrenched in power, the more it corrupts the process whereby the
alternative is generated. We find ourselves in a race against time.
Just when the alternative becomes most urgently needed, it also
tends to recede from our grasp. Conversely, precisely in the measure that it recedes from our grasp, it becomes even more urgently
needed. This dialectic is already embedded in our social existence,
but it is amplified by the deterioration of the ecosphere.

Where will we find the break—or, for that matter, Benjamin's
"brake"? The hope we must now nourish is that the sheer extremity
of the current moment will elicit responses from unexpected directions. The extremity resides not only in the ecological crisis but
also in the political face taken on by the ruling class of the world's
biggest military power. The fusion of unabashed racism and misog-
yny with a ridiculous if not symptomatic concentration of wealth at
the pinnacle of the US enforcement apparatus could galvanize the
affected popular majorities—both in the US and worldwide—into
a unity that many years of effort by activists have failed to achieve.
Signs of such an impact are already spreading within the US, as polls
show increasing support for socialism among young people[17] and
as massive protests arise on the part of women, immigrants, low-
wage workers, and prisoners (who in September 2016 launched a
work-stoppage across several states against the still unfinished

16 The potential for cooperative organizing is highlighted in recent works by Gar
    Alperovitz, Michael Lebowitz, and Richard Wolff.
17 See portside.org/2017-07-12/future-beyond-capitalism-or-no-future-all

abolition of slavery).[18] Further indicative of rising disaffection are the desertions and disclosures of whistleblowers, and even a case in which a judge has allowed the political rationale for acts of civil disobedience to be heard in court, leading to exoneration of the defendants.[19] Such particular acts hint at a wider loss of legitimacy of the established order.[20]

What has not yet developed on a wide scale is the vision of an alternative. This book is part of the search for such a vision. It seeks to go beyond the bare outlines, and to discover grounds for hope in an analysis of real conditions.

18 On the significance of prisoner organizing, see Victor Wallis, "*13th* and the Culture of Surplus Punishment," *San Francisco Bay View*, August 2017 (sfbayview.com/2017/07/13th-and-the-culture-of-surplus-punishment/).

19 On whistleblowers, Victor Wallis, "Ordeals of Whistleblowers in a 'Democracy'" (www.commondreams.org/views/2015/11/20/ordeals-whistleblowers-democracy); for the civil disobedience case, www.accuracy.org/release/drone-resisters-acquitted-juror-tells-them-keep-doing-it/

20 See Victor Wallis, "Capitalism Unhinged: Crisis of Legitimacy in the United States," *Socialism and Democracy*, 31:3 (November 2017).

1

Toward Ecological Socialism

The grotesque dance of the US political establishment around the need to reduce greenhouse emissions points to a deadly irony of our time. At the precise moment at which comprehensive democratic planning, on a global scale, has become a condition for long-term human survival, the mere suggestion that planning might be centered anywhere but in corporate boardrooms has been widely consigned—with matching witticisms—to the "dustbin of history."

The idea of ecological socialism confronts this dismissal head-on. It responds directly to the predicament that is now increasingly recognized even in the business world, namely, that the contradictions of capitalism, far from diminishing since Marx's time, have if anything intensified.[1]

Among the possible ways out of this fix, ecological socialism alone offers an approach that is comprehensive. In this preliminary discussion I propose, first, to define ecological socialism; next, to sketch the contours of an ecological socialist society; and finally, to reflect on some of the hard questions of transition.

Foundational Principles

What is ecological socialism? Or, to begin with, what are the respective goals of ecological and of socialist thought?

---

1   On the intensification of capitalist contradictions, see Ellen Meiksins Wood, "Back to Marx," *Monthly Review*, 49:2 (June 1997); on the business world's recognition of this phenomenon, see John Cassidy, "The Return of Karl Marx," *New Yorker*, 20/27 October 1997, 248.

The *ecological* goal is for humans to live somehow in balance with the rest of nature. I understand "balance" not in any absolute or timeless sense, but rather in the sense of maintaining a maximum of biodiversity while keeping toxic substances and greenhouse emissions to a minimum.[2] Such balance may be viewed as desirable both for its own sake and as a condition for the survival of the human species. There is no necessary incompatibility between these two rationales. What clashes with the goal of natural balance is not human needs as such, but only the particular structuring of human needs that has evolved in conjunction with the requirements of, or the pressures exerted by, capital. The resulting "needs"—for such things as private accumulation, a vast military apparatus, private mechanized transit, and various addictive pursuits—are purely derivative. From the standpoint of the individual human being, they are at best either instrumental or adaptive. They are not in themselves necessary to life, let alone to any kind of personal fulfillment. In the larger scheme of things, they are distinctly pathological. By contrast, basic human needs for health, creativity, and community, far from being threatened by natural balance, can only be enhanced by it.

The *socialist* goal is to bring about a society free of class divisions. Like the notion of natural balance, this vision is one that may be pursued both for its own sake and for the sake of the many other possibilities that such a society—and the struggle to attain it—would open up. These include overcoming inequities of race, gender, and region, and in general offering a favorable life-setting for every human being. Once again, there is no sharp division between intrinsic good and indirect benefits; each is in part dependent on the other. Accordingly, not all problems in these areas necessarily appear immediately in class terms, but all attempts at rational solution ultimately come up against class-based obstacles.[3] A constant

---

2   For a critique of ahistorical notions of "balance," see Daniel L. Botkin, *Discordant Harmonies: A New Ecology for the Twenty-first Century* (New York: Oxford University Press, 1990), Ch. 2. For historically informed discussion of biodiversity issues, see Yrjö Haila and Richard Levins, *Humanity and Nature: Ecology, Science and Society* (London: Pluto Press, 1992).

3   Victor Wallis, "Marxism and the U.S. Left: Thoughts for the 1990s," *Monthly Review*, 43:2 (June 1991), 9ff. The dialectical link between class-based and non-class-based concerns is discussed in Chapter 8.

theme, in any case, is the need to surmount the social injustices, the society-wide inefficiencies, the lack of accountability, and the material and spiritual hardships arising from, or intensified by, the capitalist mode of production.

Before ecological socialism can become either a movement or a social order, it must constitute a persuasive synthesis of these two sets of aspirations. Whatever the abstract potential for such a synthesis, its practical forging will depend on a dialogue between those (individuals and groups) whose initial orientations are toward each as distinct from the other of the two visions—the visions themselves being viewed, for the time being, as separate.

The ecology/socialism dialogue takes many forms. Its upshot, however, is a gradually unfolding response to the question: what does each side add to the vision offered by the other?

ADDING GREEN TO RED

Let us first consider what the ecological vision brings to socialism. Since 1917, the socialist movement has, for better or worse, been indelibly associated with the first series of announced attempts to implement socialism on a national scale. Whatever one's view as to the actual socialist credentials of the resulting regimes, one cannot usefully advance a present-day vision of socialism without situating it in relation to that widespread, though now largely terminated, "first-epoch" experience.[4]

The ecological critique begins by calling attention to the numerous and often severe ways in which those first-epoch regimes flouted ecological norms. The names of Chernobyl, Lake Baikal, and the Aral Sea have already become synonymous with environmental devastation, as have the images of Chinese city-dwellers circulating with face-masks because of the ubiquitous coal dust.

The exact manner in which such observations are associated with socialism has been a matter of debate. Limiting ourselves here to arguments that are constructive, that is, to those which do not *a priori* rule out the eventual synthesis we are seeking, a number

---

4   On the political rationale for this rubric, see Victor Wallis, "Marxism in the Age of Gorbachev," *Socialism and Democracy*, 6:2 (Fall 1990), 48.

of important "ecological" contributions have emerged. These have generally been along the lines of criticizing the productivist strands of Marxist thought (i.e., the inclination to prioritize economic growth) and reaffirming a long-term vision of free, self-sufficient, and self-regulated communities.[5]

The ecological critique thus finds common ground with a radical tradition wider than that of Marxism itself. This involves the vision of decentralized communities, principally evoked by anarchists but nonetheless compatible with Marx's view of an eventual stateless society, that is, a society in which the organization of production (and other matters) would be vested not in an instrument of class repression—the state—but rather in bodies of freely associated workers/citizens. Other aspects of the ecological/anarchist critique were more directly anticipated by Marx and Engels. These include: 1) Marx's analysis of the separation between mental and manual work, with its implicit opposition to hierarchy and support for the democratic self-organization of labor; 2) awareness of ecological dimensions to capital's destructive impact on town and country; and 3) an important tradition of respect—voiced by Marx toward the Paris Commune—for workers' capacity to act effectively on their own behalf.[6]

These dimensions of Marxism's development serve to highlight the centrality of the link between socialism and democratic control. To avoid misunderstanding, it is important to stress that this link does not exclusively define socialist history. Undemocratic practices have certainly been imposed in the name of socialism. Nonetheless,

---

5   See, e.g., Kate Soper, "Greening Prometheus: Marxism and Ecology," in Ted Benton, ed., *The Greening of Marxism* (New York: Guilford Press, 1996). Soper makes clear that productivism is only one component of Marx's legacy. John Bellamy Foster, in *Marx's Ecology* (New York: Monthly Review Press, 2000), underlines this point even further by showing that the productivist approach to nature is in fact a distortion of Marx.

6   On the anti-hierarchical theme, see Harry Braverman, *Labor and Monopoly Capital: The Degradation of Work in the Twentieth Century* (New York: Monthly Review Press, 1974), 8ff; on Marx's ecological awareness, see Paul Burkett, *Marx and Nature: A Red and Green Perspective* (Chicago: Haymarket, 2014 [1999]), as well as Foster, *Marx's Ecology*; on Marx and worker control, see Hal Draper, *Karl Marx's Theory of Revolution*, Vol. IV: *Critique of Other Socialisms* (New York: Monthly Review Press, 1990), and Assef Bayat, *Work, Politics and Power: An International Perspective on Workers' Control and Self-Management* (New York: Monthly Review Press, 1991), esp. 37ff.

the notion of workers' control offers, from within socialist thought, the basis for a thoroughgoing ecologically-oriented critique of the legacy of first-epoch socialist regimes.

Worker-control and ecological criteria converge around the goal of decentralization (which entails diversification of economic activity and of species-life within each locality). It is important to note that an authentic worker-control arrangement would eliminate the threat of unemployment which is used by capital to pit workers against environmentalists. Like the categories of worker and consumer, those of worker and environmentalist are in principle (i.e., outside the distorting perspective of capital) not only non-antagonistic; they simply represent different capacities, concerns, or activities which co-exist in each individual.

To recognize this is to see at the same time that a "green" perspective entails far more than just reminders of nature's more pristine condition. Combined with an emphasis on clearly delineated positive alternatives, it not only enriches any socialist movement; it also speaks to vital present-day concerns embracing, as we shall see, matters of public health, quality of life, and democracy.

Adding Red to Green

An equally strong claim can be made for what the socialist perspective can add to ecological thought. Although the ecological movement has never offered its critics so conspicuous a target as Soviet environmental policy, it nonetheless remains hampered by severe weaknesses relative to the scope of its mission. Competition and growth are still the invariable watchwords of economic policy in the world's leading countries, and while the presence of certain toxins has been mitigated in some regions, the general depletion of resources essential to survival—including oxygen, clean water, and cropland—continues unabated.

Thus, even though there are (at least in the US) many more self-proclaimed "environmentalists" than conscious socialists, the ecological agenda can hardly claim any great advances. If "socialism" without ecological awareness produced the disasters we have all heard about, it is equally true that environmental concern without socialist politics has left the natural as well as the human world largely at the mercy of those who are content to treat both as mere factors in their profit projections.

What, then, can socialist thought offer to the "ecologists"? To some of them, clearly, it offers nothing. I have in mind here the mainstream environmental organizations, whose corporate connections rule out any approaches that would infringe upon accepted business prerogatives. To them, environmental policy is primarily a matter of market incentives and/or regulations (under the implicitly accepted condition of minimal or non-threatening enforcement machinery).[7] Public authority is thus limited to emergency stopgap interventions; any notion of full-scale social control over production decisions is viewed as altogether unacceptable, no matter how severe the problem.

To those environmentalists who are not inhibited by such taboos, however, the socialist approach fills a major vacuum, beginning with its analysis of the role of key capitalist institutions—as discussed below—in promoting and maintaining wasteful/destructive patterns of resource consumption. A second major contribution of socialist thought is its holistic perspective on social processes. In particular, it suggests how the practices (and/or the conditions) of various sectors of society are interconnected, and it demonstrates the need for a comprehensive approach to any change of priorities. Thirdly, it offers a useful corrective to the political shortfalls of the environmental movement. In addition to exposing the ultimately deleterious role of the corporate-sponsored "green" organizations, it provides a basis on which to surmount the fragmented status of the existing grassroots environmentalist constituency.

The precise implications of these three priorities—overcoming waste, taking a comprehensive approach, and unifying disparate sectors—will emerge more clearly as we consider, in turn, the kind of society we envisage and, as a closely linked question, the process of arriving at it.

---

7   On corporate environmentalism, see Brian Tokar, *Earth for Sale: Reclaiming Ecology in the Age of Corporate Greenwash* (Boston: South End Press, 1997), 19ff, 35ff, and Joshua Karliner, *The Corporate Planet: Ecology and Politics in the Age of Globalization* (San Francisco: Sierra Club Books, 1997), Ch. 2.

Contours of an Ecological Socialist Society

Our discussion so far has disclosed an important trait common to the socialist critique of ecology and to the ecological critique of socialism. In each case, what was being introduced by the critique, far from reflecting an antagonistic starting point, actually urged its respective movement—green or red—back to a more rigorous adherence to its own underlying commitments. What was being called into question was not the essential nature of either aspiration, but rather the distortions it had undergone in the course of trying to operate within a particular set of historical constraints.

To accept this is to see immediately that the notion of an ecological socialist society is not something arbitrarily cobbled together from disparate principles but is rather, from the outset, a thoroughly coherent project. The two separate terms we use to name it are, in this sense, redundant. If we retain them both, it is only for the sake of expressing continuity with the diverse movements through which our goals were originally articulated.

An ecological socialist society is, in its simplest sense, one in which there are no class divisions and in which humans live in balance with the rest of nature.

These two requirements are vitally interrelated. Class division in its present form signifies the existence of a distinct sector of owners/managers of capital, a sector defined by the drive of each of its private or corporate constituents to maximize profits and thereby to increase the share of overall wealth that it controls. This objective takes precedence over all other concerns. It conflicts directly with any attempt at society-wide redefinition of such matters as how much of a given resource may be used, how much of a given good may be produced and by what means, how people will be educated and socialized to treat both each other and the natural world, and how the overall allocation of work and community responsibilities, individual benefits, and social services will be determined.

The breakup of a distinct class of large-property owners will allow such matters for the first time to be submitted in a meaningful way to the entire society. But why should we expect such an arrangement to offer any guarantee that ecological priorities will be observed? While the inherently anti-ecological forces may have been removed, what is to prevent their assault on the natural world from being continued under a new regime?

Here is where we have to anticipate the connection between long-range vision and the means of approaching it. Without yet going into specifics, we should remind ourselves of the sheer scope and scale of a project to dissolve the power of the ruling class. So pervasive are the institutions, the routines, and the common assumptions through which this class maintains its position, that the dissolution of this whole apparatus would be inconceivable without a correspondingly vast transformation of the attitudes, the drives, and the cultural priorities of those who would come together to make it all happen.[8]

The emergence, through this process, of a hegemonic "green" attitude cannot be assured by any formal stipulation. Commitments that are merely programmatic come and go, leaving understandably cynical constituencies. The ecological potential of any future social-ist revolution rests on firmer ground. It rests on two complementary strands of the actual movement that is taking shape: on the one hand, the felt concerns of the millions who worry daily about the physical conditions that they and their progeny will have to endure (conditions associated with illness, scarcity, social breakdown, and natural disaster), and, on the other, the conscious awareness embodied by those activists who perceive the unrelenting nature of environmental constraints and who then seek to build on such knowledge and to express it in their practical work.[9]

If this dynamic suggests why a classless society would have to be "green," it also points to why an ecologically sound society would have to be classless—which at the present stage of history means: free of the rule of capital. We have already noted the accumulation-ist drives of the capitalist class. A related impact lies in its consump-tion habits, and in its imposition of consumptionist imperatives on

---

8   See Bertell Ollman, "Market Mystification in Capitalist and Market Socialist Societies," *Socialism and Democracy*, 11:2 (Fall 1997), 30f.

9   See, e.g., Richard Hofrichter, ed., Toxic Struggles: *The Theory and Practice of Environmental Justice* (Philadelphia: New Society, 1993); Daniel Faber, ed., *The Struggle for Ecological Democracy: Environmental Justice Movements in the United States* (New York: Guilford Press, 1998).

people of lesser means.[10] Most tragically, there is the situation of the hundreds of millions—notably in Third World countries—who, having been left destitute by this whole process, are in no position to view resource use through any other lens than that of their immediate survival needs.

Both the over-extension of the capitalist class and the desperate scramble of everyone else—whether for "status" or for security or for bare survival—are thoroughly inimical to any disposition toward respect for natural limits. One cannot expect people to be able to honor such limits until they are liberated from these drives.

Natural Balance and Human Needs

In principle, natural balance and human needs are complementary, in the sense that if the human species violates natural balance—that is, violates ecological criteria of sustainability—it will only be undermining the conditions of its own well-being.

In practical political terms, however, it is not possible to speak of human needs without recognizing the way in which these needs have evolved relative to the resources available for their satisfaction. While it is legitimate to identify a large portion of "needs"—as we shall do—with the self-serving requirements of a given power system, it must also be acknowledged that the same power system has in turn generated (whether directly or indirectly) new quantitative levels of *basic* human need.[11] Where the spurious "needs" must be rejected, these new basic needs must be properly addressed, however deplorable the circumstances which produced them. I refer here, most importantly, to:

- the sheer increase in *numbers* of people, with consequent pressure on resources of all kinds;

---

10 See Paul A. Baran and Paul M. Sweezy, *Monopoly Capital: An Essay on the American Economic and Social Order* (New York: Monthly Review Press, 1966), 115ff.

11 Needs are "basic" (or universal) to the extent to which they are (*a*) essential to survival and (*b*) realizable by everyone. For further elaboration, see my "Reply" to James O'Connor, *Capitalism Nature Socialism*, 8:4 (December 1997), 52f. See also Fred Magdoff and Chris Williams, *Creating an Ecological Society: Toward a Revolutionary Transformation* (New York: Monthly Review Press, 2017), ch. 5.

  • the already severe levels of pollution, which, in combination with the tolls of military devastation, civil violence, and
systemic "accidents," as well as the effects of malnutrition and
drug-abuse (legal as well as illegal), will for a long time magnify
healthcare needs; and
  • the desolation, desertification, or flooding of certain regions,
combining with other factors (e.g., economic hardship, political oppression, war) to multiply the incidence of migration,
resulting in enormous and continuing needs associated with
displacement.

The upshot of all these developments is to narrow the limits
within which any natural balance can be arrived at. As the pressure
on available resources intensifies, it becomes more urgent than ever
to assure that all basic human needs are taken into account. The
justification for challenging those other "needs" which are either
artificial, or system-driven, or excessively costly, or defined by positions of privilege, thus becomes greater and greater all the time.

WHAT CAN WE DO WITHOUT?

Ecological and socialist criteria converge in demanding an end to
the wasteful consumption of resources and energy. The determination of what is wasteful must ultimately be a social project. Not all
instances of waste will be immediately and unanimously recognized
as such; the campaign against them will require intense education
and organizing. Deeply entrenched habits will have to be called into
question, and commercial indoctrination will have to be challenged
at every level. In place of such "conditioning" will have to come
a thoroughly democratic examination of alternative approaches.
Although no single prior vision can be expected to prevail, it is
nonetheless crucial to begin by trying to grasp the phenomenon of
waste in its totality.

  Among human activities, we may view as preeminently wasteful
those which are undertaken not in response to universal human
needs (which include spiritual or cultural as well as material objec-

tives) but rather in conjunction with institutional imperatives reflecting the power and the interests of a particular class.

A considerable portion of the energy consumption in capitalist society is precisely of this sort; that is, instead of being driven by basic needs, it arises either from the direct requirements of capital or from capital's privileges, impositions, or seductions. (It should be clearly understood here that the "impositions and seductions" encompass capital's complicity in numerous forms of racial and gender-based oppression.) At the present time, the category of superfluous energy consumption embraces most if not all of the following institutions or activities:[12]

- the advertising industry, together with private insurance, banking, stock-exchanges, and associated communications, accounting, and legal services;
- the construction, resource use, and services arising from the automobile/shopping mall/suburban sprawl complex;
- excess energy use arising from the global integration of production processes and from over-reliance on long-distance trade;
- the development of a highly specialized fuel-intensive agriculture with heavy reliance on chemical fertilizers and pesticides and, more recently, genetic engineering;
- market-based wastage of food, amounting to about one-third of global food production;
- the heavy use of disposable, non-biodegradable products, especially for packaging (an aspect of brand-related marketing);
- certain fuel-intensive, typically macho recreational addictions giving their users an artificial sense of power (car-racing, snowmobiles, all-terrain vehicles, speedboats, jet-skis, etc.);
- a growing sector of purely status-related luxuries, defined as such by (a) their frivolity—including pandering to sexist or racist

12 My discussion here builds upon the notion of the "irrational system" developed in Baran and Sweezy, *Monopoly Capital*, Ch. 11. For a fuller elaboration of my own approach, see Victor Wallis, "Socialism, Ecology, and Democracy: Toward a Strategy of Conversion," in Chronis Polychroniou, ed., *Socialism: Crisis and Renewal* (Westport, CT: Praeger, 1993); abridged version in *Monthly Review*, 44:2 (June 1992). For a discussion of methodological problems involved in the itemization of forms of waste, see "Reply" (n. 11), 55f. On food-wastage, see Magdoff and Williams, *Creating an Ecological Society*, 104f.

norms (e.g., cosmetic surgery to disguise age or ethnicity)—and (b) their highly restrictive prices;
  • the police, private protection, penal, and military services built up in response to the threat and/or the reality of challenges—whether individual (delinquent) or collective (revolutionary)—to concentrated private wealth;
  • whatever proportion of general production (and construction) or ancillary services—including healthcare—is accounted for by demands placed upon the system, or upon individuals (e.g., crash victims), by the above-mentioned practices.

It would be interesting to know the aggregate weight of these items as a percentage of overall economic activity. Even without such a figure, however, it is clear from just the range and pervasiveness of such practices that they have a vast impact.[13] To recognize this is to see that the alleged dilemma over whether to serve humanity or to respect nature is in fact a false one. One can serve *both* humanity and nature by exposing these forms of waste for what they are, and thereby building a movement to do away with them.

HOW CAN WE MAKE BETTER USE OF AVAILABLE RESOURCES?

Wasteful practices, as the above list suggests, reflect a convergence of individual impulses and structural imperatives, with each reinforcing the other. The individual dimension points to the need for some form of consciousness-raising, taking as its point of departure the popular strivings fostered by capitalism. It is important to understand this process not as one of merely replacing an old with a new set of predispositions, but rather as one of introducing

---

13 A useful effort at quantifying waste, based on a less exacting view than mine as to activities deserving of energy allocations, included the finding, as of 1987, that approximately one-third of the US labor force consisted of people whose function was confined to either actively protecting the status quo or passively constituting a reserve pool of labor power that was either unused or, in the case of prisoners, excessively cheap. Samuel Bowles, David M. Gordon, and Thomas E. Weisskopf, *After the Waste Land* (Armonk, NY: M.E. Sharpe, 1990), 195f. See also Ch. 11 of that work and Appendix D ("Estimating the Waste Burden") of its earlier (1984) edition (entitled *Beyond the Waste Land*).

a broader awareness into all the consumption/production choices that each of us is continually making. While the starting point for such awareness might be a recognition of environmental dangers, its full flowering will entail enhanced respect not only for nature but also for the human essence, that is, for both oneself and others as we might be if freed of market-driven goals or standards.

Any such evolution is inseparable from radical structural change. People will not be able to grow in social and ecological awareness unless they can have a greater sense of personal security. The latter in turn requires not just social safety-nets but, beyond this, increased access for everyone to policy-making processes, so that priorities can be defined on a new basis (and so that the gains made at one moment will not be taken back at the next). Some palpable improvement in environmental health indicators would also help. There is no way that all this can be achieved by following market-based signals. Such signals may function usefully within an already fully defined infrastructure, but when the infrastructure itself is the problem (as it is when it seamlessly generates so many wasteful practices), then conscious reorganization—planning— becomes necessary.[14]

For the sake of both prior information and eventual implementation, planning has to be democratic. So much is this so, that if our concern is with the wellbeing of society (rather than with the profits of a company), then undemocratic planning is virtually a contradiction in terms. This was the lesson of the Soviet model. Top-down directives, backed by sanctions (whether financial or penal), lead inescapably to a calculus of deception, against which the only possible check is the involvement of a greater cross-section of society, with lower personal stakes on the part of any single participant.[15]

---

14 This is not to deny that particular waste-reducing innovations may arise within a capitalist setting. For numerous creative suggestions along such lines, see Paul Hawken *et al.*, *Natural Capitalism: Creating the Next Industrial Revolution* (Boston: Little, Brown, 1999). Two fundamental problems remain, however: 1) the ecological thrust originates outside the calculus of capital, and 2) the soundness of the *part* is overridden by the unsoundness of the *whole*. For a full discussion of the limitations of "eco-capitalism," see Saral Sarkar, *Ecosocialism or Eco-Capitalism?* (New York & London: Verso, 1999), Ch. 5.

15 For further discussion and references on the Soviet planning model, see Chapter 2. For positive examples of planning (albeit on a limited scale), see Max Jaggi, et al., *Red Bologna* (London: Writers & Readers, 1977), and Molly O'Meara, "How

This idea of a much broader participation in the planning process brings us back directly to a form of present-day waste which, although every bit as severe as any of the above-listed practices, did not seem to belong in the same list. I have in mind the waste of *people*.

Much of the environmental literature treats people more as consumers than as positive agents. This reflects the roles to which people are consigned by the market. Even when they are "employed," what they are doing may have a destructive impact upon the natural environment. But their most obvious role—in common with larger economic units—is as users of nonrenewable energy sources. Hence the widespread tendency, in the tradition of Malthus, to treat people as "the problem."[16]

Whether or not people are "the problem," however, depends on how they are organized. It is well enough known that per capita energy consumption in poor countries is a small fraction of what it is in rich countries. But the figure for the rich countries also includes all the forms of waste we have noted; whatever wellbeing is enjoyed in these countries is therefore certainly not dependent on maintaining that particular total.

But the waste of the people themselves takes many forms. Whether they are unemployed, whether they are wastefully or destructively employed, or whether, because of severe deprivation, they grow up without the capacity to function as effective members of their community, in all these cases their potential is being forfeited. The irony of this situation lies in the fact that the entire ecological conversion process involves new tasks of all kinds for which people are emphatically needed. This includes not only the initial political/educational work; it is inherent also in the new organization of production. From an ecological point of view, productivity will need to be reckoned not in terms of units of labor power but rather in terms of units of nonrenewable energy that are used up (or quantities of pollutants or carbon dioxide that are released). For

---

Mid-Sized Cities Can Avoid Strangulation," *World Watch*, 11:5 (September/October 1998).

16 For a critique of late-20th-century versions of this approach, see Victor Wallis, "Lester Brown, the Worldwatch Institute, and the Dilemmas of Technocratic Revolution," *Organization and Environment*, 10:2 (June 1997).

these latter amounts to be reduced, the human input will have to grow.[17]

This expansion of the human input refers to both of its possible dimensions: both the numbers of people involved and the percentage of each individual's energy that is devoted to ecological concerns will have to increase. More time will be devoted to bio-diverse gardening; more local travel will be done on foot or bicycle; time spent in community meetings will be valorized. Such trends, to the degree that they take hold, will offer a positive scenario that could surmount the current impasse between rich and poor countries. The technological rollercoaster of the industrialized countries would no longer appear so attractive, and the hundreds of millions of un- and under-employed people in all parts of the world would begin to be viewed as a potential asset—as they could be for the vast reconfigurations of space involved in recovering paved-over soil and clear-cut hillsides.

The other changes implied by countering the items on our waste menu will augment the resources available to sustain this large population—an effect that will be further reinforced (with health-beneficial side-effects) if more crops are grown for direct human consumption rather than being used to feed livestock.

The present point, however, is that decisions on all such matters have society-wide implications, for ecological balance as well as for immediate human needs. The market has not proved to be a rational vehicle for making such decisions, for, among many other problems, its dependence on financial signals makes it increasingly incapable of responding to mass needs at a level commensurate with their urgency.[18]

The resulting disequilibria may appear tolerable if one is personally comfortable and if one disregards long-term trends. Moreover, everyone recognizes the risks inherent in revolutionary social change. What is distinctive about the ecological crisis, however, is

---

17 I owe this idea originally to Barry Commoner's remarks about synthetics in *The Poverty of Power* (New York: Bantam, 1977), 149ff.

18 On the inadequacy of market-based approaches, see Barry Commoner, *Making Peace with the Planet* (New York: Pantheon, 1990), 219, and Tokar, *Earth for Sale*, Ch. 2.

that it dramatically highlights the even greater risk that lies in keeping things the way they are.

WHAT CAN WE GAIN THAT WE DON'T HAVE NOW?

The "we" in this question refers to the entire human race. Obviously, the gains from ecological socialism would be different for different sectors, and the greatest gain would be for those who up to now have been most deprived. For them, life would clearly improve beyond recognition. But the rest of humanity would also benefit, in ways both obvious and not-so-obvious.

The central point is the one implied in the very definition of ecological socialism, namely, that material needs would be satisfied without further taxing the environment. Within this framework, interrelated problems in a variety of areas would also be alleviated. For example:

Population pressure. The immediate crisis would be eased by the greater availability of basic resources for everyone. Any tendency toward further population growth would be counteracted by the reduced fear of insecurity in old age, the greater autonomy of women, and the improved circumstances for public education.

Social breakdown. The elimination of waste would increase the number of meaningful jobs and would do away with meaningless ones. Everyone would have a positive role to play. In addition, higher levels of local self-sufficiency would reduce economic imbalances between regions, ease migratory pressures, undercut the basis for racist/expansionist drives, and thereby create more favorable conditions for the coexistence of multiple cultures.

Public health. Gains could be expected not only from the curbing of environmental toxins, but also from the elimination of poverty, the increase in personal security, improvements in diet, reduced reliance on fuel-intensive substitutes for physical exertion, control by workers over their own working conditions, (again) better public education, and, finally, a needs-based system of healthcare delivery.

The real question in all this, however, is not so much what the gains would be as it is whether the whole scenario can be implemented.

Means and Ends

Twentieth-century history established, as if never before, the inseparability of political goals from the means employed to reach them. Recognition of this indisputable fact, however, has often slid over—by largely imperceptible steps—into the assertion that revolutionary change can no longer be on the agenda.

If our argument up to this point has suggested anything, it is that a transformation of revolutionary proportions is the only way out of an otherwise hopeless social and environmental crisis. Our political challenge, then, without going back on this argument, is to suggest in what ways the ecological socialist project is constrained by its very nature to shun those means that would be inimical to its goal.

This refers in particular to the task of minimizing violence. Minimizing violence, however, does not mean rejecting revolution. The idea that it does have such a meaning rests on a deceptive argument similar to one that is often used against socialism. Just as socialism is linked simplistically to the worst of its first-epoch expressions, so revolution is identified, as though by definition, with the imposition of violence.

Of course, we would be guilty of a similar oversimplification if we were to claim that a revolution could occur completely without violence. In fact, whether one supposes a continuation of present structures or the introduction of radically new ones, whatever official violence occurs will be largely a function of the regime's incapacity to meet popular needs and thereby earn popular support.

The ecosocialist project has considerable potential for eliciting the level of support required in order to move toward its goals with a minimum of violence. Although the ultimate verdict on this will rest partly on how we build such support and partly on how the ruling class reacts to any successes we have, there are a number of grounds for affirming that the prospects for social peace will be furthered more by a committed adherence to our project than they would be either by watering down our aims or by surrendering them altogether.

What gives viability to a strong radical position is, first and foremost, the acuteness of the social/environmental crisis itself. The resulting hardship and insecurity provoke continuous outbursts of violence, even (or especially) in the absence of a purposeful social movement—and the sense of community that such a movement could engender. Such outbursts, involving everything from civil strife to mass shootings to domestic abuse, are over and above the structural violence implicit in routine material deprivation. Anyone who feels the weight of this ongoing tragedy will be ready to support a movement that offers a persuasive response. While the initially socialist component of such support would tend eventually to flow along class lines, the ecological component could broaden the support to a point at which those hostile to the movement might well find themselves isolated and severely discredited by their identification with the status quo.

It is often asserted as a kind of axiomatic truth that a "moderate" position is better suited than a radical one to build up a widespread following. This assumption may have some merit in non-crisis situations, although even then it is often based on consideration of only a limited sector of the total population (in the US case, that small portion of the adult citizenry which vacillates between voting Democrat and voting Republican). In a crisis setting, and where the whole population is affected and the level of awareness is high, the opposite dynamic comes into play. "Moderation" emerges as a form of thinly disguised resistance to change. At its very best, it is uninspiring and therefore not conducive to anything but passive support. The goals of ecological socialism, by contrast, demand not just people's passive approval but their active and sustained exertion. One does not build up such commitment by trying to compromise with those whose views have been discredited.

The best hope for keeping violence to a minimum lies in building the most solidly based, coherent, and effective movement that we can. To the degree that we (i.e., all those who share this vision) are successful, the resulting network of mobilized communities will assure that a violent response from the ruling class can only backfire and multiply our support.

Getting Ourselves Together

While there is not much room for compromise with capitalist interests, there is a great need for openness and a spirit of compromise
within the camp of politically progressive environmentalists. One of
the great merits of the ecosocialist perspective, as suggested earlier,
is its comprehensiveness. This not only provides a firm grounding
for challenges to the prevailing powers; it also offers a supportive
and stimulating framework for the working out of differences that
inevitably arise among individuals and groups who come to their
position from different backgrounds.

We noted one such difference at the beginning of this chapter:
the difference between those who seek natural balance for its own
sake (often called ecocentric) and those who do so out of concern
for human survival (generally called—sometimes derisively—
anthropocentric).[19] I have suggested that the practical difference
between the two positions may well be negligible, inasmuch as the
negative traits often attributed to anthropocentrism actually pertain
to attitudes and behaviors bearing the more or less direct imprint of
capital. If we speak not from the vantage-point of capital but rather
from that of humanity as a whole, we are doing no more than any
other species in looking out for our particular species-interests. To
the extent that our "reflective capacity" comes into play, we recognize that our being is dialectically intertwined with that of other
species, whose interests we must therefore also defend.

What this will mean in practice is nonetheless a complicated
question, as illustrated in the debates over animal rights. Even here,
though, there is a sense in which a broad overview may point the way
to common demands. For example, those who oppose in principle
the consumption of animal products also include in their argument
many references to wasteful resource use on the part of the meat
industry.[20] There they have a very strong case (as they do on a good
many other issues as well). On the other hand, however, what about

---

19 This polarity is highlighted in Carolyn Merchant, Radical Ecology: *The Search
    for a Livable World* (New York: Routledge, 1992); see my review of this book in
    Monthly Review, 45:7 (December 1993).

20 E.g., Carol J. Adams, "'Mad Cow' Disease and the Animal Industrial Complex: An
    Ecofeminist Analysis," *Organization and Environment*, 10:1 (March 1997), 39.

marginal lands that can be grazed but are unsuitable for cultivation?
What about the use of animal power and manure, in certain settings,
in preference to fuel-burning engines and chemical fertilizer? What
about the use of leather in preference to petrochemical synthetics?
And what about the practices of those indigenous peoples who,
although devoted to hunting, are second to none in their reverence
for the natural world?

This is not the place to try to resolve such questions. I mention them here in order to underline the need for an organizational
setting within which to work out a common "minimum position."
Even those who would not support a total ban on the consumption
of animal products could nonetheless join in calling for an end to
the vast scope and the severely abusive conditions (unhealthy to
people as well as to animals) which characterize meat production
in its capitalist form.

A step of this sort, however "minimal" it might appear from
one point of view, would actually be extremely radical in its overall repercussions. But the human energy required to bring it about
presupposes some intense political work in the meantime. Before
being able to supplant institutions so deeply entrenched as the
capitalist meat industry, the ecosocialist movement will need to
develop into an effective counterhegemonic organization. This
means on the one hand a massive popular presence which no
current decision-maker—whether private- or public-sector—can
ignore, but it also means, on the other hand, putting together a
coordinating mechanism which can develop long-range as well as
short-range strategies, and which is able to combine authority with
accountability.

The popular presence will take the form of protest activity,
alternative media, and various kinds of service, community, or production units. The coordinating mechanism will be something in
the nature of a political party. In any case, it will be an organization
which, while oriented toward contesting for power, does not con-
fine itself to electoral activity but rather engages at the same time in
a full span of intellectual, cultural, and mass-organizing work. Considerable activity of this sort has already been carried out, both by
Green and other alternative party formations and by the numerous

environmental justice groups.[21] The vital element lacking, however, is a unified presence.

This is, of course, the great challenge. Progress toward meeting it has in no way kept pace with the level of social/environmental breakdown. The resulting discouragement, combined with disappointment over revolutions past, has led to a widespread scaling back of aspirations. Ecological concern is widely viewed as just one "identity" among many, when in fact the interests it embraces, although clearly in conflict with those of capital, cut across all other social boundaries. The problem is that so long as capital writes the ground rules, even the most basic ecological demands divide popular constituencies into warring camps. "Environmental justice," under these conditions, means looking out for one's own community and letting the toxic wastes be shipped somewhere else. Similarly, the survival of an ecosystem is perceived as being in conflict with that of the workers who depend upon it for their livelihood.

These are dangerous assumptions, deeply implanted and not easily overcome. Worse yet, the very aspiration to overcome them is often denounced as being itself an expression of the demographic "identity" of those who put it forward.[22] The perspective of ecological socialism offers, potentially, a wealth of arguments to transcend this attitude and, with it, the destructive fragmentation that plagues progressive movements. This can only be a gradual process, however. It will grow as the particularistic groups become aware of the limits to what they can accomplish on their own.[23] The ecosocialist perspective, for its part, must be ready to enrich and adapt its vision as people from each new sector venture out into a larger world, a world of common struggle.

---

21 See note 9 above.

22 Thus, being able to think in terms of the totality is frequently viewed as being something possible only for people who come from a position of privilege. See Victor Wallis, "Socialism Under Siege," *Monthly Review*, 47:8 (January 1996).

23 Hopeful signs of such an evolution began to crystallize with the late 1999 demonstrations in Seattle against the World Trade Organization. For background, see Victor Wallis, "The U.S. Left Since 1968: Decline or Growth?" *New Political Science*, 21:3 (September 1999), reprinted and updated in Wallis, *Socialist Practice: Histories and Theories* (London: Palgrave Macmillan, 2020), 155-70. More recent developments are discussed later in this book.

2

"Progress" or Progress? Defining a Socialist Technology

It is time for socialists to reclaim the concept of progress. Progress means improvement. Under the hegemonic impact of capital, however, the concept has been steered into a narrowly instrumental/technological groove, with disastrous ecological consequences. First-epoch socialism did not challenge this understanding but mostly bought into it, thinking to overtake capitalism on its own turf. All this has led many people to view "progress" as something to be avoided. Such a response is understandable but self-defeating. A merely negative approach affords no basis on which to challenge the status quo. It moreover forfeits to the enemy a term which, despite almost two centuries of misuse, retains its positive connotation—as in the phrase "making progress"—of change in a desired direction.

Our task, then, must be to radically alter people's sense of what genuine progress would entail. This requires us, first, to review the current status of "progress" under conditions of capitalist hyper-development; second, to comment on the technological contradictions of first-epoch socialism; and third, to sketch the contours of an authentically socialist technology.

Capitalist "Progress"

Within capitalist society, progress has come to be widely understood in terms of increased levels of information and the improved execution of particular tasks (e.g., producing or moving things more quickly; targeting military objectives or establishing genetic connections more precisely).[1] Even generalized notions of progress seem to involve no more than an aggregation of such particular attainments. Thus, the greatest progress is identified with the most advanced and sophisticated machinery, irrespective of what effects it might be having either on the human species or on the natural world as a whole.

Such effects, it is further believed, may be either good or bad, depending on how the technology is used.[2] This claim of technological neutrality is indeed one of capital's strongest ideological props, and it has sharply divided the ranks of capitalism's critics. Even within Marx's own writings, one can readily find arguments for both condemning and accepting what in his time were the new forces of production. Thus on the one hand these forces stripped the workers of their humanity, but on the other, Marx found it necessary, in distancing himself from the Luddites, to distinguish sharply between the machinery itself and "its employment by capital."[3]

It is futile to ask what might have happened if, following out the Luddite scenario, capitalist industrialization had been stopped in its tracks. What is important for us now is that, once capitalism and its chronic upheavals were launched, their creative and their destructive aspects advanced together. One might well argue at any stage, of course, that the stunting or killing of human beings and the corrosion of natural goods far outweighed the benefits of whatever production took place; but from a Marxist perspective, it could also be claimed that people were nonetheless brought together in new ways and thereby became capable of tapping, through countless

---

1   For a generally enthusiastic survey and projection of such advances, see Michio Kaku, *Visions: How Science Will Revolutionize the 21st Century* (New York: Anchor Books, 1997).

2   Kaku, for example, taking into account some of the possible dangers, advocates a kind of social oversight of technology (*Visions*, 260), but treats such oversight, throughout his argument, as a purely external imposition upon technological development. Embracing a wildly productivist approach, he projects for the 21st century a global economic growth rate close to 5 percent and a rise in world energy consumption to 130 times its 1997 level! (329f).

3   *Capital*, vol. 1, trans. Ben Fowkes (New York: Vintage Books, 1977), 554f. David Noble calls attention to this passage in his *Progress Without People: New Technology, Unemployment, and the Message of Resistance* (Toronto: Between the Lines, 1995), 19. Marx addressed the dehumanizing effects of the capitalist production process in the "Alienated Labor" section of his *Economic and Philosophic Manuscripts* of 1844.

channels, new sources of creativity and self-affirmation (both individual and collective).[4]

Drawing the balance between the negative and the positive dimensions of capitalist development has always been a problem. Even if we do not question the culpability of capital (which becomes all the more glaring as we extend our gaze to take in the entire world), it remains true that the self-affirming or subversive response has often been overshadowed by some form of at least partial accommodation with capitalist "consumer society." This kind of twofold trajectory has marked progressive social movements from the beginning, resulting in situations where the gains of certain constituencies appear partly to offset the further degradation of others. How are we to weigh, for example, the improved legal status of women in some of the advanced countries against the consolidation of ruling-class impositions (economic/military/penal) on popular movements throughout the world? Obviously, the repercussions of capitalist rule are sufficiently vast to encompass certain emancipatory trends. This does not mean that the opportunities at stake could have been seized without purposeful counter-hegemonic action (in this instance, on the part of radical women's movements), but it does explain why some of the outcomes (e.g., women entering top-management positions) do not necessarily feed into a growth in revolutionary awareness.[5]

Yet, however hard it may be to gauge the extent to which progressive movements are thus coopted, our more important concern has to be with whether the underlying adaptive capacity of the established order is maintaining or losing its force. Here there is much more to be said, for even if many—especially among the members of newly assimilated groups—may be slow to question the system, the accumulating grounds for popular misgivings are evident. Some of these are of long standing, like the increasing commodification

---

4   This argument is expressed more generally in the assumption that any political project must build on the actual historical present; see Victor Wallis, "The *Communist Manifesto* and Capitalist Hegemony After 150 Years," *Socialism and Democracy*, 12:1/2 (1998), 7-13.

5   On the partial perversion of feminist gains, see Hester Eisenstein, *Feminism Seduced: How Global Elites Use Women's Labor and Ideas to Exploit the World* (Boulder, CO: Paradigm Press, 2009).

of all human activity.[6] And the desperation of the world's poorer regions has accelerated sharply under the impact of neoliberal free-trade policies, corporate land-grabs, and climate-related disasters. But even for those populations most favored by capitalist development, faith in "progress" has been severely undercut by its military applications: the massive slaughter of human beings, culminating in the specter of nuclear annihilation. Subsequently, as the nuclear war danger appeared to become less immediate, it was quickly reinforced by two threats which further strengthen the negative view of "progress": economic insecurity and environmental devastation.

Capitalism has always tended to inflict personal economic insecurity on the working class, but this "normal" tendency had been significantly attenuated in the industrialized countries—if not by the welfare state, then at least by the establishment of labor unions. It is only in relation to this latter sector that there is any social novelty in the latest round of capitalist technological breakthroughs. Layoffs, even among formerly well-off workers, have now become so routine that the very notion of a lifetime job is, for most people, a thing of the past.[7] Behind this development lies not only the pressure of competition—and in some cases mergers—but also a more general application of the capitalist drive for total control (encompassing human as well as material factors of production), a drive which has been found at times to supersede short-run considerations of cost and efficiency.[8]

The relentless substitution of technology for workers, along with the underlying striving for control, carries over directly into the environmental practices of capitalist enterprise. The price of mechanization and of increased labor-productivity is exacted in the form of "externalities." At an immediate level, this sometimes just

---

6   See for example R.C. Lewontin, "The Maturing of Capitalist Agriculture: Farmer as Proletarian," *Monthly Review*, 50:3 (July/August 1998), 72-84.

7   Hence the coining of the term "permatemp" [permanent temporary!] to describe the status of many workers in the computer industry.

8   Noble suggests in this connection, in an essay originally written in 1983, that the control-objective of capital routinely overrides cost-cutting priorities (*Progress Without People*, 91f). Jeremy Rifkin argues, however, in *The End of Work* (New York: Putnam, 1995), 6, that gains in control generate a significant bottom-line payoff to capital in the long run. For an interesting attempt at weighing such considerations, see Edmund F. Byrne, *Work, Inc.: A Philosophical Inquiry* (Philadelphia: Temple University Press, 1990), 191ff.

means wasteful procedures applied by poorly trained personnel. More systematically, it appears in the guise of a heavier-than-necessary dependence on capital goods and fuel, and in a calculated indifference to the spread of toxic wastes.[9]

Increasingly too, however, the control-imperative extends beyond the workplace to invade the actual use made of the product by its purchasers. Such has been the application of genetic engineering to agriculture, one of the few sectors that had retained, until recently, a modest sphere of productive activity outside the capitalist market. This last autonomous sphere is now in turn slated for destruction, through the development of technologies, contractual arrangements, and patenting practices designed to assure that no step of the production process could be carried out free of corporate control. The ultimate expression of this corporate sweep is the "terminator gene," which, when introduced into a seed, assures the non-renewability of the crop.[10] Here, in some ways even more transparently than with nuclear weaponry, is the reductio ad absurdum of capitalist-driven technological innovation: an invention that has a purely negative use-value, with no other purpose than to multiply sales.

The "terminator" technology is an extreme case of capital's contempt for natural processes. The more routine expression of this contempt lies in capital's underlying commitment to growth, accumulation, and profit.[11] Much has been made, in recent years, of capital's supposed capacity to respond to the ecological crisis by turning its powers in a "green" direction. This is a clear instance, however (comparable to capital's earlier accommodation with labor

---

9   See, e.g., Barry Commoner, *Making Peace with the Planet* (New York: Pantheon Books, 1990).

10 Hope Shand, "Terminator Seeds: Monsanto Moves to Tighten Its Grip on Global Agriculture," *Multinational Monitor* 20:11 (November 1998), 13-16. For a more general discussion of these issues, see Varda Burstyn, "The Dystopia of Our Times: Genetic Technology and Other Afflictions," in Leo Panitch and Colin Leys, eds., *Socialist Register 2000: Necessary and Unnecessary Utopias* (New York: Monthly Review Press, 1999), 223-42.

11 For a comprehensive critique, see Richard Douthwaite, *The Growth Illusion: How Economic Growth Has Enriched the Few, Impoverished the Many, and Endangered the Planet*, 2nd ed. (Gabriola Island, BC: New Society Publishers, 1999).

unions[12]), of making a virtue out of necessity. Whatever ecologically progressive measures might be taken by particular enterprises, the bigger picture remains unchanged. In the realm of consumer demand, ecological criteria (e.g., the preference for organic food) correspond to a niche market, which does not preclude applying contrary criteria in the rest of the economy. In the corporate sector as a whole, while it is true that certain energy-saving practices might directly enhance profitability,[13] the main stimulus to corporate "greening" derives from external factors (e.g., public pressure, fiscal incentives, government regulations). To the degree that any notion of global environmental emergency has seeped into corporate awareness, it manifests itself mainly in expressions of hope as to what others will do. The disaster-insurance business is the one sector that has encouraged—within limits, of course—the development of serious ecological alternatives. But the ostensible greening of the corporate outlook as such is no more than a public relations posture.[14] Above all, not only the corporations but also capitalist governments, without exception, remain fully committed to an overall strategy of growth.

The capitalist pursuit of "progress" thus continues unabated, combining old and new objectives. The scenario of international competition remains essentially the same, despite transient shifts of fortune from one zone to another. The only unqualified change is that the competing units—whether regional trade groups or corporate conglomerates—get bigger all the time. Oil exploration disrupts the most fragile ecosystems, while the underlying geopolitics ignites periodic military attacks and sustains long-term strategies of domination. Stakeouts of "intellectual property rights" threaten to batter down the last ramparts of natural or local autonomy.[15] Finan-

---

12 During the post-World War II period, US corporations granted wage-increases to unions in return for no-strike pledges.

13 See, e.g., Michael E. Porter and Claas van der Linde, "Green and Competitive: Ending the Stalemate," *Harvard Business Review* 73:5 (Sept./Oct. 1995), 120-34, and Paul Hawken et al., *Natural Capitalism* (Boston: Little, Brown, 1999).

14 See the case studies in Jed Greer and Kenny Bruno, Greenwash: *The Reality Behind Corporate Environmentalism* (New York: Apex Press, 1996). The special case of the insurance industry has been a frequent subject of commentary in publications of the Worldwatch Institute (see below, n. 36).

15 Vandana Shiva, *Biopiracy: The Plunder of Nature and Knowledge* (Boston: South End Press, 1997).

cial officials from all the powerful countries seek an international regime of untrammeled prerogatives for private capital.[16] Currency speculation proliferates, at the expense of the world's most vulnerable regions.[17] New "information age" technologies replace one another at an accelerating pace.[18] "Everlasting uncertainty and agitation" has never been more prevalent. And, all the while, a combination of greed, projection, and fear generates chronic pressure for higher military budgets.

Socialist Progress?

The regimes of first-epoch socialism, beginning with Soviet Russia, raised the possibility of formulating a socialist conception of progress. In the early years of the Soviet Union, thanks in part to the influence of communist visions but in part also to the goal of overcoming Russia's economic and social backwardness, the notion of progress retained a moral component which had long since been forgotten in the capitalist world. Soviet technological projects were thus, at the outset, just one dimension of a much larger design for the transformation of all aspects of human life.[19]

Such a comprehensive approach to progress, implicit in the original meaning of the term, would necessarily have to infuse any authentically socialist agenda. In the particular Soviet setting, however, given the military dangers flowing from capitalist encir-

---

16 Noam Chomsky, "Power in the Global Arena," *New Left Review* no. 230 (July/August 1998), 23ff. This process has continued with projects such as the Trans Pacific Partnership (TPP) and the Transatlantic Trade and Investment Partnership (TTIP).

17 William Greider, *One World, Ready or Not: The Manic Logic of Global Capitalism* (New York: Simon & Schuster, 1997), ch. 11, esp. 235ff.

18 For well informed discussions of this process, see Jim Davis, Thomas Hirschl, and Michael Stack, eds., *Cutting Edge: Technology, Information, Capitalism and Social Revolution* (London: Verso, 1997).

19 See William G. Rosenberg, ed., *Bolshevik Visions: First Phase of the Cultural Revolution in Soviet Russia* (Ann Arbor, MI: Ardis, 1984). I use the term "first-epoch socialism" for what came to be known as the "actually existing socialism" of the whole period between 1917 and 1989. See my essay "Marxism in the Age of Gorbachev," *Socialism and Democracy*, 6:2 (Fall 1990), reprinted as Ch. 3 of Victor Wallis, *Socialist Practice: Histories and Theories* (London: Palgrave Macmillan, 2020).

clement, the official view of technology never ceased to be conditioned by short-term requirements. Hence Lenin's portentous recourse to "scientific management," with its corollary of "iron discipline" in the workplace.[20] Such methods, as Lenin freely acknowledged, reflected a continuation of capitalist practice.[21] The debate on "Socialist man" thus remained compartmentalized. Social and cultural goals were widely discussed, but in a context that did not bear on—or admit the influence of—economic practice. Economic visions, for their part, were left to focus less on the social relations of production than on grandiose construction projects, of which the dream of "people's palaces on the peaks of Mont Blanc and at the bottom of the Atlantic"[22] was only the most extreme case.

Even as such fantasy-dimensions fell away (as visionaries lost ground to bureaucrats), a more general affinity for vast projects persisted, reflecting in part, no doubt, the daunting scope of the Soviet endeavor as a whole. The sheer rapidity of the country's industrialization both required and elicited, at certain levels, a sense that one was engaged in scaling impossible heights. Despite the intrigue, the bloodshed, and the humiliations of Stalin's rule, some of this sense remained alive even into the postwar era, although by that time its surviving traces were channeled mainly into the most narrowly technological directions, epitomized by space-flights.

Viewing the Soviet period as a whole prompts a number of reflections pertinent to any future socialist technology. The Soviet regime's most decisive shortfall, as a technological model, was its failure to breach the authoritarian structure of the productive enterprise.[23] The effects of this failure carried over into the bigger economic picture. The error, however, lay not in any rejection of

---

20 V.I. Lenin, *Collected Works* (Moscow: Progress Publishers), vol. 20 (1964 [1914]), 153f (scientific management), and vol. 27 (1965 [1918]), 271 ("iron discipline"). See also my essay "Workers' Control and Revolution," in Immanuel Ness and Dario Azzellini, eds., *Ours to Master and to Own: Workers' Control from the Commune to the Present* (Chicago: Haymarket Books, 2011) reprinted as Ch. 7 of Wallis, *Socialist Practice*.

21 Lenin, *Collected Works* vol. 27, 248f.

22 Leon Trotsky, *Literature and Revolution* (New York: Russell & Russell, 1957 [1925]), 254.

23 Harry Braverman, *Labor and Monopoly Capital: The Degradation of Work in the Twentieth Century* (New York: Monthly Review Press, 1974), 22. See esp. Michael A. Lebowitz, *The Contradictions of "Real Socialism"* (New York:

capitalist practice, but rather in not rejecting it enough. With managerial power fully preserved, an enterprise's success or failure continued to hinge disproportionately on the apparent performance of a single individual. This directly contradicted both the intent and the operation of socialist planning. The corollary to managerial power, in securing plan-fulfillment, was the assignment of financial rewards or penalties to the manager. Such incentives created powerful inducements for managers to try to protect themselves by overstating their input-needs and understating their output-targets, thereby setting in motion an intricate spiral of second-guessing, over-supervision, and corrupt shortcuts.[24] Although a planning system was nominally in force, the undemocratic structure of its components—of its outlying units as much as its central body—prevented it from functioning effectively. Capitalist-oriented critics were thus right in pointing to the system's arbitrariness but wrong in failing to see the roots of this arbitrariness in what had been left untouched from the capitalist past.

A similar pattern of contradiction underlies Soviet performance (and that of most other first-epoch regimes) with regard to the natural environment.[25] On the one hand, the same forces that encouraged capitalist-type production relations also led to a bias in favor of breakneck growth. Central planning reinforced the negative environmental impact of this bias to the degree that it encouraged oversized projects and insulated policymakers from local concerns. On the other hand, by partly freeing industry from market constraints, the system may have cushioned some enterprises against pressure toward excessive cost-cutting. Several other factors also tended to mitigate environmentally adverse practices. On the production side, the obligation to maintain full employment reduced some of the incentive to use fuel-intensive labor-saving technologies. In the sphere of consumption, certain of the characteristic

---

Monthly Review Press, 2012), and my review in *Socialism and Democracy*, 26:3 (November 2012) reprinted in Wallis, *Socialist Practice*, 88-93..

24 For background on the Soviet planning process, see e.g. Alec Nove, *The Soviet Economic System*, 3rd ed. (Boston: Allen & Unwin, 1986), as well as numerous articles by Hillel Ticktin in *Critique: A Journal of Soviet Studies and Socialist Theory*.

25 This paragraph draws heavily on James O'Connor, *Natural Causes: Essays in Ecological Marxism* (New York: Guilford Press, 1998), 257-64.

energy-wasting pursuits of late capitalism—e.g., those associated with suburbia and advertising—could be avoided. At the same time, an adequate system of social welfare preempted the environmental depredations associated with Third-World poverty. In sum, despite the well known ecological disasters of the Soviet bloc, it is possible to assert (a) that there were positive achievements as well[26] and (b) that these would have been greater were it not for the external threats. Moreover, even the admitted disasters pale in comparison with those inflicted in various parts of the world, since 1945, by US military assaults.[27]

Overall, first-epoch socialism remained unable to transcend the longstanding capitalist contradiction between technological and social progress. Such technological advances as it made were under the more or less direct stimulus of the capitalist presence, whether in the form of external dangers, financial incentives, or familiar managerial habit. Whatever counteracting influence was exercised by socialist norms was thus typically understood in its negative aspect, i.e., as the refusal to embrace certain technologies that had become commonplace in the capitalist world. In the perspective of Marx's categories, this resulted in a situation of extreme irony: a system identified with "socialism" came to be viewed as a fetter on the development of productive forces.[28] Attacks directed initially at a cumbersome planning process or at insufficient openness to new ideas escalated rapidly during the Gorbachev years (1985-91), so that by the time of his departure, an unabashed return to capitalism came to be seen as a forward rather than a backward step. The

---

26 See John Bellamy Foster, "Late Soviet Ecology and the Planetary Crisis," *Monthly Review* 67:2 (June 2015). On positive achievements, see also Richard Levins, "How Cuba Is Going Ecological," *Capitalism Nature Socialism*, 16:3 (September 2005).

27 The military dimension of environmental devastation is often left out of systematic treatments, but see Victor Wallis, "Socialism, Ecology, and Democracy: Toward a Strategy of Conversion," in Chronis Polychroniou, ed., *Socialism: Crisis and Renewal* (Westport, CT: Praeger, 1993), esp. 152f, 162, and Gar Smith (ed.), *The War and Environment Reader* (Charlottesville, VA: Just World Books, 2017).

28 Political leaders, without using this exact language, nonetheless focused continuously on institutional obstacles to technological innovation. See, e.g., Mikhail Gorbachev, *Perestroika: New Thinking for Our Country and the World*, updated ed. (New York: Harper & Row, 1988), 78-84. For an analysis along similar lines, see Manuel Castells, *End of Millennium* [vol. 3 of *The Information Age: Economy, Society and Culture*](Oxford: Blackwell, 1998), esp. 5-9, 26-37.

associated euphoria in capitalist circles gave an immense spur to capital's congenital privatizing impulses. After all, if "socialism" had failed, why not do away with all traces of its influence?

The Left's relatively weak response to this push reflects in part a hesitance—stemming in many cases from lack of expertise—to confront issues of technology. But does this then mean that all possibility of technological advance must be entrusted to capital? Does one socialist failure, even if epochal in scope, mean that no other socialist approach has a chance? Have capitalist relations somehow ceased to constitute a fetter on any technological improvement whatsoever? This can only appear to be true if socialists fail to advance their own technological goals. If we have been slow in doing this, it is partly because not enough of us have grasped the full extent to which the technology developed by capital, far from being neutral, is indeed, no matter who runs it, a preeminently capitalist technology.[29]

TOWARD A SOCIALIST TECHNOLOGY, 1

What is socialist technology? It is more than just the technology that happens to prevail in a society that is no longer capitalist. It may also include particular technologies which have existed in the form of only partly developed enclaves within capitalism, enclaves which may in turn bear the traces of precapitalist formations. This is to say that there is no such thing as a technology that is generically and exclusively socialist. What defines a technology (on whatever scale) as socialist is simply its compatibility with—and its ability to further—the overall goals of socialism. Insofar as these goals relate to technology, they emerge clearly from what remained deficient in first-epoch practice, namely, commitment to social equality and to ecological health. A socialist technology, then, is one that is

---

29 Castells, *End of Millennium*, 338ff, recognizes but downplays the capitalist foundations of "information society." For efforts to situate the new technologies in terms of the specific interests generating them, see Davis et al., *Cutting Edge*, and Robert W. McChesney, Ellen Meiksins Wood, and John Bellamy Foster, eds., *Capitalism and the Information Age: The Political Economy of the Global Communication Revolution* (New York: Monthly Review Press, 1998).

grounded in these two requirements, both of which are served by a more collective approach to production and consumption.[30]

The ecological component of socialist technology deserves to be underscored. The class power of capital has been based, from the beginning, on unrestricted access to—and often control over—natural as well as human resources.[31] The expansion of capitalism has been historically coterminous with its subjection of the natural world. The economic conquest of every country and the private or corporate appropriation of all natural resources go hand in hand. The liberation of a region or the establishment of "protected zones" (e.g., of forest) constitute similar orders of restraint so far as private investors are concerned. More fundamentally, given that human beings are themselves part of the natural world, and that the planet's carrying capacity has already been reached if not exceeded, the further expansion of capital turns every "natural disaster" into a human disaster. A technology which breaks up biodiversity thus also, by the same token, narrows the scope for human well-being. Given the tougher economic choices imposed by greater overall scarcity, egalitarian criteria increasingly become a condition for our common survival.[32]

---

30 It is worth recalling that collective approaches are by no means new; on the contrary, they have deeper anthropological roots than do capitalist individualism and capitalist-type productivism. Their socialist incarnation differs from earlier ones only in having to reckon with capitalism as its point of departure. Authentic progress, however, does not rule out the absorption or resurrection of certain precapitalist traits. Marx's whole discussion of alienation points up the aberrational character of capitalist society; in this light, a degree of overlap between socialist and precapitalist approaches should be expected, notably, in their common aversion to commodification. The relevant literature on these themes is vast, but see esp. William Morris's 1884 essay "Art and Socialism" (in A.L. Morton, ed., *Political Writings of William Morris* [New York: International Publishers, 1973], 109-33), and Dolores Hayden, *The Grand Domestic Revolution: A History of Feminist Designs for American Homes, Neighborhoods, and Cities* (Cambridge, MA: MIT Press, 1981).

31 The interpenetration of these two dimensions is forcefully highlighted in John Bellamy Foster, "The Communist Manifesto and the Environment," in Leo Panitch and Colin Leys (eds.), *Socialist Register 1998: The Communist Manifesto Now* (New York: Monthly Review Press, 1998), 169-89. See also Ian Angus, *Facing the Anthropocene: Fossil Capitalism and the Crisis of the Earth System* (New York: Monthly Review Press, 2016).

32 This is widely acknowledged even by writers who shy away from confronting class issues; thus Herman Daly, in *Beyond Growth: The Economics of Sustainable Development* (Boston: Beacon Press, 1996), 15, cites the increased need for "sharing."

To define a socialist technology in terms of what it must resist or what it may accomplish, however, is only a first step. The more difficult and politically challenging task is that of description. At this point we need to confront the problem of "expertise." The hegemony of capitalist technology rests not just on its technical feats but also on a whole ideological nexus. Part of this consists in the various patterns of dependence and addiction that the technology fosters, but a big part of it also lies in the assumption that ordinary people are incapable of seriously addressing technological questions. This assumption is nothing more than a self-fulfilling prophecy of capital, rooted in the separation of conception (which is entrusted to management) from execution (which is assigned to workers); its rejection is long overdue. I do not mean by this that technical training and expertise are unimportant; obviously they are vital to both the discussion of projects and their implementation, but this does not make expertise alone the sole proper basis for shaping social policy. No technology that requires people to change their way of life can be implemented unless the people themselves support it. The necessary participatory mechanisms need to be built, but at the same time the consideration and investigation of technological problems has to be promoted until it permeates every level of society.

A technology may be discerned in anything from a single device to a whole network of relations, involving, among other things, machines, resources, producers, and users.[33] It also encompasses particular configurations of space, such as patterns of vegetation on agricultural land or the construction layout of communities. The totality of a technology can never be neutral (in terms of its impact on social relations), but this is not necessarily the case for every particular component of the technology. Many if not most devices have a dual potential, conditional upon such questions as how numerous they are, who has access to them, and what impact their production or their use has upon the natural environment and upon human health (mental as well as physical). The automobile, for example,

---

33 For a wide-ranging treatment of these issues, see Richard E. Sclove, *Democracy and Technology* (New York: Guilford Press, 1995); for the background in Marxist theory, see Bertell Ollman, *Dialectical Investigations* (New York: Routledge, 1993).

functions in some parts of the world as the almost exclusive vehicle for local travel. In this capacity, its virtues from the standpoint of capital and its disastrous impact from the standpoints of resource-use, health, and community are sufficiently well known.[34] This does not mean, however, that the device itself is without positive potential; it means only that it must be severely circumscribed: reduced in numbers by one or two orders of magnitude, denied entry to certain zones, and placed at the disposal of a given individual or group only in accordance with certain well-defined and socially egalitarian guidelines.

The alternative technologies to that of the automobile already exist at the level of devices but not yet at the contextual level. There are bicycles, for instance, but not enough people use them routinely because the distances are too great or the routes are unsafe. There are train and bus services, but not of sufficient scope or quality (especially in North America) to accommodate needs that go beyond those satisfied by bicycles. Relative prices to the user also come into play, as do cultural preferences (e.g., the whole complex of impulses associated with being "in the driver's seat"). All such conditioning factors, however habitual or unconscious they might have become, reflect deliberate policy made at some level, whether by private or public entities (or by some combination of the two). It is important to stress that the overall technology is very much affected by decisions or assumptions which, on the face of it, are not at all "technological," for example, the very idea that one's day-to-day physical mobility should depend on one's clearing a threshold of age, dexterity, or income, or the very idea of traffic flow as a process that routinely entails intervention by the criminal justice system.[35]

To call attention to such contextual conditions is not to downplay the more narrowly technological issues; it is only to indicate that they cannot be usefully debated except with the larger setting

---

34 See, e.g., Peter Freund and George Martin, *The Ecology of the Automobile* (Montreal: Black Rose Books, 1993).

35 Scores of police-shootings of African Americans have begun with traffic-stops for petty infractions (e.g., a broken tail-light). Fines for such violations are often a major line-item in municipal budgets. See Henry A. Giroux, *America's Addiction to Terrorism* (New York: Monthly Review Press, 2016), Ch. 5.

in mind. In the present case, such issues clearly come into play in connection with the quality of the trains and buses. For example, how fast, how dependably, and how cleanly can they run? How can they be separated from human traffic? How can their space-needs be minimized so as to restore as much surface-area as possible to trees and plants?

The very idea of a transportation system without breakdowns, crashes, and highway patrols (let alone endless acreage consumed by pavement) sounds almost like science fiction; but the specific technologies it requires are already available. What is lacking is a larger framework within which those technologies could be combined.[36] The principle is simple enough. Thus, for instance, given a properly built machine, the preventive maintenance needed to avoid breakdowns is known. If the machine is owned by an individual, however (as with a private car), there is no way of guaranteeing that such maintenance will be performed. What would otherwise appear as just a technical matter thus becomes a social issue. The technical task requires for its reliable accomplishment a certain social framework. The social framework is therefore integral to the technology. It is at this level that "technology" takes on its total or global aspect, i.e., that of an entire network of relations. If the relations in question are grounded in equality and ecology, what we then have, finally, is a socialist technology.

Getting There

The implications of socialist technology, and of the struggle to attain it, are of course far-reaching. Here I offer a few summary reflections.

1. Socialist technology, taken as a whole, would give us a different world. Taken in its component parts, however, it is already present. The so-far unmet challenge of fusing those components—drawn, as we have seen, from pre-capitalist as well as capitalist times—is

---

36 For examples in areas other than transit, see Burstyn, "Dystopia" (n. 10), 234. For ongoing discussion of these topics, see https://climateandcapitalism.com/ and https://scienceforthepeople.org/

a political one. Its single indispensable requirement is the massive and organized participation of the whole population in the technological debate. So long as this fails to occur, the market will continue to rule, and people acting individually will embrace damaging practices which, as a conscious collectivity, they would be prepared to oppose.[37]

2. Much of the constructive thinking about technological alternatives has been carried out under the watchword not of socialism but of democracy.[38] "Democratic technology" efforts have opened doors, prompted useful insights, and called particular attention to a long tradition of communities committed to keeping technology as their servant rather than allowing it—or whomever controlled it—to become their master. Socialist thinking deepens the democratic vision, however, in two complementary ways. On the one hand it directs attention to the underlying precondition—the removal of class antagonism—which makes democratic collaboration possible. On the other, it reminds us, based on bitter experience, that no community is an "island"; even the most perfect local institutions can be undermined by external pressures and attacks.

3. In the effort to promote worldwide popular discussion of technological alternatives, the goal of cutting greenhouse gases is a point of departure. Within this framework, the most urgent requirement is to shift the focus of attention away from national aggregates of energy-use and toward the impact of distinct economic sectors. Then negotiators can dispense with fruitless wrangling over which countries should be granted more "pollution rights" and can directly tackle the question of which economic activities—including those of the military, financial, commercial, and advertising sectors—have greater or lesser relevance to satisfying basic human needs.[39] This

---

37 The isolated individual is largely at the mercy of the market; the organized collectivity sets limits to the market. That is why "market socialism" is a contradiction in terms. The social-psychological underpinnings to this observation are well described by Bertell Ollman in his edited collection, *Market Socialism: The Debate Among Socialists* (New York: Routledge, 1998), 83ff. See my review of this book in *New Political Science* 22:2 (June 2000), reprinted in Wallis, *Socialist Practice*, 83-88.

38 For example, Sclove, *Democracy and Technology*.

39 We examined the distinction between wasteful and needed activities in Chapter 1.

kind of approach makes the most sense not only in ecological terms but also in terms of restoring a healthy internationalism to popular awareness, given that the wasteful sectors in every country are of the same type. Since the relative weight of these sectors, however, is greater in the richer countries, curbing the activities in question would at the same time have the redistributive effect—in terms of energy-use—that is justly demanded by Third-World advocates.

4. Mass participation in technological debate is necessary in order not only to introduce new approaches but also to keep them on track. Socialist technology is indeed revolutionary, and as such requires intense popular involvement, on a permanent basis. Regrettably, "institutionalization" has acquired, like "progress," a bad reputation on the Left, because it has most often been used to consolidate hierarchical power. The alternative of controlling or limiting hierarchy, however, is no less dependent upon creating appropriate institutions. The new task will be to establish for the first time a genuine planning process. Recognizing that decentralization is desirable[40] does not mean positing that national, regional, and global coordination—particularly on environmental matters— can be dispensed with. First-epoch planning did not deserve the name because of its excessive reliance, in practice, on a speculative back-up system, based on the hoarding and release of scarce supplies. Democratically based planning, by contrast, apart from tapping people's energies and addressing their needs, would for the first time assure full disclosure of all pertinent information.

5. Taking into account the complexity of the planning process, there would clearly be a role in it for some of the specific devices of "information technology" developed under capitalism. Such devices could prove to be essential not only for the plan's initial elaboration, but also for coordinating popular inputs and for adjusting to changing circumstances.[41] In this sense, it could be said that even

---

40 As argued, for example, in Kirkpatrick Sale, *Human Scale* (New York: Coward, McCann & Geoghegan, 1980).

41 On the possible applications of computer technology in organizing this information, see Andy Pollack, "Information Technology and Socialist Self-Management," in McChesney et al., *Capitalism and the Information Age*, 219-35. On the

the most recent stage of capitalist development has had something positive to add to the groundwork for socialism. (This much may be granted independently of anything we might say about the ecological and social destructiveness that has also marked this period.) But the socialist framework would alter beyond recognition the larger network of relations within which the devices in question would be applied. Information would no longer be treated as a commodity subject to privatization and monopoly; innovation would cease to be regarded as an end in itself; and economies of labor-time would no longer be used as a weapon against the working class.[42]

6. To imagine all this happening may seem wildly ambitious, but it gives some idea of the scope available—and indeed crying out—for true progress. Recent capitalist technological advances prompted the ironic argument that humanity's first, flawed steps toward socialism were obstructing the flow of high-powered market-driven innovations (a point that for some years now has been greedily repeated with eyes on Cuba).[43] We can respond to this, however, at two levels. Conceptually, we can remind ourselves that not all innovations are healthy, and that true creativity lies in responding to the most fundamental needs rather than in devising ever-new mechanisms for amassing wealth. And in terms of practical goals, we can project the historic achievement that will be consummated if and when capital's vast and still galloping expansion of pavement—epitomized by "big box" stores with their vast parking lots—begins to retreat in the face of a massive and resolute restoration of natural diversity.

---

other hand, claims regarding computer technology's supposed conservationist potential must be treated with caution; see, in Chapter 4 (below), the section on "Information/Communication/Education."

42 See Tessa Morris-Suzuki, "Capitalism in the Computer Age," in Davis et al., *Cutting Edge*, 57-71.

43 A promotional brochure issued in 1999 by the monthly business publication *Cuba News* thus entices its prospective $399-per-year subscribers with the headline, "Get Ready for the Next Cuban Revolution." The grimness of this prospect, from our present standpoint, is underscored by the truly progressive steps described in Peter M. Rosset, "Alternative Agriculture Works: The Case of Cuba," *Monthly Review*, 50:3 (July/August 1998), 137-46. See also Richard Levins, "How Cuba Is Going Ecological," *Capitalism Nature Socialism*, 16:3 (September 2005).

3

Technology, Ecology, and Socialist Renewal

Global protests against international trade agreements, along with the World Social Forum (an almost annual event since 2001), have called attention to the urgency of developing what we might call a "people's technology." A central focus of concern has been the biotech sector, but the issues posed by information technology lie not far behind. Both can be seen, at least in their current mode of development, as instruments for expanding and deepening the control exercised by capital, over the natural world and human society alike. An alternative political/economic agenda requires an alternative technological agenda, from several angles. These include: reducing costs, absorbing labor-power, overcoming alienation, and halting despoliation of the environment.

There is no conceptual difference between a people's technology and a socialist technology. My own preference is to use the two terms interchangeably, depending on the immediate context of the discussion. The "people's" dimension reminds us that our vision is one of democratic control, while the reference to socialism reminds us that you can't have democracy, especially in an area with so profound an impact as technology, as long as a capitalist ruling class is calling the shots.

Marxism has had, from its beginnings, a defining interest in technological issues. What were, after all, the preeminent "forces of production" in Marx's time, if not the new technologies unleashed by the development of "modern industry"? And what better basis do we now have for the critique of first-epoch socialism than Harry Braverman's admonition—well before the 1989 collapse, but echoed subsequently by philosopher István Mészáros—to treat the Communist movement's long-unquestioned focus on gaining state power as a tragic detour from the task of embracing Marx's much broader assault on capitalist power-relations? And finally, what is it that drove this broader critique if not precisely Marx's analysis of the forces and relations of capitalist production?[1]

The problem, however, as Braverman and others have suggested, is that the scenario of technological transformation is too easily preempted by a fixation on achieving and exercising state power. We grow up thinking that the major outside force in our lives is the government. In the actual history of workers' movements, therefore, it is hardly surprising that the protagonists came to view the winning of state power as a climactic step along the road to a better world. The more this step eluded them and the more ferociously it was blocked, the more daunting its eventual attainment was bound to appear. And when state power did finally come into the hands of revolutionists, in Soviet Russia, what could seem more vital to them, in the face of concerted counterrevolutionary attacks, than simply to hang onto it? It was in this setting, of course, that Lenin articulated what his successors would take for granted, namely that workers' control of industry—an integral component to any notion of a "people's technology"—could not possibly be on the immediate agenda of the ruling party.[2]

At the same time, as if all this were not enough of a setback, we find in the ongoing development of capitalism a continuous process whereby the broad applications of technology are devised at an ever greater remove from the general population. The achievements of the newest technologies become ever more astounding—whether for their sophistication (e.g., communications systems) or their perversity (weapons systems, factory fishing vessels, security systems)—

---

1   Harry Braverman, *Labor and Monopoly Capital: The Degradation of Work in the Twentieth Century* (New York: Monthly Review Press, 1974), 8-24; István Mészáros, *Beyond Capital: Towards a Theory of Transition* (New York: Monthly Review Press, 1995), esp. 615ff.

2   V.I. Lenin, "On the Immediate Tasks of the Soviet Government" (April 1918), in *Selected Works*. 1-vol. ed. (New York: International Publishers, 1971), esp. 424. See my chapter "Workers' Control and Revolution," in Immanuel Ness and Dario Azzellini, eds., *Ours to Master and to Own: Workers' Control from the Commune to the Present* (Chicago: Haymarket, 2011), reprinted as Ch. 7 of Victor Wallis, *Socialist Practice: Histories and Theories* (London: Palgrave Macmillan, 2020).

while the tasks imposed at the lowest levels of the work-hierarchy, if they do not disappear altogether, become ever more limited in the demands they place on the laborer's skills. People's subjective sense of their technological competence thereupon shrinks even further, in a classic cycle of self-fulfilling prophecy.

What I want to argue is that the development of organized popular intelligence about technology is an essential component to the task of creating and maintaining a viable socialism. There are new reasons for thinking about this goal which have nothing to do with the fate of certain past regimes. These "new reasons" reflect not only recent developments in capitalism—which include heightened devastation (war), polarization, and technological displacement, as well as vastly accelerated ecological breakdown—but also some insufficiently noted achievements that belong squarely in the socialist tradition. For socialism today, therefore, there are not just fresh challenges; there is also untapped potential. To illustrate this with regard to technology, I propose to sketch out certain preliminary considerations along the following lines: 1) the nature of the technological competence that needs to be diffused; 2) prior experience of situations in which popular technological competence has been encouraged; 3) the interplay of technological issues with social or class issues in formulating sound ecological policy; and 4) what a socialist technology might achieve and how it might function.

What Kind of Technological Competence?

The popular technological competence that is now lacking can be sought in either of two directions: in the recovery of skills that are disappearing or in the acquisition of the latest new skills. Neither of these pursuits precludes the other, but they have decidedly different implications.

The "new" skills appear initially as the ones that are habitually emphasized, typically in the form of slogans like "a computer on every school-desk!" Whatever the scope of their diffusion, there remains the significant question of whether the recipients will evolve merely into users/consumers of the technology or whether they will also become its shapers. The outcome of this choice depends on the degree to which the technology is simply "handed down" to the recipients, who then receive it as isolated agents, or the degree to which, on the contrary, the technology is seized upon in an organized way and mastered as a potential power-resource. The adoption of this more purposeful approach could ultimately affect not only the use made of existing devices but also the directions taken in the invention of new ones—such as, for example, devices to reduce dependence on ecologically hazardous energy-sources.

The capacity to take such an approach depends in turn on a disposition to subordinate instrumental expertise to a larger vision. The vision in question need not initially refer to an alternative structure of economic power, although it could open the way to such a project. The starting point would more likely be some particular change in production- and consumption-patterns, of which one's own efforts are a part. While such changes are a routine component of capitalist "progress" (albeit with profit-driven parameters, as in the scenario of turning every adult into a motorist), the challenge in terms of a "people's technology" is to find them in the general population and grounded in basic needs. This is where the resurrection of "endangered skills" comes in. The best illustration of such skills is the soil-conservation practices of peasant agriculture.[3] These combine the key traits of being on the one hand broadly diffused—part of the general culture—and, on the other, clearly shaped by a commitment to provide for future generations.

In countries such as India, the peasant sector has to some extent been drawn into a conscious struggle against the forces that would skim off the fruits of those skills while destroying the matrix in which they evolved. This struggle has taken the form of protests against bio-engineered seeds.[4] By contrast, in those countries where the displacement of the peasantry occurred at an earlier time, the effort at retrieval must necessarily rely in part on what can be learned—more likely from an academic starting point—by

---

3   For my discussion of peasant agriculture, I am indebted especially to the chapter on "Agricultural Ecology" in Yrjö Haila and Richard Levins, *Humanity and Nature: Ecology, Science and Society* (London: Pluto Press, 1992).

4   Vandana Shiva, *Biopiracy: The Plunder of Nature and Knowledge* (Boston: South End Press, 1997), 124ff.

individuals possessed of a strong social awareness but lacking roots
in the culture that nurtured the original skills.

The task of recombining such expertise with the capacity to
implement it in the interests of the people is, in a sense, the classic
function of a revolutionary political organization. What is revolutionary, within the organization itself, is precisely its breaking down
of the social barriers which would otherwise separate those who
respectively embody these currently distinct kinds of skill.[5] Only
if the organization can do this now will the society be able to do it
later.

The issue is essentially one of demystifying expertise, and it
involves adjustments from both directions. On the one hand, the
highly trained people need to be extricated from the exclusive
community of their peers; they should distance themselves as much
as possible from the stereotypical experts of whom one can say
(as does one of John le Carré's characters quoted by Howard Zinn)
that they serve, in their bureaucratic "neutrality," as our jailers, our
torturers, our executioners.[6] They need instead to internalize an
ethic of responsiveness to the concerns of ordinary people, and this
can only happen if their day-to-day existence includes situations in
which appropriate—i.e., hierarchy-defying—interactions occur on
a routine basis. This is likely to point again to a role for organizations: to generate not just social situations but also specific projects
requiring the collaboration of people of diverse skill-levels.

From the side of the general population, what has to be overcome is an odd though familiar amalgam of deference and disdain.
In its place should arise a willingness to view the advanced training
with which others may be endowed simply as an instrument they
have acquired rather than as an attribute of "distinction." Otherwise, in the contorted rationalizations by which people sometimes
reconcile themselves to apathy, they will view those who have what
they lack as being in some way alien: privileged in their capaci-

---

5   Thus Richard Levins and Richard Lewontin call for "undermining the class
     barriers between full-time scientists and farmers and the mutual suspicion that
     accompanies it." *The Dialectical Biologist* (Cambridge, MA: Harvard University
     Press, 1985), 222.

6   Howard Zinn, *Declarations of Independence: Cross-Examining American Ideol-
     ogy* (New York: HarperCollins, 1995), 6.

ties—"elitists" trained in the best schools—but remote from ordinary humanity. This is the most dangerous of mindsets—the stuff of fascist appeals[7]—but in that very aspect it suggests the promise implicit in the alternative. People who can respect knowledge without being deferential to those who have it, are the ones who are capable of the kind of self-transformation that is integral to any remaking of society.

What people come to know, then, and what abilities they cultivate, are less important than the way the process comes about. Still, the revolutionary organizations must do more than just promote a culture of equality. They can introduce specific measures geared to spreading technological competence. So far as devices are concerned, they can demand that the "new" ones spawned by the existing order—notably, in the sphere of communications—be made equally accessible to all. More importantly, however, they can create settings, such as "short courses" like those offered in socialist schools or "free universities," in which people who have been trained but discarded by established institutions are given an opportunity to share their skills with others whose stake in the established order is even slimmer.[8] In a similar but less formal way, labor unions might play a role of bringing together workers from different parts of a single enterprise with the explicit purpose of having them come to grasp, as a result of their exchanges, the totality of the operation to which they have been lending their separate efforts.

All such processes, regardless of the specific skills of the people involved in them, constitute the nuclei for any eventual society-wide decisionmaking practice in matters of technology. The very range of experience reflected in the different mixes of participants is what assures—given a sufficiently grand underlying vision—that new and inspiring collective projects will emerge.

---

7   Catherine McNicol Stock, *Rural Radicals: Righteous Rage in the American Grain* (Ithaca, NY: Cornell University Press, 1996).

8   The radical political potential of this type of education is implicit in Nick Dyer-Witheford, *Cyber-Marx: Cycles and Circuits of Struggle in High-Technology Capitalism* (Urbana: University of Illinois Press, 1999), esp. his discussion of "Communication Commons," 201ff.

THE POSSIBILITY OF COLLECTIVE INITIATIVE

One of the most persistent myths about capitalism is that it is the only framework that can foster technological innovation. This assumption deserves to be challenged from several angles. In the first place, innovation is not an end in itself. This fact, obvious enough on reflection, is largely buried in capitalism's public rhetoric; it needs to be loudly proclaimed. Not only is innovation not an intrinsic "good," but many innovations are decidedly harmful. The technology of destruction is only the most blatant example, as even supposedly beneficial innovations are often overshadowed by dubious side-effects, ranging from stress or disease at the individual level to resource-depletion and pollution at the level of the ecosphere. As Richard Levins put it, "...pesticides increase pests; hospitals are foci of infection; antibiotics give rise to new pathogens; flood control increases flood damage; and economic development increases poverty."[9]

To acknowledge all this is to raise the question of the degree to which the innovation that occurs within a capitalist setting deserves to be inherently identified with capitalism. It is important not to lose sight of the long-term duality between the capitalist aspect and the human aspect of everything that goes on in capitalist society. This duality parallels and in part reflects the distinction drawn by Marx between use-value and exchange-value. Use-value, because it does not readily lend itself to quantitative measurement, was often slighted in political debate (even by socialists), but it has pursued a kind of suppressed existence which is coming back to our attention now that its classic embodiments—air, water, soil, species-diversity—are increasingly threatened.[10] With regard to innovation, the use-value dimension serves to remind us that there is an ongoing basis for creative activity that exists and flourishes *despite* capitalism and not because of it. This is important in terms of our recog-

---

9   Richard Levins, "Ten Propositions on Science and Antiscience," in Andrew Ross, ed., *Science Wars* (Durham, NC: Duke University Press, 1996), 181. The concept of such "revenge effects" is applied to a broad range of examples in Edward Tenner, *Why Things Bite Back: Technology and the Revenge of Unintended Consequences* (New York: Random House, 1996).

10 Joel Kovel, *The Enemy of Nature: The End of Capitalism or the End of the World?* (London & New York: Zed Books, 2002), 40.

nition that while innovation is not necessarily good, it may well be good in some instances. What we can then suggest is that the basis for distinguishing negative from positive innovations is precisely the *degree* to which they are—or are not—shaped by the priorities of capital.[11]

This hypothesis is of enormous importance for a socialist technology, because it reminds us that we owe historical advances in technology less to "entrepreneurs" than to artisans or professionals or skilled workers.[12] Whatever the role of private initiative, "Innovation appears now, not primarily as a single event, but rather *as a process* [, in which] interactive learning and collective entrepreneurship are fundamental."[13] Many of the most dramatic breakthroughs (especially in communications) have depended on "the role of the state [in] funding the research that is basic to the new technologies."[14] In the United States, these are of course largely military, and in their objectives they fully reflect the interests of capital. Still, their institutional setting offers certain clear advantages over direct private sponsorship. The biggest of these in practice has been superior funding. Under more enlightened conditions, however, other advantages of publicly sponsored projects come to mind, notably (1) the free exchange of ideas, unencumbered by fears of disclosing "trade secrets," and (2) the option of public accountability. These

---

11 The emphasis on *degree* is important in this formulation. No innovation under capitalism can escape the formative impact of capital, but any *useful* innovation reflects at the same time influences *other than* those of capital, whether in its conception, its elaboration, or its application. This simply restates the point that capital views innovation through the prism of profit-potential, whereas the criterion of usefulness refers to considerations independent of profit.

12 The millennial evolution of agriculture is the characteristic though not the only example of this (Lynn White, Jr., *Medieval Technology and Social Change* [Oxford University Press, 1962]). On the role of artisans, see e.g. David Landes, *The Unbound Prometheus: Technological Change and Industrial Development in Western Europe from 1750 to the Present* (Cambridge University Press, 1969), 101.

13 Bengt-Ake Lundvall, *National Systems of Innovation: Towards a Theory of Innovation and Interactive Learning* (1992): Introduction, reprinted in Ben R. Martin & Paul Nightingale, eds., *The Political Economy of Science, Technology and Innovation* (Northampton, MA: Edward Elgar, 2000), 532.

14 Ulrich Hilpert, "The State, Science and Techno-Industrial Innovation," in *idem*, ed., *State Policies and Techno-Industrial Innovation* (London & New York: Routledge, 1992), 7.

observations suggest a greater potential for non-capitalist innovation than is commonly assumed.

But the more radical notion of linking the merits of innovations with their specific socioeconomic grounding does not yet seem to have been broadly considered. The evidence I have found in its favor relates mainly to the sphere of agriculture, for which there appears to be a particularly striking contrast between, on the one hand, the ecologically sensitive innovations of peasant, communal, and organic producers and, on the other, the toxic impositions of the agro-industrial complex. Biologist Barry Commoner, for example, persistently stressed the environmental preferability of production based on such natural materials as leather, rubber, and cotton over that of the whole petrochemical sector.[15] More generally, the promise of authentically socialist innovation would appear to lie above all in bringing to the fore the most urgent human needs and in finding new ways to utilize or apply already-known devices and procedures.[16]

Capitalism's ideological appropriation of the mantle of innovation is conceptually similar to its appropriation of democracy, freedom, and individuality, but it seems to have received much less critical analysis. After all, we can readily point to examples of capitalist-sponsored repression, and also of the often legendary struggles against it—from the free-speech struggles of early US labor history to the anti-dictatorial struggles of recent decades in such countries as Chile, Guatemala, South Africa, the Philippines, South Korea, and Indonesia. But whatever the harshness of capital's political arm, who can question capital's technological prowess? And wasn't it precisely in the technological arena that first-epoch socialism met its undoing? This is the assumption that concerns us here, for there has been no end to the citation of Chinese and Soviet leaders (most notably, the Soviet Union's last president, Mikhail Gorbachev) invoking capital's supposedly unanswerable technological claims.[17]

---

15   Barry Commoner, *The Poverty of Power: Energy and the Economic Crisis* (New York, Bantam Books, 1977), 194.

16   See my entry, "Innovation," in the Historical-Critical Dictionary of Marxism; English text in *Historical Materialism* 16:3 (2008).

17   See Mikhail Gorbachev, *Perestroika: New Thinking for Our Country and the World* (Harper & Row, 1988), 78-84; Manuel Castells, *End of Millennium* [vol.

Even from the standpoint of those—especially in Russia—who now bemoan the disappearance of their personal security, there appear to be few grounds for challenging capital's supremacy in the matter of economic initiative.

Our critique in this area needs to assimilate and propagate the insights of two largely separate traditions: that of environmentalism, and that of workers' self-management. From environmentalism, we draw not only a reference-point for judging capitalist innovations, but also a network of positive projects pointing toward innovation in hitherto neglected areas. Although environmentally-grounded innovations may in certain dimensions take the form of commod-ities—such as solar-powered calculators—which respond to mar-ket-demand, the more significant innovations are likely to have an organizational component entailing shifts and displacements for which the market cannot possibly be expected to give the appro-priate signals. What market-player, for example, can signal the need for long-term replenishment of the soil? How can market-related behavior play any more than an incidental role in the hypothetical switchover from automobile-clogged conurbations to communities built around a mix of mass transit and non-motorized individual locomotion?[18]

Clearly both these projects—restoration of the soil and libera-tion of the cities—require an enormous fund of creative initiative. The technology involved will consist only to a subsidiary degree of any particular new devices. Far more important, without ceasing to be a dimension of technology, are the patterns defining the interac-tion of the various sites, devices, and agents that will make up the new system.[19] The requisite "initiative" for introducing such a system will far surpass any conceivable capitalist innovation, if for no other reason than that the latter does not need to consider as a dimen-sion of its output the totality of the social/ecological nexus. This totality is precisely the guidepost for socialist innovation. While its

---

3 of *The Information Age: Economy, Society and Culture*] (Oxford: Blackwell, 1998), 5-9, 26-37.

18 In the words of architect Paolo Soleri, "The theory that soft capitalism or 'green capitalism' will eliminate waste is wrong.... More fuel-efficient automobiles will mean more of them, more roads and more sprawl." Soleri, "The Frugal City" [interview], *New Perspectives Quarterly*, 17:4 (Fall 2000), 5.

19 See Chapter 2 of this book.

contours may be present in the imaginations of any number of individuals, its translation into concrete projects, given the manifold repercussions of each component, can only be undertaken with the active participation of every affected sector (on the understanding that some of the human participants will speak for affected species or configurations of the natural environment).[20]

This is the point at which the environmental tradition intersects with the tradition of worker control. The point of convergence is the notion of democracy as a fount of practical initiative. The potential benefits of such an approach have often been suggested even within capitalist enterprises, although abruptly terminated when they began to show that the capitalist managers were no longer needed.[21] Under revolutionary conditions, initiative from below goes further and directly promotes concerns that transcend the horizon of particular economic units. This was one of the consistent patterns in the anarchist collectives that sprang up throughout Eastern Spain during the Civil War period (1936-39). It took shape not only in the consolidation of production units (overcoming wasteful proliferation), but also in arrangements for crossover labor-time between agriculture and other sectors.[22] In the later experience of revolutionary Cuba, similarly, liberation from class constraints enabled people to perceive pro-environmental policies as being matters of universal benefit, thereby making possible "rational decisions about how to use nature."[23] In both the Spanish and the Cuban cases, whatever their institutional differences, the political setting facilitated certain indisputable advances in the use and conservation of resources.

---

20 See David M. Kotz, "Socialism and Innovation," *Science & Society*, 66:1 (Spring 2002), esp. his discussion of the fact that "Major innovations typically have victims..." (105).

21 Juan G. Espinosa and Andrew S. Zimbalist, *Economic Democracy: Workers' Participation in Chilean Industry, 1970-1973* (New York: Academic Press, 1978), 20-24.

22 Thus, as reported by Gaston Leval, "construction workers who were without work would go to help the land workers and when necessary the opposite would happen." Leval, *Collectives in the Spanish Revolution* (London: Freedom Press, 1975), 108

23 Haila and Levins, *Humanity and Nature*, 250.

TECHNOLOGICAL ISSUES AND CLASS ISSUES
IN ECOLOGICAL POLICY

The human impact on the environment reflects the sum-total of human productive activity. Ecological policy has to be understood, accordingly, not as the narrow province of state agencies explicitly concerned with things like species-protection or resource-preservation. To the contrary, it is the continuous outcome—whether intended or unintended—of the actions of every entity, be it public or "private," that affects by either its policy decisions or its practices the consumption of raw materials, the burning of fuel, or the disposal of waste. Obviously there are gradations of responsibility, and the question of scale is important. What is not important is the official rubric under which the outcomes are arrived at.

While all this may appear self-evident, it is remarkable how far removed it is from general public awareness. Insofar as people acknowledge some abstractly conceived "environmental crisis," there is almost reflex support, at least in the United States, for the most narrowly technological responses, along the lines of improved fuel-efficiency, or perhaps "alternative energy sources"—although with little attention to the level of commitment that a serious push in the latter direction would require. What is almost completely missing from public discourse is any scenario of selectively curbing those "end-uses" against whose aggregate the need for energy—whether efficient or inefficent; "clean" or dirty—is reckoned.

This deficiency reflects a productivist bias which is integral to capitalism. Capitalist ideology has always tended to legitimize any economic pursuit for which a market-demand could be found (or generated). In this light, the ecologically grounded call for prioritizing some types of production over others appears arbitrary and inadmissible—a problem that is only enhanced by the obvious difficulty of achieving consensus as to which productive activities ought to be favored. And yet how will it be possible, in the absence of such prioritization, to reduce energy-requirements in a way that does justice to the configuration of real needs?

To deliberate, in a policy context, on human need is to return to the basic framework of socialist thinking. It is to definitively reject the conflation of need with the market-oriented concept of "demand." Once need is no longer calibrated in accordance with purchasing power, however, new criteria are required. Ecological concerns can here take their place side by side with long-recognized fundamental rights in the economic, educational, and cultural spheres.[24] These will then serve as the guidelines under which productive activities are sponsored. The application of such guidelines will require that any particular project be considered in relation to the totality of other commitments and of available resources, taking into account also, of course, the variety of possible ways in which such factors can be combined. In ecological parlance, this is known as a holistic approach. In political economy, it is known as planning.

Although planning is the most natural of human activities (being virtually a defining trait of our species), its practice by public authorities, on a society-wide basis and at the national level, still suffers from a stigma deriving from a single historical experience. Stalin's repressive practice, viewed through the lens of socialism's detractors, is thought by many, even now, to hold some sort of patent on the idea of large-scale planning. This assumption is a dangerous relic of Cold War demagogy. It could permanently obstruct ecological conversion. Partly for this very reason, but for other reasons as well, the methods it evokes can be no part of the process envisioned here. Repression emerges as a tactic only when the government has no hope of getting a majority behind its policies. Radical ecological measures, by contrast, presuppose majority support as a condition for becoming real options. This is because of the link between ecological soundness and the devolution of many aspects of implementation to local, decentralized units, where it depends on the active involvement of the communities in question.[25]

Underlying this scenario is the objective interest of the majority in an ecological agenda. This interest must eventually translate into conscious support. How to accelerate that process is the permanent challenge to all Left activists. What works in their favor is the

---

24 See the Universal Declaration of Human Rights (1948).

25 For a variety of socialist perspectives on planning (rejecting both the "command" model and the "market" model), see the special issue of *Science & Society* (Spring 2002), *Building Socialism Theoretically: Alternatives to Capitalism and the Invisible Hand.*

ultimately transparent correspondence between capital's economic greed and its environmental rapacity.[26] What works against them is the impression that there can be no other framework for keeping things running. Combatting this impression depends partly on showing that this framework is leading to ruin, but more importantly on showing that those who advocate a radical alternative are not lacking in practical sense.

TOWARD A SOCIALIST TECHNOLOGY, 2

Socialist technology, as already noted, is a matter not so much of particular devices, as of a certain approach to organizing production and consumption. The devices and the organizational forms are of course, under any system, mutually dependent. This interrelationship must now be understood, however, differently from the ways in which it was imagined by the revolutionists of the early 20th century. At that time the idea of socialism still included, in the minds of its proponents, the goal of surpassing capitalism in a narrowly instrumental sense: more grandiose projects, increased mechanization, reduced toil, higher cultural levels, longer lives. The formulation entailed an odd mix of legitimate aspirations with a kind of crude quantification in their expression. The mindset underlying such an approach coincided with the one that prioritized seizing and holding state power, as opposed to transforming production relations. It was an undialectical, voluntaristic mindset, which as such manifested the continuing global hegemony of capital.

This overarching instrumentalist view of technology has by no means disappeared, but the grounds for overcoming it have become much more widely accepted over the past few decades. The very idea of *not pursuing* certain technological projects or—if they have already been implemented—of *scrapping* them (e.g., nuclear power plants, genetically modified crops), has attained a breadth of appeal which extends well beyond that of the early-19th-century machine-wreckers. The present-day critique reflects widely

---

26 This is eloquently captured in Part I of Kovel, *The Enemy of Nature*. On its centrality in Marx's thought, see John Bellamy Foster, *Marx's Ecology: Materialism and Nature* (New York: Monthly Review Press, 2000).

disparate constituencies, ranging from those of traditional religion to advocates of the most advanced ecological thinking; but as an epoch-defining prod to this new impulse, nothing can surpass the mid-20th-century development of the "ultimate weapon." This milestone gave unprecedented grounding to the contention—still not widely explored—that the merits of a system of social relations might lie precisely in its capacity to *restrain* certain technological innovations or, in more general terms, to subordinate narrowly instrumentalist projections to human and ecological priorities.

The need for restraint fits uneasily, at first glance, with the impulse to liberation, but this reflects only a one-sided view of liberation. Ecological thought reaffirms a truth long recognized in the sphere of artistic communication, namely, that the fullest range of expression corresponds to the most complete assimilation of the collective sensitivities of one's community.[27] The sensitivities reflect both experience and language, conscious or unconscious; the community is in part parochial and in part universal. What appear as defining traits or as limits, however, are precisely the constitutive elements of a freedom which, without them, would remain empty.[28]

A socialist technology is one that evolves in a manner consistent with this model. It cannot dispense with a certain type of expertise, but the expertise must be one of breadth. Nourished at every stage by interaction across hitherto inviolate social boundaries, it will no longer be tied to a fixed stratum of "credentialed" authorities. Under such conditions, those who formulate alternative scenarios would be in day-to-day contact with a range of people who, by virtue of their own positions in society, could directly articulate typical needs, while at the same time, through their very interactions, doing so in an informed and qualified way.[29] The point of this arrangement would be to move as far as possible beyond the market-grounded model, in which a multiplicity of isolated personal choices, allegedly

27 See Sidney Finkelstein, *Composer and Nation: The Folk Heritage in Music* (New York: International Publishers, 1960).

28 On this point, one of Hegel's formulations is suggestive: "It is the will whose potentialities have become fully explicit which is truly infinite, because its object is itself and so is not in its eyes an 'other' or a barrier;..." *Philosophy of Right* (1821), § 22, tr. T.M. Knox (Oxford: Clarendon Press, 1942), 30.

29 Levins: "The optimal condition for science is with one foot in the university and one in the communities in struggle..." *Science Wars*, 191.

embodying "consumer sovereignty," leaves an open field to capital at the macro level.

Haila and Levins describe agriculture as evolving "from labor intensive to capital intensive to [potentially] thought and knowledge intensive."[30] The sequence can well apply to technology in general, with the understanding (which they also make clear) that the application of thought and knowledge must be, in effect, socially intensive. Capitalist technology, for all its ingenuity, could never match such an approach for adapting production to need. Such adaptation, indeed, is not even within its purview. The perpetual feverish overhauling that marks capitalist technology is thus an illusory achievement. Far from reflecting a liberation from fetters (as some suggested following the Soviet collapse), it is itself a fetter insofar as it feeds into the systematic postponement of the much higher stage that technology could attain if it were to be reinserted, under present-day conditions of humanity and nature, into the social matrix from which capitalism artificially wrenched it.

---

30 *Humanity and Nature*, 163; also, Levins's call for "knowledge-intensive low input practices ... in which the agricultural enterprise is a planned mosaic of fields in which each has its own product but also contributes to the productivity of the other fields" ("Rearming the Revolution: The Tasks of Theory for Hard Times," *Socialism and Democracy*, 12:1/2 [1998], 64).

4

SOCIALISM AND TECHNOLOGY: A SECTORAL OVERVIEW

The discussion of socialism as a historical project—that is, as a project for which it can be argued that the necessary practical conditions exist—has from the beginning been closely linked to issues of technology. Earlier advocates of social justice (before Marx's day) had spoken in terms of timeless moral principles. Thus, leaders of millenarian movements would deliver apocalyptic religious pronouncements to peasant followers, while utopian writers, for their part, addressed all "men of good will" (though in practice this most often meant educated people who took for granted the continuation of their personal preeminence). Marx, on the other hand, linked communism—and therefore also socialism, which would be its precursor—to the rise and the eventual political organization of the proletariat (wage-workers), whose existence as a social class reflected the technology of what he called "large-scale industry."[1]

The shift from handicraft to large-scale industry entailed: 1) development of the labor market (i.e., of labor-power as a commodity); 2) reduction of the work-process to regimented repetitive motions; and 3) the bringing together of large numbers of workers under a single roof. It was this combination of traits which gave capitalism—in the form it took during Marx's time—both its destructive character and, simultaneously, the potential to generate its positive replacement.

Jumping ahead to our own time, we see that capitalism, having beaten down its challengers almost everywhere for more than a century (longer, no doubt, than Marx and his immediate successors

---

1 [*grosse Industrie*] *Capital*, vol. I, ch. 15.

could have thought possible), confronts us with a daunting paradox. On the one hand, we see that capital, viewed globally, has acted out the whole rapacious script that Marx projected for it: it has concentrated wealth at one pole and misery at another; it has tightened more than ever the mechanisms of political control, including resort to military aggression backed by the "ultimate weapon"; it has created a largely hegemonic culture in its own (commercial) image; it has aggressively rolled back many of the welfare-gains that had been won through decades-long struggles; and, with its readiness to sacrifice both soil and worker to continued unlimited growth, it has brought on an ecological crisis which puts in doubt the continuation of our species-life. All this makes more urgent than ever the task of supplanting such a system. But—and here lies the paradox—the very factors that make the rule of capital so destructive also operate to shield it against any effective effort to go beyond it.

This represents something of a change since Marx's time. For him, the concentration of capitalist power had as its byproduct the bringing together of workers and their eventual consolidation into a class that could end the rule of capital. For us, capital's even further concentration (on a global scale), together with the concomitant technological changes, has had several consequences which make this outcome appear, at least initially, much more remote. First, big capital has radically dispersed its labor force, with the result that it can undercut the potential power of the workers by shifting its operations at will. Thus, the gains won by an earlier generation of workers no longer accrue to their offspring. Second, mass media technology has been used to shrink the public sphere in favor of direct one-way communication from the centers of power (public or private) to the isolated household or individual. Third, so much environmental damage has already been done, and the infrastructure for ecologically harmful patterns of energy-consumption has become so deeply entrenched, that any reversal is bound to be both slow and disruptive. (This effect is amplified with the rise of genetic engineering, which by its very nature—since no biological organism exists in isolation—introduces uncontrollable and irreversible changes into the environment.[2]) Finally, in terms of politi-

---

2 For general discussion of this phenomenon and its implications, see Finn Bowring, *Science, Seeds and Cyborgs: Biotechnology and the Appropriation of Life*

cal discourse, the notion that a radical alternative to capitalism has already been tried and found wanting may discourage many who might otherwise be receptive to socialism.

One possible conclusion to draw from all this, is that a transformation that was conceivable in Marx's time is no longer conceivable now. Within the dominant culture, this conclusion has already attained the status of an axiom. But human beings are not automatons, and obstacles that seem insuperable may bring defections in unexpected places, with the result that what first appeared as a reinforcement to the status quo may end up being a sign of its weakness. In terms of our present focus, it is the very extremity of the current situation that could provoke people to move much further, faster, and more purposefully toward radical change than they had previously thought possible. There is, of course, nothing "inevitable" about such a response, and it is a lamentable fact that certain types of environmental damage (e.g., extinctions of particular species) cannot be undone. Nonetheless, what works in favor of a constructive response is the emerging recognition that doing nothing—letting current trends run their course—spells disaster.

The struggle to survive is indeed a powerful motivator, but it depends in turn on confidence that survival is possible. Such confidence draws partly on the solidarity that can be inspired by a vast social movement. If a movement of this kind is to grow, however, it must have theoretical underpinnings. People need to understand the potential alternative as being already implicit in conditions we can now see. Regarding technology, it is not enough to advance a notion of "what might be." Any such vision must flow in a recognizable way from "what is," granting that this encompasses not just the physical and institutional reality but also people's subjective capacity to respond.

The sphere of technology is crucial to this process, for at least two reasons. On the one hand, the capitalistic cult of innovation[3] promises to overcome all obstacles, including those posed by the absolute exhaustion of the world's resource-base. On the other

---

(London: Verso, 2003), esp. 27-57.

3   Cf. Ernest Mandel's discussion of "a permanent pressure to *accelerate technological innovation*" (his emphasis), in *Late Capitalism* (London: New Left books, 1975), 192.

hand, we know that long-term species-survival is contingent upon a nearly 90 percent reduction in the burning of fossil fuels,[4] and that the conditions for carrying out such a reduction are to a large extent already present. These conditions, consisting partly of *devices*, partly of *scientific knowledge*, and partly of *organizational experience*, are what I propose to remind us of here. As we examine them, it will become evident that the framework required for directing them toward ecological restoration is one which breaks sharply with capitalist priorities and which therefore will link up in the short run with demands reflecting working-class (or, more broadly, non-capitalist) interests, and in the long run with socialism.

Both for the economy as a whole and for each of its sectors, it is possible to outline the main features of current capitalist practice, the implicit requirements for a socialist alternative, and the degree to which the conditions for satisfying these requirements are already present. Whatever the specificities of the various sectors, a socialist approach will be understood to rest on the underlying principles of (a) social ownership and control of large-scale property, with the option of reconfiguration (including subdivision and dispersion) of production units; (b) economic decisions beyond the household seen as matters of public policy (at whatever level), to be based on criteria of physical health, social well-being, and ecological acceptability rather than of profit and the market; and (c) a revised concept of efficiency which takes into account *all* inputs and outputs of a particular productive activity (and not just those that are measured in the profit-margins of particular enterprises).

We may now consider the application of these principles to the major sectors of economic activity. The discussion here will be purely illustrative; actual implementation would require organized debate and planning on the part of all those affected.

---

4   This was the estimate for the advanced countries cited already in George Monbiot's 2007 book, *Heat: How to Stop the Planet from Burning* (Cambridge, MA: South End Press), 16.

AGRICULTURE/FORESTS/FISHERIES

The traditional practices of agriculture, forestry, and fishing—clearly the sectors most vital to our physical survival—are increasingly giving way to agribusiness, tree plantations, factory fishing, and aquaculture. Agribusiness, with its vast acres of single crops and with its factory-like regimentation of landless (often migrant) laborers, is heavily committed to fuel-intensive cultivation based on chemical fertilizer and highly toxic pesticides. Scorning age-old practices of mixed growth, it depletes both the topsoil and, through over-irrigation, the aquifers.[5] Livestock-raising is marked by similarly wasteful practices. Beef production, in particular, uses up ten times as much acreage as does grain to feed a given number of humans, and the water pollution from stockyards is prodigious.[6] Animals raised for meat are typically subjected to extreme crowding and highly unhealthy conditions, including the use of growth hormones which in turn threaten human health.[7] All such practices are carried out for the sake of guaranteeing the highest possible output and profits.

The same precepts are applied to forests and fisheries. Forests are viewed not for their roles in producing oxygen, protecting against soil erosion and floods, or sheltering many species of wildlife (including pest-predators), but exclusively as either sources of lumber or impediments to cash crops and grazing. The destructiveness of this approach is incalculable, perhaps most dramatically shown in the mudslides that beset clear-cut hillsides (frequently taking, in poor countries, hundreds of lives at a time). In terms of the capitalist bottom-line, however, all this is simply disregarded. So it is with fishing, where natural stocks are relentlessly depleted. Farm-raised fish are then bred under conditions comparable to livestock, with

---

5   Yrjö Haila and Richard Levins, *Humanity and Nature: Ecology, Science and Society* (London: Pluto Press, 1992), 157.

6   Jeremy Rifkin, *Beyond Beef: The Rise and Fall of the Cattle Culture* (New York: Penguin Books, 1992), 221. See also Christopher D. Cook, *Diet for a Dead Planet: How the Food Industry Is Killing Us* (New York: New Press, 2004).

7   Jane Akre, "The Fox, the Hounds, and the Sacred Cows," in Kristina Borjesson, ed., *Into the Buzzsaw: Leading Journalists Expose the Myth of a Free Press* (Amherst, NY: Prometheus Books, 2002), 40.

excessive crowding and consequent adverse health effects, which again are passed on to humans.[8]

Cutting across all forms of food production is the use of genetic engineering (GE). In the midst of all the controversy on this topic, a few points deserve emphasis:[9] 1. The impetus for GE comes entirely from big corporations. 2. The initial motivation for genetically modifying crops was to create captive markets for certain herbicides, to which the modified crops would be immune. 3. GE is by no means guaranteed to increase productivity; in some instances, it has the opposite effect. Productivity, however, is not the goal; the goal is to displace independent community-based agriculture with a form of production that maximizes dependence on commercial inputs. 4. It is impossible to guarantee that genetically modified plants (or fish) will not interbreed with their wild counterparts, with unknown consequences. 5. GE was introduced into US food supplies by stealth (companies blocked efforts to require labeling of GE produce); in countries where there was open discussion, GE technology has been severely restricted. 6. The attempt to impose GE has also entailed high-pressure tactics on the part of the US government, including blocking worldwide adoption of the precautionary principle (under which products have to be proven safe before they are marketed)[10] and winning a World Trade Organization ruling that declared the European Union's 6-year ban on GE foods an "unfair trade barrier."[11]

In envisaging a socialist response to all these practices, it is important in the first instance to see the practices themselves as aberrational. Far from building on the accumulated experience of food producers who understand and respect the natural setting in which they operate, capitalist agriculture—of which GE is only the most extreme expression—fixates on reaching its narrowly defined

---

8   "A Global Assessment of Organic Contaminants in Farmed vs. Wild Salmon: Geographical Differences and Health Risks" *Science*, January 2004 (summarized at www.farmedanddangerous.org).

9   See Bowring, *Science, Seeds and Cyborgs*, and, for concise introductions, Luke Anderson, *Genetic Engineering, Food, and Our Environment* (White River Junction, VT: Chelsea Green Publishing, 1999), and the 2004 film "The Future of Food" (www.futureoffood.com).

10   *Multinational Monitor*, 24:9 (Sept. 2004): special issue, "The Precautionary Principle."

11   *Washington Post*, February 8, 2008, D1.

targets "by any means necessary," in total disregard of impact on the eco-system.[12] The most urgent priority for socialism, then, is to rescue agricultural practice from the imbalances and the ravages perpetrated by capital. This implies a comprehensive approach, but one that is not wedded to intervening at any single level. What it must do is no longer treat nature's infrastructure (land, water, trees, wildlife) as a vast heap of potential commodities ready to be seized and put on the market. The challenge is not so much one of innovation as one of retrieval. Precisely how the production process will be organized—in particular, the exact mix of different scales of operations—must be determined in accordance with both the natural and the cultural traits of each locality. Specific decisions on matters such as water-use, pest-management, crop-combinations, and working conditions can then be taken on the basis of public discussion, with free flow of essential knowledge and a common commitment to long-term viability.

Nature does not recognize property boundaries. What is done in one space affects other terrains as well. Long-term viability means, on the one hand, avoiding toxins, and on the other, protecting soil quality, water availability, and species-diversity. All these objectives require a degree of mixing and complexity of plant-life. This might in turn entail, on the one hand, higher levels of labor input, and on the other, smaller outputs of any single product within a given region. Such changes can be seen as positive, however, from several angles.[13] 1. The severe rural unemployment that exists in most of the world's poor countries could be absorbed. 2. Although the output of a region's leading product might decline, this could be offset by the output of secondary products, some of which could be locally consumed. 3. Agricultural work would become—as it often used to be—more varied, more creative, more dignified, and healthier. Farming would be spread out among the whole population. More

---

12 For a powerful critique of this approach, see Vandana Shiva, *Biopiracy: The Plunder of Nature and Knowledge* (Boston: South End Press, 1997), esp. Ch. 4. Underlying this critique is the fact that peasant agriculture, which uses only 25% of the world's farmland, feeds 70% of the world's people. ETC Group [Erosion, Technology, Concentration], *Who Will Feed Us? The Industrial Food Chain vs. The Peasant Food Web*, 3rd ed. (ETC Group, 2017), www.etcgroup.org/sites/ www.etcgroup.org/files/files/etc-whowillfeedus-english-webshare.pdf

13 Based on Haila & Levins, *Humanity and Nature*, Ch. 5 ("Agricultural Ecology").

people would engage in it; fewer would have it as their exclusive occupation.

Steps in the direction of such an outcome can be discerned in a number of settings around the globe. Cuba, with what is left of its socialist framework, in some respects leads the way, as it responded to the cutoff of its external inputs (following the Soviet breakup) by carrying out an exemplary switch to organic agriculture, including large-scale promotion of urban food-gardens.[14] India has been the setting for major organizing efforts within farming communities as they have sought to defend their livelihoods against the incursion of dam-building projects and water-guzzling soft drink manufacturers. And in the advanced capitalist countries, consumer groups have established food coops and mounted educational campaigns while farmers' markets have reestablished direct links between city-dwellers and nearby small-scale food producers. However limited might be the immediate scope of such developments, they offer substantial networks on which more ambitious projects can build.[15]

INDUSTRY/TRANSPORT/ENERGY

In industry, unlike agriculture, the capitalist organization of production appears at first glance not as a possibly arbitrary superimposition upon age-old practices but rather as a structure inherent in the tasks to be performed. Large-scale industry originated under capitalist sponsorship; no earlier epoch offers an alternative model for it. Twentieth-century socialist regimes may have strengthened rather than weakened the perceived link between industrial success and the rule of capital. The reason for this is straightforward. Socialist revolutions occurred in relatively backward countries. In terms of industrial competition, therefore, the resulting regimes always appeared as laggards. It became impossible for them to shake off a fixation on overcoming this circumstance, whether the concern was to showcase what they proclaimed to be a new social order or

---

14 Peter M. Rosset, "Alternative Agriculture Works: The Case of Cuba," *Monthly Review*, 50:3 (July/August 1998), 144.

15 An expression of this is the International Federation of Organic Agriculture Movements, founded in 1972 and holding its 19th World Congress in November 2017 (www.ifoam.bio/).

whether it was to build up, in a more practical sense, the means to defend themselves against the real and continuous threat of hostile intervention. Ironically, then (as Lenin was the first to insist), they were able to contend with the capitalist powers only by largely succumbing to the rules of the capitalist game.[16] Once this pattern had become routinized, it suffused the ambitions of the Soviet ruling strata, making them easy prey for cooptation.

But the mere fact that large-scale industry was founded and propagated by capital does not in itself make capitalism the only possible framework for its existence. For reasons put forward initially by Marx, the historical evolution of the rule of capital brings problems of a new kind which capital is incapable of addressing. Capitalism's core anomaly, in comparison with earlier systems, has always been the phenomenon of overproduction. In Marx's time, overproduction came into play essentially with reference to the size of the market (in any given region) relative to the quantity of available commodities: if more was produced than could be sold, the market would collapse and the economy would go into recession. Nowadays, however, the limiting factor is not just the size of any regional market; it is also the total quantity of available resources, on a global scale. The classic capitalist desideratum of perpetual growth is thus no longer viable even in the short run, let alone as the basic measure of economic success.[17] Both *what* is produced and *how much* is produced must be decided upon in terms of an entirely new set of considerations—and hence also through a largely new set of institutions and processes.

We should note immediately that although this is formulated as a prescriptive statement, it derives its impetus from the economy's clash with objective limits, whether in the form of a peak in oil production,[18] an unsustainable increase in atmospheric carbon, a

---

16 In "On the Immediate Tasks of the Soviet Government" (1918), Lenin regretfully but firmly calls for emulating the industrial discipline of what he terms "state capitalism" as then practiced in Germany.

17 See Richard Douthwaite, *The Growth Illusion: How Economic Growth Has Enriched the Few, Impoverished the Many, and Endangered the Planet*, 2nd ed. (Gabriola, BC: New Society, 1999).

18 Richard Heinberg, *The Party's Over: Oil, War and the Fate of Industrial Societies* (Gabriola, BC: New Society, 2003), summary Table on p. 103-4. Although precise dating of the peak remains controversial, the trend toward exploiting more marginal (and hence more costly) deposits is not in doubt. See Dan Box *et al.*, "The End of Cheap Oil," *The Ecologist*, 35:8 (October 2005), 36-53; and "Peak Oil

shortage of clean water, or (as now in the case of China) an absolute shrinkage of agricultural terrain in the face of expanded reliance on private motor vehicles. What these trends imply is that an alternative set of production-parameters is a matter not just of taste or preference, but of survival.

The response of capital to this crisis is ambivalent. On the one hand, it cannot fail to recognize the threats to "business as usual," and so devotes a certain portion of its capacity to exploring, in particular, new sources of energy, most notably, the promise of "hydrogen power."[19] On the other hand, however, both in its direct corporate practices and through its political clout, it aggressively clings to an agenda of controlling and exploiting oil reserves down to the last profitable drop. While the sponsored research into devices like hydrogen cells is there to be picked up and carried further, the will to organize a timely conversion away from hazardous and unsustainable technologies is lacking. The proliferation of toxic practices continues unabated, under the assumption that the residues can always be dumped on "expendable" populations,[20] while the implementation of cleaner approaches awaits the moment—put off for as long as possible—when the market for existing practices dries up.

A socialist approach would not limit itself to inserting new energy sources into established patterns of consumption. It would seek to change those patterns both by putting an end to the power of a privileged class—with the opportunity for massive reorganization of priorities that such a power-shift would bring—and by making use of those already available approaches to production and transport that entail lower human and environmental cost than do the ones favored by capital.

More specifically, socialism can first limit the pressure on energy resources by reducing, in an organized way, the total production of goods and services. In order to minimize adverse effects, such reduction will require (a) reconfiguring economic space (tak-

Forum," *World Watch*, 19:1 (Jan./Feb. 2006), 9-24. The resulting crunch has only intensified in more recent years, with oil industry's increasing resort to offshore drilling, shale oil, and fracking.

19 Jeremy Rifkin, *The Hydrogen Economy* (New York: Penguin Books, 2003), Ch. 8.

20 See, e.g., Benjamin Joffe-Walt, "China's Computer Wasteland," *The Progressive*, 69:1 (January 2005). Prisoners within the US are also used for computer recycling. Anne-Marie Cusac, "Toxic Prison Labor," *The Progressive* 70:3 (March 2009), www.progressive.org/cusac0309.html

ing more advantage of geographic proximity), (b) promoting collective consumption (e.g., mass transit), (c) relying less on possible new inventions and more on making fuller use of existing devices (e.g., bicycles), (d) encouraging society-wide redefinition of what constitutes a "good life" (esp., reducing emphasis on possessions and discrediting exploitative lifestyles), (e) bringing immediate improvements to those who are least well off, and (f) most generally (building upon d), identifying the many currently accepted social practices (e.g., commercial, financial, bureaucratic, repressive, profligate, destructive) that can be curtailed and establishing the necessary coordination to help move people from within the affected sectors into more socially useful and fulfilling activities.

Second, the production process itself will need to be redesigned, with top priority given to its effects on those whom it directly engages. This means not only protecting workers from accidents and illnesses but also enhancing their opportunities for social interaction, diffusing control over the work process, democratizing decisions about common goals (including *what* is produced as well as how it is produced), and generally considering the mental health of the workforce (in particular, the level of well-being felt by each worker at day's end) to be as important an output of the enterprise as whatever products it sells.[21]

It is within the context of these kinds of changes that a society-wide shift to cleaner and more sustainable technologies becomes immediately conceivable. Until large numbers of people are well organized and thoroughly aware of their long-term interests, the idea of reducing carbon emissions by 90% will appear as complete fantasy. Only with the social transformation well underway will everyone be able to see through the false dilemma - "either" protect "the economy," "or" preserve the environment - propounded by those who resist even the most minimal international accords on global warming.

---

21 This goal is in part suggested by Chinese practice in the 1960s, when the enterprise was treated as a site for general cultural development of its workers. Barry M. Richman, *Industrial Society in Communist China* (New York: Random House, 1969), 723.

Information/Communication/Education

Information technology and its offshoots need to be considered from two angles. On the one hand, all the talk about a presumed shift to a "weightless economy" needs to be brought up short against recognition of the physical or material underpinnings to the supposedly "non-material" transactions that are carried out.[22] On the other hand, we must consider how the new technologies in question affect the substance of what is communicated and how this substantive dimension in turn inserts itself into either a capitalist or a socialist framework.

The common application of the adjective "virtual" to computer-transmitted images and exchanges feeds the illusion that in switching into this relatively new medium, we are somehow leaving behind the messy world of tangible objects and factory labor. This is a further extension of the rhetoric of mid-20th-century sociologists and economists who, noting the swelling of service-sector employment, popularized the term "post-industrial society" as a descriptor for contemporary capitalism. In so doing, they celebrated a supposed improvement in status of a large portion of the workforce, when in fact most of the new service workers were economically weaker than their earlier factory-employed counterparts, while the latter then saw their situation undercut by the transfer of much production work to Third World countries. The point is that the grimy/repetitive manual operations were not eliminated but were only shifted to less favorable (to the workers) settings and conditions—and to more vulnerable populations.[23]

A similar process has occurred with computerization. Both the manufacture and operation of computers as well as the uses to which they are put have heightened, rather than eased, the assault on the environment. The toxic toll of computer-manufacture is itself prodigious. As Wolfgang Sachs reports, "no less than 15-19 tons

22 Ursula Huws, "Material World: The Myth of the Weightless Economy" (ch. 9 of her book, *The Making of a Cybertariat: Virtual Work in a Real World* [New York: Monthly Review Press, 2003]). On the toxic infrastructure of the smartphone, see Adam Greenfield, *Radical Technologies: The Design of Everyday Life* (London: Verso, 2017), 18f.

23 See Michael Zweig, *The Working Class Majority: America's Best Kept Secret*, 2nd ed. (Ithaca, NY: Cornell University Press, 2012).

of energy and materials—calculated over the entire life-cycle—are consumed by the fabrication of one computer" (with 25 tons being the corresponding amount for an automobile).[24] The manufacture of a computer chip generates "about *thirteen hundred times its weight* [in] waste, some of it highly toxic—and this amount doesn't include air emissions."[25] As if these basic costs were not enough, there is the further phenomenon of perpetually accelerating obsolescence. With the intense competition over the speed, capacity, and versatility of computers, ever-new refinements are devised, and big institutions scrap and replace entire functioning systems almost without warning. Whatever the calculations that might be embodied in the first such step, the ultimate effect is to multiply real pressures to "upgrade" upon every other system that interacts with the original one. Similarly, a perfectly serviceable component of an office-complex may be rendered useless by upgrades in some other component to which it is linked.

Over and above such self-generated pressures from within the computer industry, we must take note of the frequent resort to high-tech "solutions" for problems that in themselves could be addressed more directly and effectively (and at less environmental cost) by rethinking either the infrastructure or the habits that give rise to them. The need for such rethinking tends to be overwhelmed by the mentality of the technological "quick fix," which resists disruption of existing personal habits and is positively averse to collective or structural approaches. Thus, confronted by the at-least twice-daily traffic tie-ups of major cities, instead of reducing the number of vehicles (and thereby saving not only energy but also space, materials, clean air, and sociality), one devises a computer program to detect where, at a given moment, there might be a slightly smoother flow—forgetting, of course, that if everyone does the same thing,

---

24 Wolfgang Sachs (Director of the Wuppertal Institute for Climate, Energy and Environment, in Wuppertal, Germany), "Wasting Time Is an Ecological Virtue," *New Perspectives Quarterly*, 14:1 (Winter 1997), 8.

25 Elizabeth Grossman, *High Tech Trash: Digital Devices, Hidden Toxics, and Human Health*. Revised ed. (Washington, DC: Island Press, 2007), 60 (my italics). According to another study, the ratio of fossil fuel use to product weight is roughly ten times as great for computers as for "many other manufactured goods." Eric Williams, "Energy Intensity of Computer Manufacturing: Hybrid Assessment Combining Process and Input-Output Methods," *Environmental Science and Technology*, 38:2 (2004), 6166.

the problem will be back at square one. (This is analogous to the Jevons paradox, according to which any increase in purely mechanical efficiency will encourage heightened consumption, thereby neutralizing any hoped-for reduction of total energy-use.)

A similar sort of irrationality is manifested in the educational and cultural applications of computer technology. This is not to dispute the impressive advantages conferred by such technology in matters of research and in the diffusion and filing of information. There are, however, serious concerns in terms of proportion. These have to do not only with the question of the costs of computer systems (compared with other possible allocations, such as hiring more teachers or providing more public support for the arts), but also with the degree to which *what can be done via the computer becomes a determinant of whatever tasks might be undertaken*. This latter consideration is so pervasive that its limits are hard to identify. Especially when one thinks of the addictive behavior that has developed around certain types of computer pastimes, it becomes apparent that the technology can affect human experience in a way that may shut out more than it opens up (if not quantitatively, then at least qualitatively).

The addictive dimension takes two principal forms, both of which provide a kind of shortcut to gratification. The first is computer video games, many of which involve maneuvers dangerously akin to military targeting, in which the reward is an exploding screen-image (typically, a human body). Such games isolate the direct mouse-guided act both from the human surroundings of the player and from any meaningful sense of what the image signifies. The second—and more likely long-term—form of addiction is the Internet phenomenon of Multi-User Domains (MUDs), which "provide worlds for anonymous social interaction in which you can play a role as close to or as far away from your real self as you choose."[26] Individuals readily take on multiple personae, spending up to twelve hours a day at the screen and losing any sense of their actual

---

26 Sherry Turkle, *Life on the Screen: Identity in the Age of the Internet* (New York: Simon & Schuster, 1997), 183. Later developments would carry all this even further. Turkle, *Alone Together: Why We Expect More from Technology and Less from Each Other* (New York: Basic Books, 2011), esp. Ch. 9; Adam Alter, *Irresistible: The Rise of Addictive Technology and the Business of Keeping Us Hooked* (New York: Penguin Press, 2017).

place in the world. As Sherry Turkle puts it, "the self spins off in all directions."[27] The alienation that Marx first recognized in capitalist production relations has thus taken on an added dimension, as the individual now seeks escape not (or not only) from the workplace but from the whole sphere of face-to-face interactions.[28] The further development of social media technology has only extended this trend, as people often remain captives of their smartphones even when they are in the physical presence of others.

More generally, the instant accessibility of a vast universe of facts and ideas, combined with the awareness of this accessibility, carries the danger of obscuring the painstaking creative process that underlies authentic mastery, in whatever domain. The further phenomenon of incessant updating diminishes the apparent worth of any intellectual product whose palpable form (e.g., that of a book) can be seen as fixing it at a moment that has already been superseded. In relating to bodies of knowledge that are cumulative, it becomes difficult to recognize the underpinnings of whatever stage has currently been reached. The extreme though not uncommon expression of this difficulty is the practice of plagiarism. This is of course physically facilitated by word-processing technology, but more importantly, it is made to appear ethically unproblematic by its congruence with the awareness that one can "access" any desired item of information at a moment's notice. The official condemnations of plagiarism ring hollow in view of the enormous pressures and inducements which make it attractive, and which the guardians of public morality do not call into question. But this is a familiar contradiction of capitalist culture, much like the promotion of an "abstinence only" approach to sex education in the context of commercial media that trumpet sexual conquest at every turn. In all such examples, the supposedly "moral" stance has long ago lost whatever grounding it might once have had in a genuine regard for

---

27 Turkle, *Life on the Screen*, 258. On distancing from social reality, see also Joshua Meyrowitz, *No Sense of Place: The Impact of Electronic Media on Social Behavior* (New York: Oxford University Press, 1985), esp. 317ff.

28 Marx wrote that the worker "only feels himself [i.e., feels human] outside his work" (*The Economic & Philosophic Manuscripts of 1844*, ed. D.J. Struik [New York: International Publishers, 1964], 110); we can now similarly say that the MUD addict only feels fully human outside real life, in the "virtual" world.

the quality of human interaction—the latter having been scornfully displaced in favor of market priorities.

The all-purpose target of market-appeal is the demand for instant gratification. Nowhere does this appear more sharply than in the technology of the cell-phone. Leaving aside the applications for which the mobile dimension is totally unnecessary (i.e., long conversations that could be held anytime and from anywhere), we are left with a number of distinctive applications whose desirability or necessity has to be seen in the context of alternative approaches and then weighed against the possible adverse public health consequences of blanketing the globe with the microwave fields that are required in order for cell-phones to function.[29] It is emblematic of capitalist hegemony (especially in its US guise) that, as with the imposition of the automobile-centered transportation system or of genetically modified food, the question of whether or not to build the global infrastructure for cell-phone use has never been viewed as a public policy issue—let alone as a question meriting society-wide debate grounded in full disclosure of the relevant scientific information. The purpose of such debate would be not only to bring out the risks of the proposed technology, but also to work out in great detail the alternative possible ways of meeting whatever legitimate needs the technology in question might be thought to address.

Underlying all such questions is the issue of control. Should technology be democratically controlled, or can its development be safely left in the hands of capital (and/or of governments constituted by capital)? In view of the costs and dangers of the new technologies (as well as their complexity), choices on their adoption have implications far beyond what can be perceived or contemplated by the prospective individual consumer. If this is true of already known

---

29 Arthur Firstenberg, "Killing Fields," *The Ecologist*, 34:5 (June 2004), 22-27. See also Paul Brodeur, *The Great Power-Line Cover-Up: How the Utilities and the Government Are Trying to Hide the Cancer Hazard Posed by Electromagnetic Fields* (Boston: Little, Brown & Co., 1993), esp. Ch. 19. Recent findings on carcinogenic effects are discussed in Igor Yakimenko et al., "Oxidative mechanisms of biological activity of low-intensity radiofrequency radiation," *Electromagnetic Biology and Radiation* 35:2 (2016), 186-202, dx.doi.org/10.3109/15368378.2015 .1043557. The psychological effects of cell-phone dependence are explored in Hannah Rippin, "The Mobile Phone in Everyday Life," *Fast Capitalism* (www. fastcapitalism.com) 1:1 (2005).

technologies, it will apply with even greater force to the new nanotechnology, which involves particles so tiny and capable of so many
permutations that the means to contain them have not yet been
devised.[30] The protection of human beings, not just as "consumers"
(i.e., buyers) but as involuntary recipients of particles with unknown
properties, has become very much a collective responsibility. Hence
the need for social control over production. Only within such a
framework can public debate be made a precondition for major
production decisions. In the case of information technologies, the
task will be to avoid harmful or wasteful applications while at the
same time exploring what positive role these technologies can play
in democratizing all aspects of society and politics. Here their contributions could range from breaking down knowledge-barriers to
addressing the more intractable problems of coordination that arise
in any society-wide planning process.

SURVEILLANCE/REPRESSION/MILITARY

The non-neutrality of technology deserves particular emphasis
when we look at technologies of repression. In the sectors we
have examined so far, the task has been to identify and preserve
the components that can serve human needs (consistent with ecological concerns), while at the same time recognizing and curbing
the components that are wasteful and/or dangerous. With the technologies of repression, however, and in particular with those of
military destruction, we confront a set of applications that is inherently negative and whose adoption can at best claim only the most
transient and circumscribed justification, in contexts of territorial
self-defense.

It is important to begin by noting the military dimension of capitalism itself. Like the growing of food, the fighting of wars pre-dated
capitalism, but capitalism added its own distinctive stamp which,
evolving through history, has created a whole new level of high-

---

30 Peter Montague, "Welcome to the NanoWorld: Nanotechnology and the Precau-
    tionary Principle Imperative," *Multinational Monitor* 25:9 (Sept. 2004), 16-19.
    On the current status of such uncertainties, see the continuously updated Wiki-
    pedia articles on "Nanotechnology" and "Nanotoxicology."

tech mass killing. In the military sphere, the concentration of capitalist power has reached a previously unimagined level, where the agenda of global domination has become an article of consensus within the ruling class of the world's most powerful country. The specific expression of this agenda is the self-proclaimed prerogative of the US government to intervene militarily, at its own discretion, in any country at any time.[31] A long record of such interventions makes clear that what motivates them has no necessary connection with any threat of physical attack against US territory or, despite invocations about "expanding liberty," with whether or not the targeted regimes or movements have the support of the local populations.[32] What unites the interventions, rather, is a pair of preoccupations central to the rule of capital, namely, 1) maximizing the sphere of corporate economic operations (now focusing especially on oil) and 2) blocking, punishing, and ultimately destroying any attempt to chart an independent—especially if socialist—course of development.

The technology that has evolved in carrying out this agenda goes far beyond any device that could conceivably be needed for territorial protection. It now extends to the domination of space, as the US claims exclusive sway over the shield from which one can exercise surveillance—backed by the threat of instant attack from above—anywhere on the planet.[33] On the ground, the goal of intervening with impunity while minimizing the risk of US casualties has prompted a major thrust toward replacing infantry soldiers with robots.[34] It would be hard to imagine a more definitive acknowledgment than this, that one is sending one's forces where they are not

---

31 See esp. Section V ("Prevent Our Enemies from Threatening Us...") of the US National Security Strategy statement of September 2002 (georgewbush-whitehouse.archives.gov/nsc/nss/2002/).

32 See esp. William Blum, *Killing Hope: U.S. Military and CIA Interventions Since World War II* (Monroe, ME: Common Courage Press, 2003).

33 Howell M. Estes, *U.S. Space Command Long Range Plan* (Colorado Springs: HQ, U.S. Command, 1998), 65, as cited in Matthew Mowthorpe, *The Militarization and Weaponization of Space* (Lanham, MD: Lexington Books, 2004), 200.

34 Tim Weiner, "A New Model Army Soldier Rolls Closer to the Battlefield," *New York Times*, February 16, 2005, A1. The subsequent development of drone warfare, of course, made it possible to dispense with ground combat altogether. Medea Benjamin, *Drone Warfare: Killing by Remote Control* (London: Verso, 2013).

welcome. In order for the shielding effect to be complete, however, the robots must acquire an increasing capacity to make life-and-death decisions on their own, without nearby humans to type in the computer-commands. The dominion of machines over humans, described by Marx as the control of living labor by dead labor,[35] would thus reach a new level of impregnability.

On the domestic front, the mission of crime-control blends almost seamlessly into that of political repression. Criminal activity can of course itself take on a high-tech character, especially in information-related matters that shade over into routine financial practices like currency trading. The targets of surveillance and of high-tech weaponry, however, are most likely to be officially marginalized populations of one kind or another, ranging from prisoners to radical activists. There are now monitoring mechanisms of every description, from barcode/credit-card links to surgically implanted computer chips.[36] Stun guns and other allegedly "non-lethal" weapons have been used by law enforcement personnel with reckless indifference to their effects. "Crowd control" at demonstrations has often become a pretext for police assaults, especially against people carrying video equipment;[37] more generally, local police forces in the US tend increasingly to adopt military-scale weaponry.[38] In the prison system, stun guns serve as backup to the increasingly vindictive official regimen that has been imposed under the pretext of fighting terrorism.[39]

It is clear that the disposition to use these technologies—along with the more traditional "quick fix" of relying on bullets—will

---

35 *Capital*, vol. I, Ch. 10, sec. 1.

36 For a recent overview, see Robert O'Harrow, *No Place to Hide: Behind the Scenes of Our Emerging Surveillance Society* (New York: Free Press, 2005).

37 Eyewitness accounts of the November 2003 demonstration against the Free Trade Association of the Americas; Ben Manski, "Massacre in Miami," *Socialism and Democracy*, 18:1 (Jan.-June 2004), 250.

38 Radley Balko, *Rise of the Warrior Cop: The Militarization of America's Police Forces* (New York: Public Affairs, 2013).

39 On the introduction of these devices, see Anne-Marie Cusac's reports in *The Progressive*: "Stunning Technology" (July 1996) and "Shock Value" (September 1997). A further twist in surplus punishment, with a financial payoff, is the growing practice of replacing in-person prison visits by pay-per-minute "video visitation." Bernadette Rabuy and Peter Wagner, "Screening Out Family Time: The For-Profit Video Visitation Industry in Prisons and Jails" (2015), static.prisonpolicy.org/visitation/ScreeningOutFamilyTime_January2015.pdf

tend to increase as the policies of the sponsoring regime become more oblivious to mass needs, rendering it less capable of gaining acceptance on the basis of any real services it might provide. At a more mundane level, the same indifference to popular needs has fed into the elite's growing propensity to circumvent the electoral process by, among other things, techniques that rely on the manipulability (and potential impenetrability) of computerized voting.[40] Whether by violence or by subterfuge (along with quiet complicity on the part of those who are not the direct perpetrators), the ruling class thus routinely shields itself from any priorities but its own. Ultimately, this may heighten people's awareness of the need for radical change. At the same time, however, any such repudiation of the status quo will only magnify the insecurity and consequent repressiveness of the regime. This raises, among other things, severe tactical problems for advocates of an alternative order.

The issues go beyond anything that can be fully resolved here, but they have to be mentioned because the core issue for socialism is the extent to which it can dismantle the structures and practices that have discredited its predecessor. Nowhere do these appear more intractable than in the domain of repression. What gives the repressive machinery added tenacity—an added appearance of inevitability—is the fact that it is directly used (whether internally or internationally) against any socialist movement that even approaches the possibility of taking power. How then can a socialist movement break free of this kind of defining circumstance?

It should not be expected that such a break can be instantaneous. Capital has made, and will continue to make, war on any regime (or movement) that defies it, no matter how legal or democratic the challenger might be.[41] Indeed, such grounds for legitimacy could make the defiance even more sharply felt (because ultimately

---

40 See Mark Crispin Miller, *Fooled Again! How the Right Stole the 2004 Election and Why They'll Steal the Next One Too (Unless We Stop Them)* (New York: Basic Books, 2005), and Greg Palast, *The Best Democracy Money Can Buy: A Tale of Billionaires and Ballot Bandits* (New York: Seven Stories Press, 2016), esp. 183-90.

41 Witness the continuing US efforts to undermine Venezuela's Bolivarian Revolution, despite its repeated electoral legitimation (Hugo Chávez's victory in the 2004 recall vote, for example, was both more decisive and less tainted by fraud than was the victory of George W. Bush in US elections the same year -- www.cartercenter.org/documents/2020.pdf).

more embarrassing) than would be the case with a regime lacking in these qualities. For defensive arms to become outdated, therefore (on the part of regimes moving toward socialism), an international popular movement of enormous scope, especially within the imperial center, will have to act as a restraining force against intervention. In that process, and as its outcome, a number of restraints on military technology will have to evolve. Given that the imperial power is the one that exercises military initiative (and also has the more advanced military technology), it is on *its* part that restraint will first need to be felt. Once such restraint has become manifest, then the leadership of a country in revolution will have the space to reduce its own military orientation—a step that it would welcome insofar as it is committed to prioritizing social improvements.

The ultimate goal would be a society in which the armed forces dissolve into a reserve of mobilized citizens whose primary orientation is no longer combat but rather social/ecological reconstruction projects of various kinds. As for the high-tech forms of surveillance that have developed under late capitalism, they would become increasingly superfluous as private financial transactions shrink in scope, as international economic polarization declines (reducing pressure at border-crossings), and as secretive practices of accumulation (including criminal activity—or what is officially stigmatized as such) give way to a revival of face-to-face collaboration on a wide scale. The point of immediate concern, however, is that in the military/repressive sector more than in any other single domain, the transformative steps that can be taken within a socialist framework are severely limited by the degree of external threat that continues to face any society in revolution.

PUBLIC HEALTH AND HEALTHCARE SERVICES

Capitalist medical technology, like its counterparts in the communications and military spheres, can boast extraordinary achievements. At the same time, both the disorders it has to address and the selection of its beneficiaries reflect a failure to achieve its purported objective—public health—in more direct, effective, and universal ways. It is widely accepted, except in mainstream US political discourse, that the costs of healthcare can only be reasonably and universally met if they are averaged out over the entire population, as is done in many national health plans even in otherwise capitalist countries. What is less commonly recognized is the role of capitalist priorities in creating health problems which should never arise in the first place, and to which high-tech treatments are applied selectively and (often) only when it is too late.[42] The greatest of these problems are those associated with *poverty*. Hunger, like war, is older than capitalism, but many of the present-day manifestations of poverty reflect market-based priorities. These include the disproportionate exposure of poor people to unhealthy working conditions, bad air, tobacco culture, and factory-processed food, combined with insufficient access to relaxation, exercise, and simply the knowledge of what is beneficial. More specific burdens on the healthcare system arise from various forms of *systemic violence*, ranging from car crashes (which, viewed in the aggregate, are predictable and therefore not accidental) to individual acts of violence and, beyond this, to war casualties. Finally, healthcare resources (including high-tech) are also diverted to *cosmetic surgery*, the demand for which arises from the quick-fix mentality applied either to physical problems (like obesity) or to psychological problems (reflecting internalization of degrading stereotypes associated with age, sex, or ethnicity).[43]

A socialist approach would not do away with high-tech treatments but would reduce the need for them by raising the general level of public health (mental as well as physical). This approach—based on ending the poverty, violence, unhealthy habits, environmental toxins, and stereotyping culture that account for excess healthcare demands[44]—would be both cheaper for the healthcare system and more beneficial for the people. It would signify, however,

---

42 Vicente Navarro, *Medicine Under Capitalism* (New York: Neale Watson Academic Publications, 1976), esp. 82ff; Samuel Epstein, "Cancer: It's a Growth Industry" [interview], *Z Magazine* (October 2003), 39-42.

43 For an interesting discussion of the pressures in question, see Carl Elliott, "Enhancement Technology," in David M. Kaplan, ed., *Readings in the Philosophy of Technology* (Lanham, MD: Rowman & Littlefield, 2004), 373-79.

44 See Richard Wilkinson, *The Impact of Inequality* (New York: New Press, 2005), and also the medical research papers of Nancy Krieger (www.hsph.harvard.edu/nancy-krieger/publications/).

a radical reconfiguration of social priorities. All the sectors we have discussed would evolve along lines such as those here suggested. With regard to healthcare services in particular, we can go beyond sketching imaginary systems, because current Cuban arrangements already embody a thoroughgoing preventive approach—based on an ambitious level of training, an ethic of service, and routine house-calls by family doctors—resulting in public health indicators on a par with those of much richer countries.[45] The mental or psychological dimension is of course more complicated, but there can be no doubt that a society in which everyone's basic needs are acknowledged—both at the community level and in public policy—will free its people from the stresses associated with the pervasive capitalist stereotype of "the loser."

A SOCIALIST TECHNOLOGY?

While some devices may be more compatible than others with socialist principles, the devices required for life under socialism pre-exist any socialist formation.[46] The distinctive contribution of socialism lies not in any particular inventions that might emerge but rather in the reorganization of society in such a way that technological choices are no longer made (as we noted at the outset) on the basis of marketability and profit-potential, but rather on the basis of compatibility with the overall requirements of humanity and the natural world. The process of identifying those requirements will of course be a matter for debate, but the guiding principles for any decisions will be, on the one hand, the concern for long-term species-survival, and on the other, the assumption that no portion of the human race is entitled to deny any other portion of it, on any pretext, the conditions for a decent life.

45 See e.g. Richard S. Cooper, Joan F. Kennelly and Pedro Ordúñez García, "Health in Cuba," *International Journal of Epidemiology* 35:4 (2006), ije.oxfordjournals. org/content/35/4/817.full.

46 See above, Chapter 2; see also my entry, "Innovation," in the Historical-Critical Dictionary of Marxism; English text in *Historical Materialism* 16:3 (2008).

5

CAPITALIST AND SOCIALIST RESPONSES TO THE ECOLOGICAL CRISIS

The global ecological crisis sprang forth full-blown at roughly the same historical moment that global capital—welcoming the collapse of the Soviet bloc and the decay of the revolutionary process in China—was claiming a definitive victory over socialism. The irony of this historic convergence lies in the fact that there could be no more decisive a refutation of capitalist precepts than their long-term incompatibility with species-survival.

Unfortunately, the steamroller effect of capital's short-term political triumph has shown itself in unexpected places. Corporate hype about technological fixes has meshed conveniently with certain applications of the postmodernist "production of nature" thesis to lend credibility, even in leftist quarters, to the idea that while we might reject and challenge capitalism in matters of democracy and social justice, there is not much that we have to offer when it comes to decisions about production and consumption.

Precisely at the moment that the growth-principle has reached its limits, in the sense of having turned from a creative into a largely destructive force, precisely at this moment, the very milieus of political thought which are most attuned to formulating a radical alternative find themselves in part seduced by the sheer bluster and braggadocio of a system committed to perpetual technological upheaval and ready to beat down any effort to bring its practices under social control.

The ecological crisis is a complex mix of dangerous trends. Capitalist ideology characteristically views the components of this crisis piecemeal, thereby obscuring its systemic nature. The buildup of greenhouse gases and the consequent specter of a climatic "tip-ping point" have been widely if reluctantly acknowledged within the US ruling class, although for the most part without any match-ing sense of urgency (witness how little serious attention is paid to this prospect in mainstream campaign discourse).[1] But the other—not unrelated—dimensions of the crisis tend to be viewed either as local problems or, more alarmingly, as opportunities for future profit. I refer here to the spread of toxins, the depletion of vital goods (notably, fresh water and biodiversity), and the increasingly intrusive and reckless manipulation of basic natural processes (as in genetic engineering, cloud-seeding, changing the course of rivers).

An adequate response to the crisis will ultimately involve addressing all these dimensions. Given the range, the widespread acceptance, and the presumed normality of the existing power-pat-terns, however, such a response will require an unprecedentedly thoroughgoing process of mass political education. We are still only in the earliest stages of the necessary awareness. This means that we must first address convincingly the arguments of those who would downplay the depth of the transformation that long-term species-survival will require. One part of this task—responding to those who deny human agency in the climate crisis—is a matter of pitting straightforward scientific reasoning against assertions made principally by representatives of corporate capital.[2] But another challenge to socialist ecology comes from those on the left who, out of a misplaced sense of what is politically "realistic," put forward the view that the only feasible "green" agenda is a capitalist one. We need to examine (in context) some of the more recent expressions of this view before returning to address the larger practical chal-lenges that capitalism of whatever hue is incapable of meeting.

---

1   Politicians who deny climate-change provide convenient cover for an agenda of perpetual economic expansion which is pursued even by those corporate lead-ers who acknowledge climate-change.

2   See John W. Farley, "The Scientific Case for Modern Anthropogenic Global Warming," *Monthly Review*, 60:3 (July-August 2008).

Green Capitalism?

Among the many possible illustrations of "green capitalism" in practice, a small news-item in the financial section of the March 7, 2008 *New York Times* (page C6) provides a useful lead. Captioned "Gore Gets Rich," it reports that former Vice-President Al Gore, fresh from winning the Nobel Peace Prize for his cautionary filmed lecture about global warming, "recently invested $35 million with Capricorn Investment Group, a firm that Bloomberg [News] says puts clients' assets into hedge funds and invests in 'makers of environmentally friendly products.'" The article also notes that Gore has flourished from his business ties to Apple and to Google, and that "he was recently made a partner at Kleiner Perkins Caufield & Byers, the top-tier Silicon Valley venture capital firm." The Capricorn Group's website, which I visited just after reading that report, carried stories about the various projects in which its funds had been invested, one of which was Mendel Biotechnology Inc., which was working with BP and Monsanto—supported by a $125 million grant from the US Department of Energy—to "find a way to propagate miscanthus [a potentially more efficient fuel-producing plant than corn] for quick plantings and maximum yields."

This is quintessential capitalism. Its only green attribute is the notion of crop-derived fuel as offering (in the words of the Web report) a "clean and green" form of energy. Core aspects of the ecological crisis, however, remain unaddressed if not aggravated in this scenario: (1) Although biofuels may produce less greenhouse gas than petroleum, their aggregate impact—in terms of air and water pollution, soil degradation, and food prices—may be more severe.[3] (2) No recognition is given to the need to reduce the total amount of energy-consumption or of paved surfaces. (3) Large-scale use of cropland as a fuel source impinges on food-crops without reducing pressure on the world's water supply. (4) Agribusiness practices, whatever the product, have a negative impact on biodiversity. (5) Monsanto is implicated in the coercive imposition of genetically modified organisms (GMOs). (6) Silicon Valley (Gore's

---

3   See Fred Magdoff, "The Political Economy and Ecology of Biofuels," *Monthly Review*, 60:3 (July-August 2008).

other reported financial interest) is at the cutting edge of capitalist hyper-development (accelerated innovation and obsolescence; generation of vast quantities of toxic trash). (7) The US government continues to provide subsidies to corporations rather than supporting efforts to directly address long-term human needs.

Of course, the more familiar image of green capitalism is one of small grassroots enterprises offering local services, solar housing, organic food markets, etc. It is true—and promising—that as ecological awareness spreads, the space for such activities will grow. We should also acknowledge that the related exploration of alternative living arrangements may contribute in a positive way to the longer-term conversion that is required. More generally, it is certainly the case that any effective conservation measures (including steps toward renewable energy) that can be taken in the short run should be welcomed, whoever takes them. But it is important not to see in such steps any repudiation by capital of its ecologically and socially devastating core commitment to expansion, accumulation, and profit.

To remind ourselves of this core commitment is not to claim that capital ignores the environmental crisis; it is simply to account for the particular way it responds to it. This is partly made up of direct corporate initiatives and partly made up of measures taken by capitalist governments. At least in the United States, however, the former thrust predominates. The accepted self-designation of this approach is "corporate environmentalism"—defined in an authoritative text as "environmentally friendly actions not required by law"[4] and thereby signifying explicitly that the corporations themselves are setting the agenda.[5] The most tangible expression of corporate environmentalism is a substantial across-the-board jump, through the 1980s, in the numbers of management personnel assigned to deal with environmental issues.[6]

---

4 Thomas P. Lyon and John W. Maxwell, *Corporate Environmentalism and Public Policy* (New York: Cambridge University Press, 2004), 3.

5 Andrew J. Hoffman, *From Heresy to Dogma: An Institutional History of Corporate Environmentalism*, expanded edition (Stanford, CA: Stanford University Press, 2001), 3. Ironically, this thoroughly corporate-oriented Stanford Business Books publication was awarded a prize in memory of Rachel Carson.

6 Hoffman (ibid., 127) cites as emblematic the case of Amoco, whose Environmental Department staffing increased by a factor of approximately 8 between 1978 and 1993.

On the basis of both theory and performance, and viewing the corporate sector as a whole, we can say that this new emphasis has made itself felt in two ways. On the one hand, corporations have been alert to opportunities for making environmentally positive adjustments where these coincide with standard business criteria of efficiency and cost-reduction.[7] On the other hand, more importantly, corporations have acted directly on the political stage, with an exceptionally free hand in the US case. Both by lobbying and by direct penetration of policymaking bodies, they have molded regulatory practices, censored scientific reports, and shaped a defiant official posture in the global arena (exemplified by US withdrawal from the Kyoto accords). In addition, they have undertaken vast public relations campaigns ("greenwashing") to portray their practices as environmentally progressive.[8] From outside as well as within the United States, they have attempted—with considerable success—to define in their own interests the internationally accepted parameters of "sustainable development": initially, through the World Business Council on Sustainable Development driving the agenda of the 1992 Earth Summit in Rio, and subsequently, through the continuing activity of the World Trade Organization as well as via corporate partnerships with United Nations development agencies.[9]

None of these efforts embodies the slightest change in basic capitalist practice. To the contrary, they reflect a determination to shore up such practice at all costs. The reality of green capitalism is that capital pays attention to green issues; this is not at all the same as having green priorities.[10] Insofar as capital makes green-oriented

7   Michael E. Porter and Claas van der Linde, "Green and Competitive: Ending the Stalemate," *Harvard Business Review* 73:5 (Sept./Oct. 1995).

8   Jed Greer and Kenny Bruno, *Greenwash: The Reality behind Corporate Environmentalism* (New York: Apex Press, 1996).

9   Kenny Bruno and Joshua Karliner, *earthsummit.biz: The Corporate Takeover of Sustainable Development* (Oakland, CA: Food First Books, 2002). The corporate tendency to downplay the extent to which atmospheric carbon must be reduced in order to stave off catastrophic climate change is exemplified in the influential *Stern Review*; see the critique in the Editors' Introduction to *Monthly Review*, 60:3 (July-August 2008), 3-6.

10   See, for example, critiques of Wal-Mart at changewalmart.org/; also, "Green—Up to a Point: Some Companies Send Mixed Messages," *Business Week*, March 3, 2008. A particularly common expression of allegedly green concerns is the call for greater use of nuclear power. For a wide-ranging summary of the dangers of

adjustments beyond those that are either directly profit-friendly or advisable for PR purposes or protection against liability, it is because those adjustments have been imposed—or, as in the case of wind-turbines in Germany, stimulated and subsidized—by public authority.[11] Such authority, even though exerted within an overall capitalist framework, reflects primarily the political strength of non- or anti-capitalist forces (environmentalist organizations, trade unions, community groups, grassroots coalitions, etc.), although these may be supported in part by certain sectors of capital such as the alternative energy and insurance industries.

As this whole current of opinion becomes stronger, advocates of green capitalism pick up on the popular call for renewable energy, but accompany it with a vision of undiminished proliferation of industrial products.[12] In so doing, they overlook the complexity of the environmental crisis, which has to do not only with the burning of fossil fuels but with assaults on the earth's resource-base as a whole, including for example the paving over of green space, the raw-material and energy costs of producing solar collectors and wind-turbines, the encroachment on natural habitats (not only by buildings and pavement but also by dams, wind-turbines, etc.), the toxins associated with high-tech commodities, and the increasingly critical problem of waste disposal—in short, the routine spinoffs from capital's unqualified prioritization of economic growth.

Proponents of green capitalism respond to this by saying that economic growth, far from being the problem, is what holds the solution. Environmentalism, on this view, is a purely negative response to the ecological crisis, giving rise to unpopular practices like regulation and prohibition. Hence the singular "green

---

nuclear power, see Public Citizen, "The Fatal Flaws of Nuclear Power" (2016), www.citizen.org/Page.aspx?pid=2183.

11 On business considerations prompting green practices, see Peter Thayer Robbins, *Greening the Corporation: Management Strategy and the Environmental Challenge* (London: Earthscan Publications, 2001), 93. On Germany and wind turbines, see Naomi Klein, *This Changes Everything: Capitalism vs. the Climate* (New York: Simon & Schuster, 2014), 130ff.

12 Thus Robert F. Kennedy Jr., in his May 2008 manifesto, "The Next President's First Task" (www.vanityfair.com/politics/features/2008/05/rfk_manifesto200805), says that the United States could be powered entirely by solar, wind, and geothermal energy "even assuming every American owned a plug-in hybrid."

capitalist" caricature of environmentalists: "All of them direct our attention to stopping the bad, not creating the good."[13] The "good," from this perspective, is a scenario of jobs, material abundance, and energy independence—understood, however, within a characteristically capitalist competitive framework. While the need to cut greenhouse gases is recognized, the challenge is posed in narrowly technological terms. Attempts to resist consumerism are belittled, on the assumption that innovations, along with massive public investment, will solve any problem of scarcity (the vision is emphatically centered on the United States, with China invoked to signify that the drive to growth is unstoppable). The very existence of an environmental nexus is called into question, on the grounds that the category "environment" can only be conceived either as excluding humans or as being synonymous with "everything," at either of which extremes it is seen to make no sense.[14] The biological understanding of the environment as a matrix with interpenetrating parts is not entertained.

Ultimately, "green capitalism" is a contradiction in terms—the one pole referring to a complexly evolving equilibrium encompassing the ensemble of species-life, and the other, to the unchecked or cancerous growth of one of its particular components.[15] Ironically, however, the core capitalist response to ecological crisis is a further deepening of the logic of commodification. It is in this regard that capitalist practice has come to pose not just a material threat to ecological recovery, but also an ideological threat to socialist theory and, by extension, to the prospects for developing a long-term popular movement with an inspiring alternative vision.

---

13 Ted Nordhaus and Michael Shellenberger, in their *Wall Street Journal*-praised book, *Break Through: From the Death of Environmentalism to the Politics of Possibility* (Boston: Houghton Mifflin, 2007), 6. See also Shellenberger, "The Coming Bursting of the Green Bubble," April 22, 2008, thebreakthrough.org/blog/2008/04/its_china_stupid_why_kristof_g.shtml. Cf. Richard Douthwaite, *The Growth Illusion: How Economic Growth Has Enriched the Few, Impoverished the Many and Endangered the Planet*, rev.ed. (Gabriola, BC: New Society, 1999).

14 Nordhaus and Shellenberger, *Break Through*, 8

15 See John McMurtry, *The Cancer Stage of Capitalism* (London: Pluto Press, 1999), esp. 113f.

STRUGGLE OVER THE MEANING OF "NATURE"

The ideological response of capital to the environmental crisis has been to reaffirm faith in the market. At the most immediate level, this entails arguing that as any kind of good becomes scarce, its price will go up and the demand for it will consequently shrink. A problem arises, however, when the goods in question are, like air, water, soil, or forests, essential to survival. But the logic is relentless: supposedly there is nothing on which a price cannot be set, and price in turn implies ownership—a good thing, on this view, since only with ownership comes a sense of responsibility (never mind what the goals of the owner might be). The field of application for this principle is unlimited. A 1991 text thus proposed that whales "be 'branded' by genetic prints and tracked by satellites, providing another way to define property rights."[16] Once prices are set on so-called "natural capital" there follows a market in "rights to pollute," which, among other effects, allows for offsetting any technological improvements with production increases.

One extension of this whole market-driven approach has been the idea that the way to preserve tropical forests or natural wetlands is simply to offer compensation for their being kept untouched. A cash value is thus apparently placed on "nature." It is from this observation that the leftist ecological debate has now been joined by arguments questioning the effectiveness of a socialist approach to species-survival. In the words of Neil Smith, "If still incompletely, the market has now retaken and recolonized environmental practices.... This represents a sweeping political co-optation and victory for capital and a defeat for environmental-cum-socialist politics."[17]

The assumption underlying this assessment is signaled by Smith in the preceding paragraph, where he writes, "The explosion of ecological commodification has significantly deepened the production of nature." It is this "production of nature" concept that Smith considers to be insufficiently recognized in ecosocialist thinking.

---

16 Terry L. Anderson and Donald R. Leal, *Free Market Environmentalism* (San Francisco: Pacific Research Institute for Public Policy, 1991), 34.

17 Neil Smith, "Nature as Accumulation Strategy," in Leo Panitch and Colin Leys, eds., *Coming to Terms with Nature: Socialist Register* 2007 (London: Merlin Press, 2006), 26.

He characterizes the latter as adhering to an oversimplified dichotomy between society and nature, where "nature" is viewed in quasi-mystical romanticized terms as something pristine, untouched by the human imprint. In an earlier essay, Smith summarizes the superiority of his own position in these terms: "The argument of the 'production of nature' has the advantage, in that it gets beyond the powerful fetishism of 'nature-in-itself' to focus on the social relationship with nature."[18]

In fact, of course, the latter focus in itself is no different from that of ecosocialists; it flows logically from recognizing, with Richard Lewontin, that "the environment," insofar as it is imagined as being untouched by any of its constituent organisms (notably, the human species), "does not exist."[19] Marx already made the same point when he noted that pure nature untouched by human beings, as depicted by Feuerbach, "no longer exists anywhere (except perhaps on a few Australian coral islands of recent origin)."[20]

Why should Smith have jumped, however, from an incontestable acknowledgment that the environment is generated (in part) by humans to an implicit assertion that the only available framework for remedial measures is the one imposed by capital? This can only derive from a one-sided emphasis on the "production of nature" by society (in this case capital) and a failure to understand Marx's more complex dialectic of the human metabolism with nature, according to which human beings do not create nature, but only transpose it from one form into another, often with unforeseen consequences. Thus, Marx quoted Pietro Verri as saying, "All the phenomena of the universe, whether produced by the hand of man or indeed by the universal laws of physics, are not to be conceived of as acts of creation but solely as a reordering of matter." For this reason nature can only be "produced" by means of nature itself and in conformity with natural laws. The failure to understand or to follow these laws

18   Neil Smith, "The Production of Nature," in George Robertson et al., eds., *Future Natural: Nature, Science, Culture* (London: Routledge, 1996), 50

19   Richard Lewontin, "Genes, Environment, and Organisms" (1997), in Richard Lewontin and Richard Levins, *Biology Under the Influence: Dialectical Essays on Ecology, Agriculture, and Health* (New York: Monthly Review Press, 2007), 234.

20   Karl Marx and Friedrich Engels, *Collected Works* (New York: International Publishers, 1975), vol. 5, 40.

leads to ecological crises, with nature, as Engels observed, thereby taking its "revenge."[21]

What Smith appears to have done, in rejecting the notion of a pristine nature, is to have gone to the opposite extreme: if "nature" as such is a figment, then the only real nature is what has been "produced" by humans; as he says at one point, "universal nature is every bit as much a capitalist as a pre- and post-capitalist project."[22] In other words, there would appear to be no qualitative difference, in his view, in the claims of different social formations to represent natural relations. Any objective process that might occur within a natural ecosystem independent of society is thus equally obliterated by all societies—pre-capitalist, capitalist, and post-capitalist. The environment is thus mere grist for bourgeois economics, which is seen as holding the cure to all its ills. Hence Smith's remarkable statement, in his *Socialist Register* chapter, that "the central use value of the restored wetlands is precisely their ability to garner exchange value under the new conditions of created scarcity."[23]

This view of nature as having no existence apart from that which has been conferred upon it by the human species is in the tradition of a long line of idealist thought whose most recent expression has been postmodernism. Smith signals his intellectual debt to this mode of thought with a pertinent quote from Michel Foucault: "In fact, power produces: it produces reality; it produces domains of objects and rituals of truth."[24] In the present context, the capitalist market assigns value to natural resources and processes, and this

---

21 Karl Marx, *Capital*, vol. 1 (London: Penguin, 1976), 133-34, 647; Karl Marx and Friedrich Engels, *Collected Works* (New York: International Publishers, 1975), vol. 25, 461; Paul Burkett and John Bellamy Foster, "Metabolism, Energy, and Entropy in Marx's Critique of Political Economy," *Theory and Society*, vol. 35 (2006), 109-56.

22 Smith, "The Production of Nature," 46.

23 Smith, "Nature as Accumulation Strategy," 18. For an in-depth critique of this type of thinking, see John Bellamy Foster, *Ecology Against Capitalism* (New York: Monthly Review Press, 2002), esp. Ch. 2 ("The Ecological Tyranny of the Bottom Line"). Foster's insight is extended to more recent writings in his 2016 book (co-authored with Paul Burkett), *Marx and the Earth: An Anti-Critique* (Leiden: Brill).

24 From Foucault, *Discipline and Punish* (1979); quoted in Smith, "The Production of Nature," 51. On the political impact of postmodernist thought, see Timothy Brennan, *Wars of Position: The Cultural Politics of Left and Right* (New York: Columbia University Press, 2006).

alone determines the degree to which they will appear and function as needed.

And yet it is precisely the non-commodified substratum of life which governs the processes by which soil is renewed, aquifers replenished, botanical diversity maintained, insect species and their predators nourished, hillsides protected from erosion, and much else as well.[25] Money values are as little applicable to any of this as they are to the life of a particular person or community. To affirm otherwise is to reject the basic sinew of resistance to ecological devastation. It is almost to deny that ecological devastation is real. The currently fashionable form taken by such denial is the contention that so long as a massive program of energy-conversion is carried out (with or without nuclear power as one of its components), productivist assumptions can remain unchallenged. Smith largely buys into this approach. While he opposes GMOs and calls for "a truly democratic production of nature," he indicates his affinity with the capitalist approach by urging us in the same passage "to think how nature ought to change"![26]

Underlying this is a notion of human beings as somehow outside of nature, i.e. existing as independent agents "producing" nature but not themselves subject to it. Hence the human species is thought capable not only of using and molding natural resources, but also (at least implicitly) of changing or even producing/creating nature's modus operandi—in supposed defiance of physical and biological dynamics. This reflects a peculiar mix of fantasy, alienation, and hubris. It is at one, however, with the overall current response of capital to the ecological crisis it has unleashed, a response which, in its more extreme forms, has imagined offsetting global warming by

---

25 For persistent and eloquent reminders of these "gifts of nature," see the works of Vandana Shiva, e.g., *Earth Democracy: Justice, Sustainability, and Peace* (Cambridge, MA: South End Press, 2005). The processes in question are referred to by Marx as "metabolic restoration" (Foster, "The Ecology of Destruction," *Monthly Review* 58:9 [February 2007], 11). For critique of attempts to attribute market-value to such processes, see Ch. 2 ("Values in Ecological Value Analysis") of Paul Burkett, *Marxism and Ecological Economics* (Leiden: Brill, 2006).

26   Smith, "Nature as Accumulation Strategy," 34. This concluding section of Smith's *Socialist Register* chapter draws on Nordhaus & Shellenberger (above, note 13), whose work he cites. For a basic critique of productivism/developmentalism, see Yrjö Haila and Richard Levins, *Humanity and Nature: Ecology, Science and Society* (London: Pluto Press, 1992), 162-167.

such stratagems as shooting heat-reflecting mirrors into the upper atmosphere.[27]

More immediately, in terms of debates on the left, the notion that we must surrender to capitalist logic tends to foster an accusatory identification of radical ecological demands with a supposedly unwarranted sense of urgency—as in the statement, "it is important to try to avoid an anxiety-driven ecological catastrophism...."[28] In fact, one does not even have to be on the left to recognize the accelerated pace—reinforced by feedback loops—at which natural phenomena are spinning out of their accustomed patterns and at which certain species, including the human inhabitants of vulnerable zones, are already paying the ultimate price.[29] Yet, given a socialist perspective, we are equipped to match the justified feeling of urgency with a correspondingly radical approach to the underlying causes of the problem. This is something, however, that Smith wishes to deny, declaring that environmentalism "is dead...as an anti-capitalist movement."[30]

Green Goals beyond Capital

People arrive at a socialist position from many different starting points or initial concerns. The particular attribute of an ecological focus—whether it comes early or late in a person's political awakening—is that it addresses basic survival-interests which affect everyone. More specifically in relation to socialism, the ecological theme points sharply to the need for structural changes that are both deep and wide-ranging.

Our present discussion has so far indicated the basic sense in which corporate capital is both disinclined and unsuited to pursue

---

27 See Ch. 6 ("Dimming the Sun") of Klein, *This Changes Everything*.

28 Preface to Panitch and Leys, *Socialist Register 2007*, x. This collection also contains a chapter by Daniel Buck ("The Ecological Question: Can Capitalism Prevail?") which is notable for its suggestion that capitalism's aptitude for sweeping technological transformation equips it to resolve the ecological crisis. Ibid., 64f.

29 Thus Bill McKibben, in *Deep Economy* (New York: Henry Holt, 2007), offers a biting critique of the growth-obsession but no attribution of responsibility for it; he explains agricultural consolidation by saying that "we [sic] have substituted oil for people" (67).

30 Smith, "Nature as Accumulation Strategy," 32.

an ecological agenda. But we have yet to bring out the full span of ecologically requisite tasks for which capitalism falls short. The economic growth issue requires further discussion in relation to its most recent expression in the form of high-tech innovation and toxic trash. Closely related to this problem are two further requirements for a green economy, both of which go far beyond the constraints of the capitalist paradigm. One is an end to militarism and imperialism; the other is a cultural transformation that would make possible a new consensus as to the social/economic requirements for a good life.

Capitalist Hyper-Development, Toxic Trash, and the Commons

A major issue in challenging the goal of economic growth is that this inescapably calls consumption-levels into question. It is remarkable, however, how little effort is routinely made to disaggregate the "consumption" category. Common parlance, reinforced by the typical framing of cross-national statistics, links consumption to the satisfaction of individual needs or wants, whereas in fact, as an ecological category, it refers to all throughput of materials and energy, for whatever purpose. Much of the appeal of "green capitalism" would vanish if people could focus on how much of its ever-expanding production went into goods and services that are useless if not destructive.

Capital seeks always to produce and sell as much as possible. Ecology posits the need for massive cutbacks in throughput, but the market offers no opportunity to target such cutbacks on the basis of any rational assessment of need. Instead, it constantly drives businesses to create new "needs" in order to maintain a perpetual cycle of innovation, obsolescence, and upgrading. Although this has long been a familiar phenomenon, it has accelerated markedly with the new waves of digital and instant-communication devices.[31] Hence there has been an extraordinary proliferation of toxic trash (especially heavy metals), which has led to growing recognition

---

31 See Jon Mooallem, "The Afterlife of Cellphones," *New York Times Magazine*, January 13, 2008; for earlier analyses: Paul A. Baran and Paul M. Sweezy, *Monopoly Capital* (New York: Monthly Review Press, 1966), Ch. 5; Ernest Mandel, *Late Capitalism* (London: New Left Books, 1975), 192.

that responsibility for final disposal of such items can no longer be simply left with the consumer. The concept of "extended producer responsibility" (EPR) is now gaining wide acceptance, although it is not yet strictly and universally applied, relying instead on modest financial incentives to purchasers, flavored with appeals to ecological civic-mindedness.[32]

In terms of the "green capitalism" debate, EPR practice can be seen as an outcome of public pressure on the producers, but with the side-benefit to them of reducing their dependence on a constant re-supply of materials. Potentially more consequential, however, are the implications of this process for the whole question of private versus public ownership. A rigorous interpretation of producer responsibility would necessarily make inroads on private ownership not just in the sphere of production but also in regard to certain categories of personal consumption, especially those involving land, scarce and/or toxic materials, and high levels of energy-use. Ownership would become more akin to stewardship, creating a much wider constituency of accountability for the earth's raw materials. While the most immediately compelling examples arise from the need to contain dangerous substances, the same logic would govern the imperative to protect vital resources (water, soil, trees, fish, etc.).

If such reasoning should concern the private individual who is getting rid of an old computer or TV, how much more crucially does it apply to the manufacturer who might wish to render obsolete a whole line of products! Now that awareness is spreading of the social impact of even individual consumption, how much easier it should be to persuade people, finally, of the social—and therefore socially accountable—character of production. And indeed, only a relatively small further descriptive step would now be needed to cast in socialist terms the environmentalist recognition that every "private" act of combustion (of whatever scale) imposes a burden on the atmospheric commons. The parallel argument has already

---

32 Elizabeth Grossman, *High Tech Trash: Digital Devices, Hidden Toxics, and Human Health* (Washington, D.C.: Island Press, 2007), 159f. On the broader political economy of trash, see Heather Rogers, *Gone Tomorrow: The Hidden Life of Garbage* (New York: New Press, 2005).

been sharply formulated for the world's water-supply;[33] it could similarly extend to every other natural resource, including not only those which are "consumed" but also those which, whether benign or toxic in themselves, help constitute the necessary substratum for other vital processes, both within and outside the circuit of social production.

Addressing Militarism and Imperialism

Given capital's sacrosanct commitment to growth, it is understandable that mainstream environmentalist organizations are loath to deconstruct the phenomenon of consumption. To distinguish between useful and wasteful (or harmful) consumption would be to defy the precept that all such determinations should be made through the workings of the market—except where government acts directly on behalf of capital.

The military sector of production and "service" is of particular relevance here, because it does not arise in response to any kind of direct mass demand. Within the advanced capitalist countries, the military performs an instrumental function which is truly vital only to the ruling class. This is especially the case with the US military, which, since 1945, has been the unrivalled global enforcer of capitalist interests.[34] US military operations—including training and weapons-development as well as actual fighting—occupy a distinctive position in economic/ecological terms, in that their very mission of protecting capital releases them from any possible restraint that might impinge on enterprises competing with one another (let alone any restraint arising from organized popular pressure). This applies as much to private military contractors as it does to the official armed forces. What is decisive is that both are underwritten by the "employer of last resort," which in this issue-area transmits the consensus of corporate capital reflected in the governing political duopoly.

---

33 Maude Barlow, *Blue Covenant: The Global Water Crisis and the Coming Battle for the Right to Water* (New York: New Press, 2008), 164ff.

34 For a thorough analysis, see John Bellamy Foster, *Naked Imperialism: The US Pursuit of Global Dominance* (New York: Monthly Review Press, 2006).

The free rein enjoyed by the military/paramilitary consists not only in the unchallenged funding of its massive worldwide operations but also, more specifically, in the protection it enjoys, grounded in "security" arguments, against political questioning of its toxic practices, such as the pervasive use of dioxin in Vietnam and of depleted-uranium shell-casings in Iraq[35]—not to mention the continuous prodigious consumption of petroleum which prompted the observation (by Michael Klare) that a major consideration behind US occupation of oil-rich lands is to assure a sufficient fuel-supply to sustain the military activities themselves.[36]

The larger imperial drive underlying the acceptance of such a self-perpetuating cycle remains for the most part outside the sphere of public debate. Mainstream politicians conveying disquiet about the Iraq occupation thus spoke of "redeploying" US troops rather than questioning their interventionist role as such. This reflects the extraordinary degree to which imperialist assumptions pervade the full bipartisan spectrum of US politics, constituting the central obstacle to any critical rethinking of the goals of production and consumption.

The separation of the growth issue from the question of militarism and imperialism reflects the ideological parameters of US political discourse. Growth is an issue of "the economy," which is defined as a "domestic" matter; militarism, global projection, and war come under the heading of "foreign policy." This compartmentalization is entirely spurious; its deeply ingrained status is a major block to working-class/popular awareness. The ecological crisis—as illustrated in the threat posed to all coastlines by the melting of polar icecaps—is at once a global and a "domestic" issue. Its adequate explication could help shatter, once and for all, popular acquiescence in one of the key blinders erected by bourgeois ideology.

---

35 See William Thomas, *Scorched Earth: The Military's Assault on the Environment* (Philadelphia: New Society Publishers, 1995), Seth Shulman, *The Threat at Home: Confronting the Toxic Legacy of the US Military* (Boston: Beacon Press, 1992), and Gar Smith, ed., *The War and Environment Reader* (Charlottesville, VA: Just World Books, 2017).

36 See Michael Klare, *The Race for What's Left: The Global Scramble for the World's Last Resources* (New York: Metropolitan Books, 2012).

Popular Cultural Transformation

To challenge the militarism/imperialism/growth agenda is to call into question not just policies but also emotions—both civic and private—whose resonance extends far beyond the confines of the capitalist class. The civic aspect is associated with the rhetoric and symbols of national grandeur; the private aspect, with the whole mindset of individualism and consumerism. Mainstream environmentalism, with its emphasis on competitive prowess, has left the civic aspect unchallenged. Insofar as it has addressed the private aspect (as for example in the Al Gore film), it has done so essentially in the form of appeals to conscience.

Where the private and the civic dimensions would merge would be in developing a full-scale class analysis of responsibility for the current crisis and, with it, a movement which could pose a systemic alternative. The steps so far taken in this direction have been limited. Exposés like Gore's have called attention, for example, to the role of particular oil companies in sponsoring attacks on scientific findings related to climate change, but the idea that there could be an antagonism between capitalism and the environment as such[37] has not yet made its way into general public debate. Until this happens, the inertial impact of the prevailing ideology will severely limit the scope of any concrete recuperative measures.

The situation is comparable to that surrounding any prospective revolution: until a certain critical point has been reached, the only demands that appear to have a chance of acceptance are the "moderate" ones. But what makes the situation revolutionary is the very fact that the moderate or "realistic" proposals will not provide a solution. What gives these proposals a veneer of reasonableness is no more than their acceptability to political forces which, although unable to design a response commensurate with the scale of the problem, have not yet been displaced from their positions of power. But this very inability on the part of those forces is also an expression of their weakness. They sit precariously atop a process they do not understand, whose scope they cannot imagine, and over which

---

37   As expressed, e.g., in: Foster, *Ecology Against Capitalism*; Joel Kovel, *The Enemy of Nature: The End of Capitalism or the End of the World?*, 2nd ed. (London: Zed Press, 2007); and Klein, *This Changes Everything*.

they can have no control. (Or, if they do sense the gravity of the situation, they view it with a siege mentality, seeking above all to assure their own survival.[38])

At this point, it is clear that the purchase on "realism" has changed hands. The "moderates," with their relentless insistence on coaxing an ecological cure out of a system inherently committed to trampling everything in its path, have lost all sense of reality. The question now becomes whether the hitherto misgoverned populace will be prepared to push through the radical measures (by now clearly the only realistic ones) or whether its members will have remained so encased within the capitalist paradigm that the only thing they can do is to try—following the cue of those who plunged us all into this fix—to fend individually for themselves.

This is the conjuncture that all our efforts have been building for; it will provide the ultimate test of how well we have done our work. In order for the scope of the needed measures to be grasped by sufficient numbers of people, an intense level of grassroots organizing will already have to be underway. However, the measures themselves, if they are to accomplish their purpose, will have to further advance the very process that put them on the agenda to begin with. A characteristically revolutionary mix of persuasion and coercion will necessarily apply—the balance of these two methods depending partly on the effectiveness of prior consciousness-raising and partly on the window of time available for the required steps.

No dimension of life will be untouched. From our present vantage point we can only begin to envisage the specific changes, which will primarily involve a reversal or undoing of the more wasteful and harmful structures bequeathed by prior development. Fortunately, however, it will not be a matter of starting from scratch. Many historical lessons have already been learned, and not all of them are of things to avoid. There are positive models as well.

---

38 Thus, in the Pentagon's climate-crisis planning, "the US effectively seeks to build a fortress around itself to preserve resources." David Stripp, "The Pentagon's Weather Nightmare," *Fortune*, February 9, 2004 (money.cnn.com/magazines/fortune/fortune_archive/2004/02/09/360120/index.htm).

GREEN SOCIALISM: PRECEDENTS AND HARBINGERS

If "green capitalism" is a contradiction in terms, then one might naturally regard "green socialism" as a redundancy. In the long run, this is certainly the case, in the sense that green policies presuppose the curbing of expansionist drives, which in turn requires that economic decisions be grounded in a wider social (socialist) consensus as to how resources may or may not be used. In the short term, however, there is nothing automatic in the link between green and red policy-measures. Historically, the two agendas have been more in conflict than in harmony. Having addressed the reasons for this problem in Chapters 1 and 2, I note here some cases which give grounds for hope.

The first example emerged from the Russian Revolution. The Soviet leadership's continuing focus on growth was partially offset, during the early years of the regime, by an extraordinary interest in creating a more advanced level of mass culture and, with it, an approach to development that, compared to its capitalist counterparts, would be more firmly anchored in an awareness of natural limits. It was in this context that Lenin signed (in 1921) a law establishing, over widely dispersed areas in the Soviet Union, "the first protected territory anywhere to be created by a government exclusively in the interests of the scientific study of nature."[39] Although these areas (*zapovedniki*) were subsequently dissolved (under Stalin), what is important to us in their brief history is what it suggests about the capacities and potential initiative of socialist leadership, as well as the early sensitivity of some of the Russian Marxists—long before the current crisis—to the fragility of the ecosphere.[40]

The second example pertains to power exercised at the municipal level, within an otherwise capitalist framework. It is important, however, for what it suggests about the processes involved in any full-scale ecological conversion. I refer to the Italian city of Bologna during the period of its elected Communist government in the mid-1970s. At the heart of its urban reform was the exclusion of private

---

39 Douglas R. Weiner, *Models of Nature: Ecology, Conservation, and Cultural Revolution in Soviet Russia* (Bloomington: Indiana University Press, 1988), 29.

40 Ibid., 230. See also John Bellamy Foster, "Late Soviet Ecology and the Planetary Crisis," *Monthly Review*, 67:2 (June 2015).

automobiles from most of the city's central residential and business district. It achieved this outcome partly through a relatively cost-effective switch to free rush-hour bus service and partly through several exhaustive rounds of neighborhood meetings to decide upon zoning.[41] Although the capitalist class maintained its hold on the traditional levers of power, setting tight limits on the scope of possible change, the participatory approach to policymaking was shown to be effective. A collective history of such efforts, which work especially well in addressing universally recognized problems such as those having to do with the environment, is part of the preparatory process for eventual popular rule.

The third and perhaps most impressive application of socialist ecology is that of Cuba. The initial effect on Cuba of the Soviet collapse (1991) offers a foretaste of the difficulties that will hit many other countries when their resource-base is cut off. Although Cuba would later (after 1999) receive significant oil-shipments from Venezuela, it lacked such a collaborative supplier in the early 1990s. Its immediate predicament then was comparable to that which any oil-dependent country will experience in the post-peak oil era. The country's response was radical, creative, and, above all, green.[42] Confronted with a fuel shortage, the government imported massive numbers of bicycles. Unable to run tractors and lacking chemical fertilizer, the government promoted a full-scale return to organic farming methods. Its reforestation program was cited as a model of its kind, and Cuba now offers the only remaining habitat to many of the Americas' tropical species. Finally, encouraged by appropriate land-grants, planning laws, and seed houses - "the only nationwide infrastructure for urban agriculture in the world"—Cubans planted urban gardens on a large scale (more than 30,000 in the city of Havana as of 2003).[43]

These examples should give us confidence in affirming that we must not be satisfied with the fall-back scenario of an imagined

---

41 Max Jaggi, "Free Fares Were Only the Beginning," in Jaggi et al., *Red Bologna* (London: Writers and Readers, 1977).

42 See Richard Levins, "How Cuba Is Going Ecological," *Capitalism Nature Socialism*, 16:3 (September 2005).

43 Raquel Pinderhughes, *Alternative Urban Futures* (Lanham, MD: Rowman & Littlefield, 2004), 212, 213.

green capitalism. Of course, we should both press for and implement ecological measures without delay—making demands at the national level and acting directly at the local level (where popular control is possible)—even while capital still reigns. But we should not expect to achieve anything close to a long-term environmental solution unless and until a society-wide democratic planning structure, capable of properly targeting and implementing the full agenda of transitional investments (including the reconfiguration of cities), is in place.[44]

The development of such a structure, like that of the ecological agenda itself, is not an all-or-nothing matter. As the Bologna example suggests, participatory planning for certain dimensions of policy can be initiated prior to the full transfer of state power from one class to another. Further instances of such practice have been offered since the 1970s by a number of Brazilian cities which have instituted participatory budgeting.[45] However, as the Cuban experience shows, it is also possible—not only in the matter of urban gardens but also for day-to-day economic decisions more generally—that popular participation can be introduced as a matter of deliberate policy by a revolutionary government.[46] In other words, there is no fixed trajectory for the link between instituting a socialist framework and developing the particular mechanisms (and cultural traits) that will allow it to work.

This preeminently dialectical process will unfold in distinct ways in each national setting, in full awareness of prior worldwide experience. It may be generally observed that first-epoch socialism showed the difficulty of transforming a society without having in place an already existing network and culture of grassroots political participation. It is noteworthy that the revolutionary ferment of the early 2000s in Latin America featured a strong emphasis on local popular networks, whether evolving with the encouragement of

---

44 For wide-ranging discussions of this process, see *Science & Society*, 66:1 (Spring 2002) (special issue: *Building Socialism Theoretically*, ed. Pat Devine).

45 Gianpaolo Baiocchi, "Brazilian Cities in the Nineties and Beyond: New Urban Dystopias and Utopias," *Socialism and Democracy*, 15:2 (Fall 2001).

46 See for example the first-hand account in Peter Roman, "The Law-Making Process in Cuba: Debating the Bill on Agricultural Cooperatives," *Socialism and Democracy*, 19:2 (July 2005).

the state (as in Venezuela's Bolivarian process) or in the face of its hostility (as in Mexico and in Bolivia).[47]

The integral link between the ecological and the socialist dimensions of this process lies in the common demand for decommodification. In ecological terms, this requires expansion of the natural commons—the fount of life-giving replenishment. In economic policy terms, it consists of reducing the sphere within which market-exchange (the law of value) prevails and expanding the scope for the direct satisfaction of need—both individual and social.

An emblematic instance of what is currently lacking was reported in a *New York Times* story headlined "As Prices Rise, Farmers Spurn Conservation."[48] The price-rise reflects heightened demand for cash crops, including corn for ethanol. The income from sale of such crops greatly exceeds the government subsidies received by the farmers for keeping land out of production for ecological purposes (species habitat, water conservation, etc.). Of course, the government could theoretically increase the subsidies, but the pressure would continue over time, threatening an unending cycle, in which more and more public funds would be allocated simply to offset the farmers' absolute legal right, under capitalism, to decide how "their" land should be used.

Since the ecological priority will then be expressed in a constantly rising outlay of tax dollars for the subsidy payments, it will become natural to put the question: why shouldn't ecologically informed management of the land—and therefore the necessary legal power over it—reside directly in the public sphere in the first place? Why should such a vital matter be decided on the basis of acquisitive drives and market pressures?

These questions are longstanding, but here—as with the issue of toxic trash—the ecological crisis has raised them to a heightened level of urgency. By the same token, it has added new weight to the argument for socialism.

---

47 For detailed coverage, see *Socialism and Democracy* issues of November 2005 (19:3, special issue, *The Reawakening of Revolution in Latin America*, ed. Gerardo Rénique); July 2007 (21:2, special section on Oaxaca); and November 2007 (21:3, article by Roger Burbach and Camila Piñeiro on Venezuela). For an overview, see D.L. Raby, *Democracy and Revolution: Latin America and Socialism Today* (London: Pluto Press, 2006).

48 *New York Times*, April 9, 2008, front page.

6

BEYOND "GREEN CAPITALISM"

A disdain for the natural environment has characterized capitalism from the beginning. As Marx noted, capital abuses the soil as much as it exploits the worker.[1] The makings of ecological breakdown are thus inherent in capitalism. No serious observer now denies the severity of the environmental crisis, but it is still not widely recognized as a *capitalist* crisis, that is, as a crisis arising from and perpetuated by the rule of capital and hence incapable of resolution within the capitalist framework.

It is useful to remind ourselves that although Marx situated capitalism's crisis-tendencies initially in the business cycle (specifically, in its downward phase), he recognized at the same time that those tendencies could manifest themselves under other forms—the first of these being the drive to global expansion.[2] Such manifestations are not inherently cyclical; they are permanent trends. They can be sporadically offset, but for as long as capitalism prevails, they cannot be reversed. They encompass 1) increased concentration of economic power, 2) increased polarization between rich and poor, both within and across national boundaries, 3) a permanent readiness for military engagement in support of these drives, and 4), of special concern to us here, the uninterrupted debasement or depletion of vital natural resources.

---

1 Speaking respectively of "large-scale industry" and "industrially pursued large-scale agriculture," Marx wrote, "the former lays waste and ruins labour-power and thus the natural power of man, whereas the latter does the same to the natural power of the soil." *Capital*, vol. 3, tr. David Fernbach (London: Penguin Books, 1991), 950.
2 *Communist Manifesto*, section I.

The economic recession of 2008, widely recognized as the most severe since the post-1929 depression, has been variously interpreted on the Left in terms of whether or not capital can overcome it by in effect restoring the remedial measures—including bank regulation but also labor protections—that it had accepted (in the United States) in the 1930s. To the extent that such remediation is viewed as possible, the crisis is seen as undermining only the neoliberal agenda and not capitalism as such.[3] In that case, we would be witnessing a perhaps cyclical return to a period of greater governmental regulation (including greater responsiveness to limited working-class demands).

But what is not at all cyclical—and what most sharply distinguishes the present crisis from that of the 1930s—is the backdrop of aggravated environmental devastation. The reign of capital has now been thrown into disarray not only by financial chaos, but also by the shrinkage and disruption of the natural infrastructure which serves not only the survival needs of the human species but also the particular requirements of the capitalist ruling class. The immediate grounds for ruling-class concern arise along several major axes: a) rising raw-material and energy costs, b) losses from catastrophic climate events, and c) mass dislocation, popular disaffection, and eventual social upheaval.

It is this set of preoccupations that drives the political agenda of "green capitalism." While there are obvious points of convergence between different green agendas, it eventually becomes clear that any full merger between an agenda that is insistently capitalist and one that accentuates the green dimension is impossible. On the other hand, immediate pro-ecology steps are urgently needed, irrespective of their sponsorship. The resulting dilemma is one that the Left must face without delay, as an integral step in developing whatever more radical strategy might be possible for the longer term.

---

3   Rick Wolff, "Economic Crisis from a Socialist Perspective," *Socialism and Democracy*, 23:2 (July 2009), 3.

THE "GREEN CAPITALIST" AGENDA[4]

At a conceptual level, it is clear that "green capitalism" seeks to bind together two antagonistic notions. To be green means to prioritize the health of the ecosphere, with all that this entails in terms of curbing greenhouse gases and preserving biodiversity. To promote capitalism, by contrast, is to foster growth and accumulation, treating both the workforce and the natural environment as mere inputs.

Capital is no stranger to contradiction, however. Just as it seeks to balance market-expansion with wage-restraint, so it must seek to balance perpetual growth with preservation of the basic conditions for survival. Despite the ultimate incompatibility of these two goals, therefore, capital must to some extent pursue both at once. Although green capitalism is an oxymoron, it is therefore nonetheless a policy-objective. Its proponents thus find themselves in an ongoing two-front struggle against, on the one hand, capital's more shortsighted advocates and, on the other, the demand for a far-reaching ecologically grounded conversion of production and consumption.

The green capitalist vision is sometimes associated with small enterprises, which can directly implement green criteria by, for example, using renewable energy sources, avoiding toxic chemicals, repairing or recycling used products, and minimizing reliance on long-distance shipment for either supplies or sales. But the scope of such practices is likely to be severely limited by market-pressures. The aspect of local self-sufficiency is most widely seen in the food-services sector, especially in farmers' markets, which have experienced a notable resurgence in recent years in industrialized countries. This corresponds more to what Marx called "simple commodity production," however, than to capitalist enterprise. Agribusiness allows residual space for it, but at the same time undercuts it through a) economies of scale facilitated by technologies of food processing and storage, b) political clout, resulting in subsidies to

---

4   This section is drawn from my report written for the Rosa Luxemburg Foundation (www.rosalux.de), entitled "The 'Green Capitalist' Agenda in the United States: Theory, Structure, Alternatives," published in English as an Appendix to Stephan Kaufmann and Tadzio Müller, *Grüner Kapitalismus: Krise, Klimawandel und kein Ende des Wachstums* (Berlin: Karl Dietz Verlag, 2009).

itself, and c) reliance on a typically migrant workforce that receives less than a living wage. Because of the resulting cost-differences (as well as inconveniences of access), patronage of farmers' markets is likely to remain primarily a political choice until much more is done to offset the artificial competitive edge enjoyed by the food-industrial complex.

Focusing now on the dominant corporate sector, we find the green capitalist agenda expressed partly by the enterprises themselves, partly by industry associations, and partly by government. For the corporations themselves, "green" practice takes essentially three forms: 1) energy-saving and other cost-cutting measures which are advantageous to them in any case; 2) compliance with whatever regulations may be enforced by a government in which they normally have a large voice; and 3), most importantly, public relations (PR). The industry associations further amplify the PR aspect, playing an especially vital role on the global stage, where they strive to establish the common assumptions underlying international agreements. They have worked extensively to influence the United Nations Development Program, and they also carry out large-scale lobbying campaigns to set negotiating parameters for the periodic Earth Summits (Rio de Janeiro 1992, Kyoto 1997, Johannesburg 2002, Copenhagen 2009, Paris 2015). The Business Council for Sustainable Development thus came into being in the run-up to the Rio conference, declaring in its charter that "economic growth provides the conditions in which protection of the environment can best be achieved." Under its influence, the monitoring of global environmental measures was entrusted to the World Bank, which in the ensuing decade paradoxically invested more than 15 times as much in fossil-fuel projects as in renewable energy.[5] The Kyoto conference advanced similar criteria five years later by enshrining emissions-trading as the strategy for battling global warming. This practice, under the rubric of "cap and trade," has become the centerpiece of governmental proposals in the United States. It posits an incentive-based approach to corporate policy, under which enterprises participate in a market in pollution-credits. Because of the

---

5   Kenny Bruno and Joshua Karliner, *earthsummit.biz: The Corporate Takeover of Sustainable Development* (Oakland, Cal.: Food First Books, 2002), 30.

political clout of the corporations, however, the initial cost of these credits may be reduced to zero. At the same time, the most severe industrial offenders are allowed to "offset" their damages elsewhere (e.g. by funding reforestation programs) rather than directly curtailing them.

Cutting across all corporate insertions into the environmental debate is the assumption that the basic instruments for responding to ecological crisis are technology and the market. The technological fixation has been a constant of capitalist development. Initially focused on maximizing labor productivity, it is continuously replenished by ever more miraculous applications, especially in the spheres of communication and genetic engineering. The unending proliferation of innovations—a hallmark of late capitalism[6]—lends credence, in public perception, to the idea that there is no challenge that technology cannot overcome. The unstated premise behind such claims is that the selection of any technology will continue to reflect corporate interests, which in turn reflect the goals implicit in market competition, i.e., profit-maximization, growth, and accumulation. While green technologies—e.g., renewable energy sources—may attract some degree of corporate investment (thanks mainly to social/political pressure), nothing short of a change in the basic locus of economic decision-making will stop certain corporations from continuing to pursue established [non-green] lines of production. Insofar as they must nonetheless try to present themselves in green clothing, they will not hesitate to misrepresent the questions at stake and to invoke technological "solutions" that have little chance of being successfully implemented.

A revealing and economically important illustration of this dynamic is the advocacy of so-called "clean coal." To begin with, much of the coal industry's PR emphasis is placed on the removal of specific impurities (such as sulfur and particulates) from coal-burning emissions, overlooking the fact that the biggest problem is the combustion process itself and the resultant rise in atmospheric concentration of carbon dioxide. When this unavoidable "bottom line" can no longer be ignored, the industry, not wishing to be restrained even by such modest disincentives as a carbon tax, will

---

6   Ernest Mandel, *Late Capitalism* (London: New Left Books, 1975), 192.

assert, with CEO Steven Leer of Arch Coal Inc., that "the enabling technology for stabilizing carbon dioxide levels in the atmosphere is carbon capture and sequestration. There is not another option."[7] Carbon capture and sequestration (CCS), however, is an unproven technology, with problems not unlike those associated with any toxic byproduct that has to be disposed of in very large quantities. While it is possible to isolate CO2 emissions and to pump them into out-of-the-way sites (whether underground or perhaps even under the ocean), the potential blowback from such undertakings, once they exceed a certain threshold, is uncertain, incalculable, and potentially catastrophic.[8] Restoring carbon to the soil via regenerative agriculture is at once safer, cheaper, and healthier, but its large-scale application would require a holistic approach not distorted by market incentives.[9]

The desirability of shifting to certain inexhaustible or renewable energy sources is obvious. What is not so widely recognized, however, is that these sources too have their costs—in terms of installation, collection, maintenance, and transmission—and therefore that none of them, despite whatever abundance may characterize their occurrence in nature, can offer unlimited accessibility for energy supply.[10] Some of the alternative sources, such as hydrogen and biomass, themselves require significant if not prohibitive energy inputs. Biomass (obtaining fuel from crops) also threatens to reduce the land-area available for growing food. Hydrogen, for its part, carries the danger of leakage and of rising to the stratosphere,

---

7   Alvin Powell, "Mining Exec: Coal Vital to Energy Mix." *Harvard University Gazette*, February 9, 2009.

8   CCS is, even apart from its unpredictable dangers (including suffocation by massive CO2-inhalation in the event of a sudden accidental release), very costly and energy-intensive. For detailed study and discussion, based on the Dutch experience, see Philip Vergragt, *CCS in the Netherlands: Glass half empty or half full?* (Boston: Tellus Institute, 2008).

9   On regenerative agriculture, see Chapter 9.

10 The summary that follows is based in part on Tom Blees, *Prescription for the Planet: The Painless Remedy for Our Energy and Environmental Crises* (self-published, 2008), 63-86. Blees' critical summary is useful irrespective of his pro-nuclear-power perspective. As Fred Magdoff and Chris Williams point out, "each renewable technology comes with its own drawbacks and requires energy and other resources, many nonrenewable, in order to construct facilities" (*Creating an Ecological Society: Toward a Revolutionary Transformation* [New York: Monthly Review Press, 2017], 263).

where it could destroy the ozone layer. Tapping geothermal energy can, in certain regions, risk provoking seismic disturbances; in addition, there may be high costs associated with the depth of requisite drilling, and the emerging heat may be dissipated and lost in various ways. Wind energy, despite its clear positive potential, is limited by materials and space requirements, as well as by the irregularity of its source in many locations. Tidal power is more continuous than wind energy, but in addition to the high installation cost of its requisite barrages or underwater turbines, it poses—as do wind turbines—certain dangers for resident or migrant wildlife. Solar energy, finally, is extraordinarily promising in direct localized applications, but for power-generation on a large scale, it would risk impinging on space required for other purposes. As for solar collectors situated in otherwise unused desert regions, their dust-free maintenance in such sites would require the long-distance trans-shipment of vast quantities of water.

All these technologies, with the partial exception of biomass, avoid adding to the net concentration of CO_2 in the atmosphere. The same might perhaps be said of nuclear power, provided that, as the more up-to-date versions promise, it does not entail further large-scale mining and refinement of fissionable material. Nuclear power has other problematic implications, however, beyond its daunting startup costs in both time and money. Even if we were to suppose that the problem of waste has been minimized via repeated re-use (until there is hardly any radioactive material left),[11] there still remain the safety concerns epitomized by disaster scenarios such as that of 2011 in Fukushima. Finally, nuclear power is linked to the

---

11 Blees argues, in *Prescription for the Planet*, that this can be accomplished by the new generation of Integral Fast Reactors. The support expressed for nuclear power by former NASA climatologist James Hansen (e.g., in "The Threat to the Planet," *New York Review of Books*, July 13, 2006) gives unexpected reinforcement to such contentions. But even in the absence of severe mishaps, the underlying risk of accumulated radiation effects on workers and, through them, on the wider population, remains. See John W. Gofman and Arthur R. Tamplin, *Poisoned Power: The Case Against Nuclear Power Plants Before and After Three Mile Island* (Emmaus, PA: Rodale Press, 1979), www.ratical.org/radiation/CNR/ PP/. The Union of Concerned Scientists (UCS), which is open to nuclear power, acknowledges that the waste problem has not been solved. Further, "UCS opposes reprocessing because it increases proliferation and terrorism risks while actually adding to the waste problem rather than reducing it" (www.ucsusa.org/ nuclear-power/nuclear-waste).

potential for making bombs, and no disarmament process is underway. The imperialist governments will therefore not allow nuclear
power to be diffused on a scale sufficient to match the potential
global demand for it. The longer-term ecological and political
solution would be not to lift such restrictions, but rather to impose
them on the imperialist powers themselves, as part of a full-scale
conversion process.

The upshot of all these considerations is that the question of
how to supply the world's currently growing energy demand without continuing recourse to CO2-producing fossil fuels—coal, oil,
and natural gas—has not yet been solved.[12] In view of the problems
associated with all of the alternative energy sources, a radical and
comprehensive reconsideration of the demand side of this equation would seem to be called for. This is the essence of the socialist
response: while encouraging the use of various safe-energy alternatives, it can accept the fact that these alternatives are ultimately
limited in their total power-generating capacity, and therefore that
the world's aggregate energy-consumption will actually have to be
reduced. Once this is understood, one can then focus on the interrelated issues of how to identify and prioritize real needs and how
to correspondingly reorganize society, in such a way as to assure
everyone's well-being. This is beyond the purview of capitalist thought, whatever its level of awareness of the environmental
danger.

THE POLITICS OF REDUCED ENERGY CONSUMPTION

The ecological movement, as it has so far developed, has not yet
been able to mount a socially persuasive agenda for reducing
energy consumption on a large scale. Broadly speaking, critique of
the capitalist growth-model has advanced along two paths which,

---

12   David Schwartzman has suggested that solar power will be able to overcome all
     energy shortages (see his "Beyond Eco-Catastrophism: The Conditions for Solar
     Communism," in Leo Panitch and Greg Albo, eds., *Socialist Register 2017*, New
     York: Monthly Review Press, 2016). I hope he is right, but even if enough clean
     energy can be generated to theoretically satisfy all human needs, the remaining
     limitations of available materials and of space will still require a radical reduction
     of throughput.

although complementary in their ultimate thrust, have tended to clash politically. On the one hand has been the tradition identifiable with the "small is beautiful" slogan, associated with localism, rural-ism, and (in varying degrees) rejection of "industrial society." This tradition understands the danger of growth but tends to link it with the general condition of modernity, including modern technology, population increase, and urbanization.[13] On the other hand is the socialist tradition, which, drawing on Marx, sees growth not in terms of human evolution as such, but rather in terms of the specific drives unleashed by capital. In its political expression, however, this tradition has been associated with revolutionary regimes arising in countries of widespread poverty where the top priority was its alleviation through a form of "socialist growth." As a result of this association—buttressed by real or ascribed failings of the regimes in question—critics of growth tended also to become critics of social-ism, which they saw as sharing the major negative traits of capital-ism. Conversely, those who felt the urgency of emerging from pov-erty rejected the anti-growth posture, viewing it as an ideological expression of sectors whose needs were already satisfied and who would unfairly deny similar satisfaction to others.

A theoretical resolution to this antagonism already exists. It is implicit in Marx's dual focus on nature and man as sources/creators of wealth and as objects of capitalist depredation. The link has been discussed in depth by, among others, writers such as Paul Burkett, John Bellamy Foster, Joel Kovel, and Richard Levins. Foster's book *Marx's Ecology*, in particular, refutes the productivist stereotype of Marx's thinking, and Levins has presented a concise yet wide-rang-ing refutation of developmentalist assumptions, informed by a blend of dialectical thought, biological expertise, and his own farming experience.[14] Reading this literature, one can see implicit

---

13 An influential expression of this tradition is Herman E. Daly and Jonathan B. Cobb, Jr., *For the Common Good*, 2nd ed. (Boston: Beacon Press, 1994); see also Clive Ponting. *A New Green History of the World* (New York: Penguin Books, 2007).

14 John Bellamy Foster, *Marx's Ecology: Materialism and Nature* (New York: Monthly Review Press, 2000); Yrjö Haila and Richard Levins, *Humanity and Nature: Ecology, Science, and Society* (London: Pluto Press, 1992), Chapter 5 ("Agricultural Ecology"). (Productivism and developmentalism alike give priority to economic growth, thereby perpetuating a core feature of capitalism.)

in the Marxist critique of capital a call for undoing high-tech agri-culture, restoring biodiversity, drastically reducing the volume of long-distance trade, and generally bringing technology under social or community control. These are the same goals enunciated by the zero-growth activists (who stress lifestyle choices and local actions over challenges to state power), but the realization of those goals is, for Marxists, clearly linked up with class struggle. The basis for this link is simply that without successful class struggle, the major vectors determining trade patterns and technological development will continue to be those of the capitalist market.

There is thus a clear theoretical symbiosis between ecological thinking and the anti-capitalist critique. Two major strands of radi-cal activism are thereby poised to function as one, in the sense that the ecological movement, in seeking to override market dictates, is at its core anti-capitalist, while the critique of capitalism is, in its rejection of the growth/accumulation imperative, inherently ecological.[15] The resultant socialist ecology or ecological socialism constitutes a full-blown alternative to the dominant ideology. Its political potential, moreover, should be greatly enhanced by the 2008 financial collapse, which showed up the hollowness of cap-italist "prosperity." Yet there remain huge obstacles to *popular* rec-ognition of the link between ecology and socialism, and hence to popular support for an agenda of collectively planned, society-wide reduction in energy-use. What are these obstacles, and how can they be overcome?

Although the growth-imperative at the macro level is specific to capitalism, it is not without some grounding in longer-standing human traits. Indeed, this is what makes possible the very idea of seeing growth as an inherent human pursuit. Like all such general-izations, it has a strand of accuracy which is then amplified to the point of blotting out the truth of the whole. It is legitimate to say that there is a natural human striving for improvement and even for perfection. This is evident in various forms of artistic expression throughout the ages, as it is also in the care of artisans—whether individually or as part of a team—to make the best possible product.

---

15 See, in addition to Chapter 1 above, Michael Löwy, "Eco-Socialism and Dem-ocratic Planning," *Socialist Register 2007* (New York: Monthly Review Press, 2006).

The goal of growth intersects with such striving in a qualified way. A healthy plant, animal, or human must grow to full stature. One can even say something similar of a community, which, unless it reaches a certain threshold of size and productive capacity, cannot expect to provide the range of services and diversions required in order to offer a satisfying life to each of its members.

But in any such unit of growth, one must distinguish optimum from maximum. Optimum growth for any living entity is part of what constitutes fulfillment of its potential. Anything above optimum, however, is pathological: the organism, whether an individual or a community, suffers disequilibrium either among its component parts or between itself and its environment (or both).

Capital's growth-impulse is inscribed in its credo of accumulation. Its objective limits are determined, in the short run, by saturation of the market and, in the long run, by exhaustion of resources. When its productive potential is stymied, it turns to financial speculation, which only increases the gulf between the capitalist class and the rest of the species. Because of imperialist relations, deprivation is particularly vast, widespread, and seemingly intractable in countries of the global South. This has the ironic effect of creating a constituency which, although desirous of revolutionary redistribution, may at the same time be receptive to calls for growth as a kind of compensatory entitlement, as its members seek to overcome the huge gap between their own consumption-levels and those prevalent within the imperial metropolis.

Insofar as the world's poor—and/or those who purport to speak for them on the global stage—retain this longing to ape the extravagant US-advertised lifestyle, the US leadership will continue to invoke the poor countries' demands as a pretext for rejecting its own ecological responsibility. The governments of the United States on the one hand and of countries such as China and India on the other will remain locked together in a dance of death, in which each partner invokes the other's intransigence to justify its own. The impact of progressive ecological steps taken in other countries will be severely limited, and most of the world's peoples will be reduced to the status of spectators if not victims of the ongoing environmental breakdown. This is the dynamic that regularly plays out at environmental summits.

An alternative to this bleak scenario, if there is to be one, will depend primarily on the impact of popular movements around the world. There are promising steps in this direction, from both the South and the North, although the idea of a policy-link to socialism—let alone of a politically powerful organization to articulate and embody such a link—remains elusive. The incipient efforts deserve our attention, as does the question of how to surmount the conceptual impasse that frustrates international negotiations.

IN SEARCH OF A MASS MOVEMENT FOR ECOLOGICAL SOCIALISM

The most massive expressions of radical environmental awareness have arisen among the peasants and indigenous peoples of the global South. For these populations, the capitalist/productivist plunder of the environment—in the form of deforestation, reckless or deliberate pollution, sea-level rise from global warming, and misuse of fresh water (flooding by dams or depletion of aquifers)—is a direct assault on their homes and livelihoods.[16] Their sense of outrage and desperation is beyond measure. It is, moreover, a *community* sentiment on the part of people who are being stripped of everything and whose plight leads them to consciously reject the entire agenda of the invasive force. One would have to return to the early days of capitalism to find elsewhere a comparable unanimity of antagonism to the agencies of exploitation.

Yet while the anger and its justification are not unprecedented, the basis for the current movement distinguishes itself from that of earlier resistance in at least two ways, one of which makes it weaker but the other of which could give it greater strength. The weakening factor has to do with dispensability. Through all its phases, capi-

---

16 Numerous cases from Latin America are analyzed in *Nacla Report on the Americas*, 42:5 (Sept.-Oct. 2009) and in Gerardo Rénique, ed., *Latin America: The New Neoliberalism and Popular Mobilization*, special issue of *Socialism and Democracy*, 23:3 (November 2009). See also Joseph Berlinger's 2009 documentary film on the struggle in Ecuador, *Crude: The Real Price of Oil* (www.crude-film.com/).

tal has sought limitless supplies of its necessary inputs, including human labor power—for which its early recourse to open slavery has given way in more recent times to the large-scale abuse of migrant laborers and in some countries also of prisoners. Alongside this element of continuity, however, has come, with labor-saving technological advances, a markedly increased propensity on the part of capital to view certain populations as altogether expendable. Insofar as these populations exist on the margins of capitalist production, they lack economic leverage, and their demands—much less their sufferings—therefore carry no political weight. So far as capital is concerned, they can thus be consigned with impunity to sickness, dispersion, or death.

Where then lies the potential strength of this constituency? They do indeed hold one card which was not available to their exploited counterparts of an earlier age. Their direct tie to the long-term sustainability of the land, at a time when such sustainability is being everywhere undermined, gives them in fact a strategic placement which contrasts diametrically with the supposed super-fluity to which capital has relegated them. Their own "parochial" needs embody the collective need of the entire human species— not to mention other endangered life-forms—to stop the relent-less destruction of the ecosphere. Ironically, therefore, although such peoples are among the world's poorest not just by capitalist standards (personal possessions) but also in terms of access to the means of mass communication, they have been thrust into a van-guard position, on a par with that of Cuba,[17] in the global ecosocial-ist movement.

Visible expressions of this leadership role have so far been sporadic, beginning with direct, on-site confrontations— in India, Latin America, and North America (most recently, at Standing Rock, North Dakota)—but progressing to the world stage via international conferences of indigenous peoples,[18] interventions at the United

---

17 Cuba's special significance as an ecological model, including its shift to 80% organic agriculture with large-scale urban gardening, is well brought out in the 2006 documentary film, *The Power of Community: How Cuba Survived Peak Oil* (www.communitysolution.org/mediaandeducation/films/powerofcommunity/).

18 See for example materials on the 4th Continental Summit of Indigenous Peoples (May 2009) in Puno, Peru, which drew 6500 delegates from 22 countries (cum-brecontinentalindigena.wordpress.com/).

Nations,[19] and participation in the annual gatherings of the World Social Forum (WSF). From such platforms they have been able to remind a worldwide audience how arbitrary has been the whole historical development underlying commonly held assumptions about the way our species should live. Their WSF declaration at Belém in 2009 included this statement:

> Modern capitalism was initiated centuries ago and imposed in America with the invasion of October 12, 1492. This gave way to global plundering and invented theories of "races" to justify American ethnocide, the incursion in Africa for its slave trade, and the plundering of other continents....
>
> ... what is in crisis is capitalism, Euro-centrism, with its model of Uni-National State, cultural homogeneity, western positive rights, developmentalism and the commodification of life....
>
> We belong to Mother Earth. We are not her owners, plunderers, nor are we her vendors, and today we arrive at a crossroads: imperialist capitalism has shown [itself] to be dangerous not only due to its domination, exploitation and structural violence but also because it kills Mother Earth and leads us to planetary suicide, which is neither "useful" nor "necessary."[20]

This perspective is clearly one that speaks for a bigger constituency than that of its immediate exponents. Indigenous peoples, numbering approximately 300 million worldwide, constitute less than 5% of the total human population. From a sociological standpoint, they are simply an ethno-linguistic category, distinguished above all by their immemorial roots in a particular locality. But in terms of their collective message in an epoch of environmental breakdown, they express, more completely than any other demographic group, the common survival interest of humanity as a whole.[21]

---

19 UN interventions culminated in 2007 with the General Assembly's overwhelming ratification of the Declaration of the Rights of Indigenous Peoples (www.un.org/esa/socdev/unpfii/documents/DRIPS_en.pdf), which includes in its Preamble a clause "*Recognizing* that respect for indigenous knowledge, cultures and traditional practices contributes to sustainable and equitable development and proper management of the environment."

20 www.europe-solidaire.org/spip.php?article14007.

21 This role has been dramatically illustrated in the convergence of Native American nations in 2016-17 to resist construction of the Dakota Access Pipeline.

Our theoretical challenge is to define an arena of negotiation, and eventually a political strategy for reconciliation, between the global perspective of the indigenous peoples and the ongoing, though in part disputable, needs of the much larger population—in its majority, the international working class of the 21st century—that has been drawn into a mode of life far removed from the one that the indigenous are striving to preserve.[22]

From our earlier discussion it is clear that total energy-consumption must be drastically reduced. To this end, indigenous communities can offer inspiration in several respects. They tend to be exemplary in their reverence for the natural world, as also in their material self-sufficiency, their rejection of individual property-rights, their egalitarianism, and their sense of mutual accountability.

But how can these virtues, embodied in defiantly autonomous communities, with a way of life in many cases defined by low population-density, be acquired on a massive scale by the other 95% of the world's people?—the majority of whom inhabit large urban settlements in which they have become alienated from the natural world and acculturated to livelihoods characterized, at one end of the spectrum, by energy-intensive services and comfort and, at the other, by a desperate and competitive scramble to stay alive.

This question is, in essence, the present-day form taken by long-standing enigmas of revolutionary transformation. From the beginning of the capitalist epoch, the challenge has centered on attaining class-consciousness, a key component of which is the process by which wage-workers come to recognize that their interests are better served by mutual cooperation than by competition (which, in terms of contending wage-claims, has always entailed a race to the bottom—whether with one's immediate co-workers or

---

22 In many countries experiencing large-scale urban migration, one cannot draw a sharp distinction between indigenous and non-indigenous populations. People who have left their original territories may preserve much of their culture, as in the city of El Alto, Bolivia (see Adolfo Gilly, "Bolivia: A 21st-Century Revolution," trans. Victor Wallis, *Socialism and Democracy*, 19:3, November 2005). The global figure of 300 million indigenous could in this respect be viewed as an underestimate. In addition, the communication boundaries between indigenous and non-indigenous may sometimes be more porous than this apparent dichotomy suggests.

with others in distant locations). The progression from a competitive to a cooperative or solidaristic mindset is a cultural shift. As such, it weakens or undercuts ingrained defenses and prejudices. It prefigures, albeit on a limited scale, the new constellation of attitudes associated with the socialist project.

Such an initial step in the process of transformation—namely, the formation of labor unions—has been an experience common to most countries. Its benefits have typically been offset, however, and in many instances reversed, by the enormous economic impact of transnational corporations. Previously powerful labor movements have suffered dramatic declines in membership, and their surviving leaderships have often been forced to accept humiliating concessions, always under the threat of an even worse alternative. Their readiness to acquiesce was forged, in the US case, during the post-World War II period of labor's direct partnership with global capital. Now, in their weakened position, US labor leaders are less capable than ever of challenging capitalist priorities. Instead, often in defiance of programmatic demands of their membership, they give unconditional support to one of the country's two capitalist governing parties.[23]

In the wake of this evolution, any revival of the latent working-class predisposition to solidarity will have to come at least in part on the basis of a whole new set of cultural influences. These can be drawn from a mix of sources. Looking again at the US case (no doubt the most resistant to such change), one possible source of fresh perspectives may be the arrival of immigrant workers with experience of class struggle in their home countries.[24] Another may be the impact of various social movements, including those of radical youth, from outside the workplace. But a very important additional source, sooner or later, will be awareness of the environmental crisis: in particular, the understanding that it cannot be adequately addressed merely by a mass of individual responses.

---

23 See Kim Moody, *Workers in a Lean World: Unions in the International Economy* (London: Verso, 1997).

24 For a suggestive example of such impact, see Héctor Perla Jr., "Grassroots Mobilization against US Military Intervention in El Salvador," *Socialism and Democracy*, 22:3 (November 2008).

At this point, the collective nature of the response put forward by indigenous communities could resonate within an otherwise disoriented and dispirited working class. Most especially, if the struggles of those communities were to become widely known, they could further energize the current revival of worker self-management initiatives. Thus, recent chains of bankruptcies—in Argentina in 2002 and in the United States following the financial meltdown of 2008—gave workers new inducements to take over their factories.[25] In Venezuela, a similar process has evolved in response to economic sabotage by capitalist opponents of the Bolivarian Revolution.[26] The potential for ecologically informed redesign of production processes could generate added motivation for such initiatives: workers not only can see at first hand where materials and energy have been wasted; they also identify as a matter of course with the nearby population's non-negotiable interest (and their own) in eliminating or neutralizing toxic emissions.

Complementing such workplace-grounded developments are those which may occur in the neighborhoods. Again, the indigenous models would have to be made known through every possible channel. But the manifest breakdown in the supply of fresh produce to poor urban communities will create an opening for new (or in some sense much older) solutions. People could begin to ask themselves why common food-items need to be shipped great distances, via countless intermediaries. The farmers' markets are a first step in breaking out of this circle; a second step, already gaining traction in some places, is urban gardens. All such practices restore a level of direct interaction among people, promoting collective autonomy and undercutting the impact of commodification. The infrastructure required for the necessary cooperative arrangements will be conducive also to political education, which is integral to the overall

25 On Argentina, see Laura Meyer and María Chaves, "Winds of Freedom: An Argentine Factory under Workers' Control," trans. Victor Wallis, *Socialism and Democracy*, 23:3 (November 2009). On the US, see Immanuel Ness and Stacy Warner Maddern, "Worker Direct Action Grows In Wake of Financial Meltdown," *Dollars & Sense*, no. 284 (Sept.-Oct. 2009), and also Michael Moore's documentary film, *Capitalism: A Love Story* (2009).

26 A useful general analysis is Iain Bruce, *The Real Venezuela: Making Socialism in the 21st Century* (London: Pluto Press, 2008), esp. Ch. 4, reprinted as Ch. 5 of Victor Wallis, *Socialist Practice: Histories and Theories* (London: Palgrave Macmillan, 2020).

process. Here again, the experience of indigenous peoples could be brought into play—perhaps even by direct contacts—to combine practical advice with wider inspiration.[27]

The larger picture here is one of a vast learning process. This is something that revolution has always entailed, but with distinct contours in each period. The present conjuncture is marked by a core paradox. Capitalism is superannuated. This is not just a wishful assertion that it "should have" been superseded; it is recognition of the verifiable fact that its accelerated resource-depletion has out-paced the regenerative capacities of the ecosphere. Under these conditions, the most advanced technological achievements of the capitalist era are, taken as a whole, outdated.[28] They are not collec-tively sustainable over the long term. As a result, they are now force-fully challenged by a perspective which rejects them altogether.

Relatively few, on a world scale, would consciously choose "business as usual" (worst-case scenario for the *Stern Review*)[29] over species-survival. But the vast majority of the non-indigenous 95% are caught up in structures—many of them internalized—which impede our efforts to build a new paradigm. Mere exhortation will not induce us to jettison these relics of a nefarious mode of produc-tion. As a species, we will have to liberate ourselves "strategically" from the associated habits, by focusing on scale and on degrees of urgency, framing equitable criteria for restricting or eliminating one or another practice—be it a given form of transport, a given item of

---

27 Although I here emphasize what indigenous peoples can teach the rest of us, the theoretical dialogue will need to go in both directions, inasmuch as certain spokespersons for the indigenous (e.g., Ward Churchill) and for a "subsistence" approach (e.g., Maria Mies) have popularized a severe misreading of Marx, ascribing to him the very interpretation of value—as excluding nature—that Marx had identified as a major fault of capital. For a critique of such misreadings, see John Bellamy Foster and Brett Clark, "The Paradox of Wealth: Capitalism and Ecological Destruction," *Monthly Review*, 61:6 (November 2009), 7-10.

28 See the discussion of agriculture in Chapters 2-4 of this book.

29 *The Economics of Climate Change: The Stern Review* (Cambridge University Press, 2006), a British government report prepared under the direction of Nich-olas Stern, is perhaps the most comprehensive formulation of the "green capi-talist" perspective. For a critique, see the Introduction by John Bellamy Foster et al. to *Monthly Review*, 60:3 (July-August 2008), 3-6.

long-distance trade, or a particular energy-intensive amenity of any kind.[30]

In carrying out this process, those who do not belong to indigenous communities will have much to learn from those who do. The indigenous communities' lives are being threatened, however, and their members may be understandably reluctant to visit "alien" territory. But they may also begin to recognize that their own survival depends on whether a transformation takes place in that outside world. If they can contribute to such a revolution, they would thus be serving their own interest as well.

Breaking the Impasse on the World Stage

The emergence of indigenous peoples as an organized presence on the world stage presents an extraordinary opportunity to the rest of humanity. We have already noted the traits which have earned these peoples a leadership role in terms of ecological practice, and how those traits are linked to their rejection of the property regime that underlies capitalism's growth-impulse. Of equally great importance is the fact that neither the indigenous population as a whole nor any community within it constitutes a nation-state. To the contrary, such a formation would violate their very essence. Instead, the world's indigenous peoples are spread out over many countries and regions. Only in exceptional cases have their interests attained even limited expression in any national government.[31] They therefore act at the global level as a kind of transnational pressure group, advocating for their own interests but, in so doing, serving also as a moral force reminding international organizations of a shared responsibility for the preservation of life.

This new element in the global equation matches the ecological issue itself as a phenomenon transcending national boundaries. It

---

30 For a fuller exposition of this point, see my essay, "Vision and Strategy: Questioning the Subsistence Perspective," *Capitalism Nature Socialism*, 17:4 (December 2006).

31 Where they do attain such representation, as in Bolivia with Evo Morales, the government is inescapably subjected to conflicting pressures (in particular, over the exploitation of energy resources), as a result of which tensions arise between it and its indigenous base.

gives us the possibility of rethinking the entire framework of representation that currently exists for addressing matters of worldwide concern. The frustration that has attended international negotiations over environmental policy is well known. National governments speak for the dominant interests in their respective countries; their stances on ecological issues are only as good as they have been pressured to be by each society's working-class and progressive movements.[32] Moreover, the aggregate global outcome tends routinely to reflect the position of the ecologically most retrograde of the major powers, which, given the parameters of capitalist competition, are likely—in part precisely because of their ecological negligence—to be the ones with the greatest commercial advantage and therefore the biggest impact. Given this dynamic, the ambitious ecological proposals that may be put forward by other governments will go nowhere.[33]

It is within this arena of inter-government negotiations that the deadly standoff between the most profligate "developed" economy (the United States) and the most populous "developing" countries (China and India) is sustained. The dynamic at work here is reminiscent of the fear of "mutually assured destruction" (MAD) that for decades sustained the nuclear arms race between the United States and the Soviet Union, in that in both cases the logic of competition tends to block any concessions. That earlier dance of death ended only with the disintegration of one of the two partners. The present race to environmental oblivion is unlikely to be restrained without a series of political collapses of comparable scope. When the Soviet Union disappeared, the progressive forces in the United States had no conception of what it would take to implement the anticipated "peace dividend" (re-directing military expenditure to social reconstruction), because they failed to recognize that, for the forces driving US global military projection, the alleged threat of an

---

32 This does not mean that working-class movements necessarily have progressive positions on ecological issues; what it does mean is that only when they *do* have progressive positions do the latter carry significant weight.

33 Ironically, the European governments, which took stronger ecological stances than the US during the Bush administration, slipped back during the Obama presidency to supporting a US approach of leaving emissions-reduction targets up to individual countries. Naomi Klein, "Obama's Bad Influence," *The Nation*, November 2, 2009.

equivalent Soviet thrust had never been more than a pretext[34]—for which some substitute would quickly be devised.

At the global level, discussion over how to respond to the environmental dangers requires a new framework. The non-state contours of the worldwide indigenous movement offer a hint as to where to begin. In the environmental debate among states, those opposing the status quo proceed on the assumption that every national unit has equal entitlement (on a per-capita basis) to deplete the earth's resources. This seems fair enough so long as we accept the nation-state as the basic agent of policy, with the implication that the particular earmarking of environmental costs *within* each nation-state is beyond the purview of international scrutiny. Yet this is precisely where the problem lies. Each national aggregate encompasses its own mix of necessary and wasteful expenditures—with the proportion of the latter tending to vary directly with a country's economic and military power-position (as well as its acquired patterns of excess consumption). Certain types of resource-use must be curbed *wherever* they occur; the fact that they are more prevalent in the richer countries will itself reinforce the concern for seeking equity between richer and poorer regions.

But the global community will now have to promote such equity not only *between* regions, but also within them. Such an externally driven reorientation will of course be fiercely resisted, initially with the argument that it violates sovereignty. National sovereignty, however, is properly understood not to supersede basic human rights, which are what is ultimately at stake in the environmental debate. The irrelevance of national boundaries to the spread of environmental devastation is well known, but the corresponding political conclusions have yet to be widely drawn. This is a clear case where the whole world has a legitimate interest in the measures that may or may not be taken—whether by government or by the private sector—within any given country. Although the formal means to imple-

---

34 US global interventionism long pre-dated the growth of Soviet military power. When the Soviet Union collapsed, US military strategists immediately formulated a new rationale for global supremacy, known as the Wolfowitz Doctrine. See Patrick E. Tyler, "U.S. Strategy Plan Calls for Insuring No Rivals Develop," *New York Times*, March 8, 1992, and, more generally, John Bellamy Foster, *Naked Imperialism: The U.S. Pursuit of Global Dominance* (New York: Monthly Review Press, 2006).

ment this interest are at present very weak, the political potential of such universally formulated criteria has been amply demonstrated in connection with historic struggles against racism (e.g., the United States in the 1960s and South Africa in the 1980s)

In the sphere of environmental policy, the worldwide debate about emissions needs to undergo a radical shift, from a national to a *sectoral* focus. The first sector to be challenged will of course be the military. For each of the sectors that is addressed, however, the key issue to be resolved, through informed, society-wide debate, is: how much of the activity in that sector—and hence, of the resources it consumes—is directed not at the satisfaction of human need but rather at pursuits reflecting the priorities of capital and its ruling class?

It would be illusory to expect such a process to yield a universally accepted set of criteria that could be quickly applied. Like all revolutionary processes, its realization will be beset by obstacles and contingencies. But the challenge of identifying and eliminating social waste could prove to be a powerful unifying force for the vast majority, as it seeks simultaneously to restore the environment and assure the satisfaction of its own needs. The process also readily lends itself to defining short-term targets—particular categories of energy-waste—while nonetheless enabling activists to spell out the full scope of the longer-term task.

7

THE SEARCH FOR A MASS ECOLOGICAL CONSTITUENCY

More than four decades into the global environmental movement, and with species life-support unraveling at an accelerated pace, the US corporate bulldozer, wrapped in its usual political and media extravaganza, grinds on as if it could keep doing so forever.

Broad curbs on corporate priorities have been imposed to varying degrees in certain countries. Some of them have developed extensive grids of renewable energy; many have resisted genetically modified agricultural products; and even greater numbers have demanded binding international controls on greenhouse gas emissions. But the impact of all such steps will remain limited until there arises an irresistible popular outcry, worldwide in scope, that can overwhelm the anti-ecological fixation on growth which drives global capital and which frames to varying degrees the policies of all the major powers—though none more fully than the United States, which in 2017 became the only country to officially defy the global consensus on the need to combat climate-change.

The challenge is clear. The US economy has a disproportionate environmental footprint; the US political system exercises disproportionate global power; and the US population, except for a relatively small minority, remains unorganized and passive in the face of imminent devastation.[1] An effective initiative to change all this must

---

1   The gravity of the threat is a scientific assessment (see, e.g., James Hansen, *Storms of My Grandchildren*, New York: Bloomsbury USA, 2009; Ian Angus, *Facing the Anthropocene: Fossil Capitalism and the Crisis of the Earth System*, New York: Monthly Review Press, 2016). Some (e.g., Sasha Lilley et al. *Catastrophism: The Apocalyptic Politics of Collapse and Rebirth*, Oakland, CA: PM Press, 2012) have denounced such notions of extreme danger as "catastrophist" and counterproductive. The latter charge is linked to the unfounded assumption

come from below; this much is widely recognized. But the question of what can inspire such an initiative has yet to be answered.

A whole new language and culture grounded in environmentalism will have to come into being. Every economic decision, at every level, will need to be considered in its environmental dimension. In order to implement this principle, people will have to examine the full ecological ramifications of practices that they have hitherto viewed as either pleasurable, beneficial, routine, or inescapable. And they will also need to pinpoint—again, at every level—who or what is responsible for perpetuating whatever component of those practices is unnecessary and therefore wasteful.

This is a task both for individuals and for organizations. Thinking ahead, it is also a task for governments. No government has yet come close to embracing such a mandate, but the US government, with its total commitment to profit-driven growth, is further from doing so than is that of any other country. Putting in power governments ready to define and enforce limits would itself mark a major advance.

But it would not be enough. We would still need to completely transform our attitudes and standards in matters of production and consumption. With a government promoting rather than obstructing such transformation, the task would be less forbidding, but the goal for each of us as individuals would also be higher. We would then each be able to reduce our impact on the natural environment more than is possible for even the most conscientious person functioning within the parameters of daily life under capitalism—where, for example, many of us would prefer not to use cars (or planes except for going great distances) yet remain reluctantly dependent on them.

To specify an alternative in abstract terms is not immediately useful. The outlines of an alternative—putting people and nature before profits, or, more pointedly, emancipating humanity and nature from the rule of capital—have long been known and discussed.[2] What has not yet been achieved, except at fleeting moments,

---

that advocacy of drastic or systemic change precludes support for less sweeping near-term demands. We return to this issue in the final section of this chapter.

2   For a useful synthesis, see Fred Magdoff and John Bellamy Foster, *What Every Environmentalist Needs to Know about Capitalism* (New York: Monthly Review

has been to turn these ideas into the watchwords of mass struggle. How can masses of people come to be gripped by the urgency of the ecological crisis, by awareness of the scale of the changes it must call forth, and by a commitment to act on those insights?

Expositions of the urgency are manifold and authoritative. What is perhaps most striking is that danger signals which have been evident for decades—severe climatic events; species-loss; the melting of glaciers and of polar ice—have been multiplying or accelerating faster than anticipated.[3] The trends in question are recognized not only by those who would welcome the necessary radical response, but also by many who wish to continue business as usual, and who therefore, although admitting that greenhouse gases must be cut back, promote insufficiently drastic curbs. The latter approach is that of the more strategically alert sectors of international capital, and was well expressed in the 2007 *Stern Review*.[4] These sectors, represented at the 2015 Paris Climate Summit by the major capitalist governments, fully acknowledge the severity of the environmental crisis but, because of their economic priorities, deliberately advocate doing less than is necessary to meet the challenges it poses.

As for the scale of the required changes, this is grudgingly acknowledged by these same interests, but only to say that the consequent shake-up is unacceptable. Ironically, as Naomi Klein has emphasized,[5] the capitalist class has a stronger awareness of the subversive implications of a truly ecological approach than do most of the established (politically liberal) environmentalist organizations. Where these implications have been powerfully and directly articulated, by contrast, is within the Marxian framework, in which profit-driven calculation would ultimately give way to collective control over economic decisions and hence, finally, to full prioritization of human and environmental requirements.

Press, 2011).

3   Bill McKibben, *Eaarth: Making a Life on a Tough New Planet* (New York: Henry Holt, 2010), 4-10, 20-23.

4   Nicholas Stern, *The Economics of Climate Change* (Cambridge, UK: Cambridge University Press, 2007).

5   Naomi Klein, *This Changes Everything: Capitalism vs. the Climate* (New York: Simon & Schuster, 2014), Ch. 1.

But, while the urgency of the problem and the scope of the necessary response are clear, the question of how such awareness can come to permeate our daily lives remains unanswered. In Chapter 6, we looked at populations for whom an environmentalist philosophy is already central, namely, the world's indigenous peoples. Indigenous people living in their traditional manner not only have a non-exploitative relationship to the natural world; they also have brought their approach to the international arena, where they have invoked it as a direct response and alternative to that of imperialist capital. But how can the message of the indigenous intersect with and spread to the political projects of other constituencies?

Our common starting point is the multiplicity of popular demands in a country such as the United States. Together, the constituencies for these demands comprise a vast majority of the national population, but as political entities, they remain largely separate. The survival-needs called into question by the environmental crisis cut across all other demands. Our task is to identify the organic links between the constituency-specific demands and the universal perspective implicit in environmental exigencies.

THE ENVIRONMENT AS A CLASS ISSUE

The effort to define an explicit link between constituency-specific demands and a universal perspective goes back to Marx. Before his time, philosophers easily spoke in terms of universals, from which vantage-point they sometimes put forward, as in the case of Rousseau, radical critiques of the established order. But such critiques were cast in the language of abstract ethical principles—denouncing corruption, hypocrisy, and social injustice. The denunciations implied empathy, perhaps, with those who were collectively victimized by such evils, but they did not endow the victims with agency. Agency remained unspecified. At a society-wide level, it thus belonged, by default, to members of the dominant class.

Marx argued that the working class that had been brought into being by capitalism had become—because of the degree to which its members had been stripped of all capacity for human fulfillment— the key protagonist in the struggle for universal emancipation. Not only did it constitute society's "immense majority"; in addition, its eventual passage from a condition of alienation to one of collective self-awareness could not occur without shaking existing structures to their foundations and thereby generating an entirely new basis for social organization.

This projected historic transition carries the key to ecological conversion. Ecological conversion signifies, at its core, rejection of the capitalist growth-imperative.[6] A new locus or agent will be needed to guide economic decisions, which will have to be taken out of the hands of the capitalist class and its political operatives. Although the need for this power-transfer can be expressed in universalistic terms, the step itself requires the intervention of a particular socially defined protagonist. The latter cannot be found in any mere statistical aggregate (such as "the 99%"); it must arise from a concretely grounded and consciously articulated community of interests. This is the fundamental sense in which the ecological challenge is a *class* issue.

The working class is the implicit, if not explicit, embodiment of ecological sanity—just as it is the implicit bearer, more generally, of an approach to economic policy that rejects the goals of profit and accumulation. This affirmation is still far from being embodied, however, by existing labor organizations in the United States. The current labor hierarchy, with its stress on "jobs" and hence (because of the capitalist framework) its support for "growth," could hardly be further from exercising the kind of leadership necessary to transcend the ecological status quo. This point was dramatically underscored by the AFL-CIO's virtual endorsement, in February 2013, of the Keystone XL pipeline. More recently, at its 2017 convention, the AFL-CIO passed a resolution in support of alternative forms of energy, but it has yet to denounce the continued reliance on fossil fuel production.[7] But working-class activism is not limited to what is expressed at the leadership level of the labor movement.

---

6   John Bellamy Foster and Brett Clark, "The Planetary Emergency," *Monthly Review* 64:7 (December 2012).

7   The text of the resolution is at aflcio.org/resolutions/resolution-55-climate-change-energy-and-union-jobs; a useful analysis is at www.labor4sustainability.org/wp-content/uploads/2017/10/AFLResolution.pdf

There are several dimensions to the overlap of working-class demands with pro-ecological positions. The most direct convergence is in the issue of occupational safety and health. Toxic products—and toxic production processes—result in sick workers. A second type of convergence lies in the fact that environmentally problematic technologies, because they are energy-intensive rather than labor-intensive, have the effect of destroying jobs. Third, we should remind ourselves that common class experience goes beyond the workplace to encompass the full range of conditions in which working-class people live, and while environmental breakdown ultimately affects everyone, it hits working-class communities first—and with the greatest impact.

All these dimensions of the class-configuration of environmental issues have been evident since the earliest years of capitalist development. The crippling impact of coal dust and other toxins on workers—both on the job and in their neighborhoods—is vividly described in Engels' classic 1844 work of urban anthropology.[8] Marx's *Capital*, in addition to documenting the direct damage inflicted on factory workers, includes bitter observations on the fouling of waterways and depletion of soil.[9]

In recent decades, the "jobs" argument has often been successfully deployed to pit workers against environmentalists (by claiming that if companies are forced to bear the cost of environmental regulations, they will go out of business). But more positive countercurrents have emerged as well, and some of these have arisen within the labor movement. Also, as organized labor continues to lose ground in the face of globalizing capital, working-class resistance to environmental devastation increasingly takes on a neighborhood- and community-centered character.

It is at once paradoxical and fitting that the first grassroots challenge to capital's environmental despotism should have arisen among workers directly involved in the most toxic industries—the Oil, Chemical and Atomic Workers (OCAW): paradoxical because the workers' livelihoods were tied to the very sector whose profits

---

8   Friedrich Engels, *The Condition of the Working Class in England* (available in
     many editions).
9   John Bellamy Foster, *Marx's Ecology* (New York: Monthly Review Press, 2000),
     163.

they were threatening, but at the same time fitting because of how closely exposed they were to the dangers that had to be targeted. The links are highlighted in the work of Anthony Mazzocchi, whose career as an organizer spanned the entire existence of OCAW, from its 1955 birth in one union-merger to its 1995 demise in another.[10]

The figure of Mazzocchi is important for a combination of reasons. Within the labor movement, he was the first radical environmentalist. He identified environmental danger in its most direct and immediate manifestations, both inside and outside the workplace; he understood this danger as an imposition arising from capitalist production priorities; he was a union activist with organizational skills and without status-ambition; and he placed a high value on education. It was under his leadership that labor support was generated—in the early 1970s—to enact the strongest US environmental measures to date: the Environmental Protection Act, the Clean Air and Clean Water Acts, and the Occupational Safety and Health Act. Of course, the ground for these advances was also prepared by the wider popular movements of that period, as well as by the influential writings of Rachel Carson and Barry Commoner and the highly effective consumer organizing drives of Ralph Nader. Still, the labor-organizing dimension was important in overturning stereotypes of narrowly economistic popular attitudes, and also for grounding an explicitly anti-capitalist mass constituency.

With the subsequent weakening of the US labor movement—epitomized in the deindustrialization crisis of the early 1980s—and with the concurrent growing general awareness of ecological breakdown, the locus of radical organizing on environmental issues shifted away from specific concentrations of toxins and toward the larger task of preserving the ecosphere. This did not diminish the underlying class issues at stake, but it made them less obvious. For example, saving old-growth forests was a universalistic demand, which initially appeared to clash with the interests of those employed in logging them.[11] What would ultimately matter,

---

10   Les Leopold, *The Man Who Hated Work and Loved Labor: The Life and Times of Tony Mazzocchi* (White River Junction, VT: Chelsea Green Publishing Co., 2007).

11   Fred Rose, *Coalitions across the Class Divide: Lessons from the Labor, Peace, and Environmental Movements*. Ithaca, NY: Cornell University Press, 2000), 44.

however, was the sustainability of any harvesting. The profit-drive of the timber companies encouraged clearcutting, whereas long-term employment for local workers dictated forest-preservation. The long-term interests of those hired as loggers therefore lay more with the environmentalists' agenda than with that of the timber companies. The environmentalists, however, would need to speak to this reality, which meant reminding the forest workers of their class position vis-à-vis the companies.

This is exactly the approach that was taken by northern California Earth First! activist Judi Bari. As she explained in an interview,[12] she herself, before becoming an Earth Firster, had been a woodworker. She challenged from both directions the assumption that the interests of workers and environmentalists were antagonistic. Addressing environmental activists, she offered a workshop on union organizing in the timber industry and, significantly, a critique of eco-sabotage tactics that put workers' lives at risk. Addressing workers, she exposed anti-worker practices of the timber companies and advocated a sustainable approach to logging. Judi Bari was critically injured by a car bomb in 1990 and died prematurely seven years later. Her being targeted was bitter testimony to the potential force of the labor/environmental alliance to which she had been committed—an alliance grounded in the inherent commonality of human and natural priorities, but for this very reason a threat to capitalist interests.

The anti-toxics and anti-clearcutting struggles can be viewed as models. They cannot yet be considered typical of either the labor or the environmental movement as a whole, but they are important for having crystallized an implicitly socialist theoretical understanding in broadly popular stances. The underlying insight is that the supposed "dilemma" whereby people are expected to choose between keeping their jobs and preserving the environment—and often also (as with coal mining and petrochemicals) protecting their own health—is artificially created, reflecting the terms under which capital chooses to operate. If investment decisions were made socially, i.e., by the affected communities and workforces rather

---

12 Interview by Douglas Bevington, in Daniel Faber, ed., *The Struggle for Ecological Democracy: Environmental Justice Movements in the United States* (New York: Guilford Press, 1998), ch. 8.

than by corporate management, then the adverse conditions could be minimized as a matter of policy—by avoiding certain types of production and/or (as with forest-management) by using sustainable production methods.

Other examples of such an approach can also be cited. In Wisconsin in 1997, an environmentalist coalition stretching from Native American tribes to sport-fishing organizations and labor unions secured overwhelming passage of a strict Mining Moratorium Law.[13] During the 1999 demonstrations in Seattle against the World Trade Organization, labor and environmentalist groups (dubbed "Teamsters and Turtles") joined forces to uphold protective regulations that the WTO, representing the interests of capital, sought to dismantle. And the United Steelworkers in recent years have maintained a steady interest in promoting wind-turbines as an energy alternative and also in exploring cooperative ownership as a basis for assuring steady and meaningful employment.[14] The people who have joined these various struggles have been intellectually and culturally prepared to defy prevailing assumptions as to who are the real guardians of their interest. Such preparation is not easy to achieve. In its intellectual aspect it reflects educational work; in its cultural aspect, a supportive community. But both these dimensions are increasingly handicapped by low union-density (now at less than 7% in the private sector) and by the typically segmented/specialized character of issue-oriented groups.

Overcoming this difficulty has come to depend in part on shifting the locus of working-class organization from the workplace to the community. Here, too, the challenge is to develop constituencies which, while firmly anchored in an array of practical demands, can recognize the underlying configuration of class power that stands in the way of their realization, and then, on the basis of this, formulate a vision going beyond their immediate concerns. This is where we

---

13 Holly Nearman, "This Week in History: Mining Moratorium Bill Passed in 1997," ThirdCoastDaily.com (Milwaukee), March 12, 2012, thirdcoastdaily. com/2012/03/this-week-in-history-mining-moratorium-bill-passed-in-1997/ See also Al Gedicks, "Mining Industry Targets 'Prove It First' Law." *Z Magazine* 26:2 (February 2013).

14 See Victor Wallis, "Workers' Control and Revolution," in Immanuel Ness and Dario Azzellini, eds., *Ours to Master and to Own: Workers' Control from the Commune to the Present* (Chicago: Haymarket Books, 2011), 29.

find one of the strongest material bases for a popular environmentalism, of which a signal model has been the work of the Labor/Community Strategy Center of Los Angeles and its founding director, Eric Mann.[15] While the most sustained focus of the Strategy Center's agitation has been for immediate services to the city's bus riders (who are mostly poor and people of color), it also undertook a major spatial study of air pollution[16] and, addressing the global issue of greenhouse gases, has issued repeated calls for measures to curb the overall use of automobiles. Although begun as a local group, the Strategy Center thus increasingly articulates a national agenda.

Existing US organizations around the environment have been slow to develop a class perspective. To be sure, with the accelerating alarm over greenhouse gases, there is increasing militancy, exemplified in the turn to direct action by climate scientist James Hansen and in the waves of massive civil disobedience starting in 2011 (with more than 1200 arrests) in protest of the Keystone XL pipeline, and continuing in 2016 with the convergence of indigenous peoples and their allies at Standing Rock, North Dakota, to resist the Dakota Access pipeline. A socialist presence in environmental organizing—one component in the 300,000-strong September 2014 demonstration at the United Nations—is beginning to develop, under the slogan "system change not climate change." But so long as the movement as a whole fails to stress the class-implications of its demands, it will have trouble translating popular dissatisfaction into an alternative policy framework.

TOWARD ECOLOGICAL CLASS CONSCIOUSNESS

The components of a class perspective on the environment are already present. Indeed, at a theoretical level, they are highly developed, in the sense that the clash between capitalist and environmental priorities is widely recognized—not least, as we have noted, by capitalist interests themselves. Our concern here, however, is to

---

15   See www.thestrategycenter.org/

16   Eric Mann, *L.A.'s Lethal Air* (Los Angeles: Labor/Community Strategy Center, 1993).

go beyond this recognition, which has already been dramatized by the perverse spectacle of business leaders rejoicing in the melting of the polar icecap on the grounds that it will facilitate stepped-up commerce and oil exploration in the Arctic!

In light of this impulse to ramp up the very practices that have generated the crisis, what we must identify, gather, and try to synthesize are all the disparate expressions of a popular response. Up to this point, our focus here has been on the more explicit expressions of an ecological class-consciousness. Now we must explore those expressions which have arisen and articulated themselves on the basis of other, "non-class" identities and ethical principles. The reason for seeking to bring these together in relation to class, is that class is the irreducible factor underlying the dominant agenda of uninterrupted growth and accumulation. No human constituency benefits from or favors species-loss or catastrophic climate change, but there are clear interests that oppose the measures necessary to halt such outcomes, and those interests reflect the common class-position of capital.

What, then, are the components of an alternative class-position—one that, when put together as a political force, could directly and comprehensively confront capital's anti-ecological thrust?

On a global scale, we begin, as noted earlier, with the distinctive and principled stance of the indigenous movements. More generally, however, there are countless movements of local popular resistance which have been characterized—often by their own spokespeople—under the watchword of *environmental justice*.[17] A notable feature of EJ movements is that their very existence refutes the longstanding stereotype (common in the US) of environmentalism as a "middle class" or "elite" issue. EJ movements, especially in the Third World but also in the United States itself, typically arise among the most oppressed sectors of the population, for whom the environmental assault compounds the pre-existing burden of poverty.[18] Examples include: the disproportionate concentration of

17 See Richard Hofrichter, ed., *Toxic Struggles: The Theory and Practice of Environmental Justice*. Philadelphia: New Society, 1993), and Faber, *The Struggle for Ecological Democracy*.

18 Perhaps the most egregious instance of such assault was the 1984 disaster at the Union Carbide plant in Bhopal, India, where the release of methyl isocyanate gas

toxic waste-dumps in poor and minority communities, the failure
to curb toxic emissions affecting those same communities (resulting
in high rates of asthma and cancer), the destruction of community
water supplies by such procedures as mountaintop removal and
fracking, the destruction of fishing grounds by mining operations,
the destruction of biodiversity in agricultural regions by the use of
pesticides and genetic engineering, and the draining of community
water supplies for industrial purposes. All such practices have provoked popular protest, but what has been missing, at least in the
United States but for the most part elsewhere as well, has been a
political formation that could at once amplify such protest, coordi-
nate strategies and tactics, and raise the political awareness of both
activists and the public.

In thinking about this lack, it may be helpful to examine some of
the ways in which EJ demands and environmental issues generally
have intersected—or could intersect—with the interests and views
of various particular constituencies.

Bridging the Racial Divide

One of the most potent charges, eliciting the strongest reactions,
has been that of environmental racism. This phenomenon forces
us to sharpen our understanding of the class divide. The concentration of toxins in communities of color is longstanding.[19] What's
in question, therefore, is not whether race constitutes a pretext for
assaulting communities (which it indisputably does), but rather the
political nature of the mechanisms that have led to its being cast in
that role.

Here we come face to face with the class basis of racial oppression. Beyond the historic implantation of "racial" classifications to
divide the working class,[20] there is the stark present-day fact, in the
United States, that the prevalence of working-class occupations or
statuses (including low-rank military, unemployed, and incarcer-

---

and other chemicals resulted in thousands of deaths and many more injuries.

19 See Robert D. Bullard, "Anatomy of Environmental Racism," in Hofrichter, ed.,
    Toxic Struggles.

20 See Theodore W. Allen, *The Invention of the White Race*. 2nd ed. (London: Verso,
    2012).

ated) is substantially higher among black people—as well as most Latino and some Asian ethnicities as well as Native Americans—than it is in the population as a whole. At the same time, race-based thinking routinely serves the academic and media establishments as a surrogate for recognizing the impact of class. This has been particularly true in the post-civil rights era, as targets for attaining institutional "diversity" have been met in large part by tapping the proportionately minuscule privileged sectors of oppressed ethnic groups.[21] The majorities within those groups, meanwhile, gain no improvement. Policies to hold them down continue to be implemented, via mass criminalization and incarceration associated with the "war on drugs."[22] With a black president in office for two terms beginning in 2009, it became increasingly evident that class takes precedence over race as the key external variable framing one's life-chances.

This argument points to the likelihood that communities oppressed on what have hitherto been perceived as racial grounds may now become more receptive to a class analysis of their condition. Steps in such a direction are among the side-effects of the current particularly harsh prison-regimen in the United States. While the targets of such repression are disproportionately black, a common practice of appointing black wardens to administer the process—yet another instance of "black faces in high places"—again points to the reality that the underlying priorities are those of class interest. From that vantage-point, there is a clear drive to obstruct steps that might be taken "from below" toward transcending racial barriers among prisoners.[23] More generally, a class-based critique of the Obama administration received its most widely diffused articulation in the "poor people's campaign" conducted during the 2012 presidential race by African American opinion leaders Tavis Smiley and Cornel West. Such developments reflect and encourage an increasing readiness within oppressed "racial"

---

21 Walter Benn Michaels, *The Trouble with Diversity: How We Learned to Love Identity and Ignore Inequality* (New York: Henry Holt, 2006).

22 Michelle Alexander, *The New Jim Crow: Mass Incarceration in the Age of Colorblindness*, revised ed. (New York: New Press, 2012).

23 See Kevin "Rashid" Johnson, "Political Struggle in the Teeth of Prison Reaction: From Virginia to Oregon," *Socialism and Democracy* 27:1 (March 2013).

communities to understand the power exercised over them as being a function of class—a perspective which makes it easier for them to find common ground with a class-oriented ecological movement.[24] The plausibility of such an understanding has only been amplified under the Trump presidency, which, while fostering unabashed racism, embodies the fusion of environmental denialism with open embrace of the most extreme class-privilege.[25]

Learning from Feminism

The ecological movement has been particularly enriched by feminist thought. In a way parallel to anti-racism, though more sweeping, feminism calls into question all relationships of domination. Whereas racial oppression is a particular manifestation of class domination, feminism extends the critique of domination beyond class to encompass the historically evolved stance of the human species in relation to the natural world as a whole. While the link between exploitation of humans and plunder of the natural world had been recognized by Marx,[26] it was with the feminist movement that this link began to be widely noted in radical discourse, as the subjugation of nature became personified in the institutions of male supremacy.[27]

In terms of building a unified class-conscious environmental movement, the challenge is to acknowledge the negative patterns evoked in this analogy, but then to envisage and map out the dialectic by which they will be overcome. Feminist criticism punctured what were thought to be the distinctively male attributes of toughness and aggressiveness while vaunting the correspondingly paradigmatic "feminine" traits of compassion and cooperation. While at that level feminism could veer into a kind of essentialism (i.e., ste-

---

24 See Keeanga-Yamahtta Taylor, *From #Black Lives Matter to Black Liberation* (Chicago: Haymarket Books, 2016).

25 See John Bellamy Foster, *Trump in the White House: Tragedy and Farce* (New York: Monthly Review Press, 2017).

26 See Victor Wallis, "Species Questions: Humanity and Nature from Marx to Shiva," *Organization & Environment* 13:4 (December 2000), reprinted as Ch. 5 of Victor Wallis, *Socialist Practice: Histories and Theories* (London: Palgrave Macmillan, 2020).

27 Ynestra King, "Feminism and Ecology," in Hofrichter, ed., *Toxic Struggles*.

reotyping based on sex), at another level it called into question all received assumptions that would allocate dispositions and talents as a function of sex. Feminism has thus played a dual role. On the one hand it has posited a historic need for the affirmation, in relation to matters of public controversy, of approaches traditionally derided as soft or conciliatory. On the other hand, it has insisted that the full range of human behaviors—from warlike to nurturing—is within the capacity of each person, irrespective of sexual identity.

Feminist understanding is thus central to the transformation of human nature which is, in turn, integral to the ecological agenda. In its ethical dimension, feminism elevates cooperation over competition; as social critique, feminism reminds us that the capacity of each of us to act appropriately is not constrained by any biological traits. Contrary to the classic binary, then, biology is not destiny. Applied to the environmental crisis, this tells us that in relating to nature we have the potential, as a species, to overcome the drives instilled in us by the whole culture of capitalist consumerism.

Although an influential strand of feminism shuns this kind of radical critique, that attitude—aptly expressed in Hillary Clinton's presidential ambitions—represents a departure from the core feminist principle of resistance to *all* forms of domination. This original approach, articulated in reverence for "Mother Earth," in critiques of capitalist patriarchy, and in visions of a higher level of humanity, has lost ground in the United States, compared to the emphasis on women moving into roles previously reserved to men—a kind of feminism which "patriarchal capitalist institutions are comfortable with ... and encourage"[28] Feminism's indispensable role in the ecological movement will depend on the degree to which it recovers its earlier radical thrust. As it does so, it will be able to reclaim for the movement as a whole a primordial commitment to life, expressed in our collective responsibility to bequeath the world to future generations in at least as good a condition as the one in which we came into it.

---

28 Ariel Salleh, *Ecofeminism as Politics: Nature, Marx, and the Postmodern* (London: Zed Books, 1997), 104; see also Hester Eisenstein, *Feminism Seduced: How Global Elites Use Women's Labor and Ideas to Exploit the World* (Boulder, CO: Paradigm Publishers, 2009).

Other Dimensions of Commonality

The feminist critique of inequality is replicated in other spheres. People's individual capacities and traits may vary independently not only of sex but also of sexual orientation. They may also vary independently of certain physical disabilities, especially if the necessary logistical accommodations are made available as a matter of right.[29] These observations have now attained a wide degree of acceptance. What is striking, however, is that this entirely positive development has not carried over into a general revulsion against vast social and economic inequality. The ignorance surrounding this core feature of US society[30] and the consequent air of inevitability attributed to it—especially in light of the heightened sensitivity to disrespect vis-à-vis all the "particular" identities—is a remarkable expression of the cultural hegemony of capital.[31] Although vast inequalities are becoming increasingly difficult to ignore, the thrust of political discourse is to view them as matters of policy rather than as a reflection of systemic forces.

The ecological movement we are seeking will by its very nature have to address this condition. At the same time, it will grow stronger to the degree that it is successful in doing so. What is required can be expressed almost as a matter of common sense. If racism, sexism, and homophobia can be discredited, why can't there emerge an equally negative aura around the attitudes and practices tied to extreme social inequality? Going beyond the common-sense understanding, however, we can observe in all these spheres that moral condemnation is not enough. A common pattern of hierarchy points to a common underlying disposition, which carries over from one sphere of activity to others.

One of the essential insights of ecological thought is that consumption—including the occupation of space—is not a purely private matter. What each of us does with the earth and its resources

---

29 See Ravi Malhotra, "Expanding the Frontiers of Justice: Reflections on the Theory of Capabilities, Disability Rights, and the Politics of Global Inequality," *Socialism and Democracy* 22:1 (March 2008).

30 A Harvard Business School survey of over 5,000 Americans in 2013 showed a dramatic contrast between supposed and actual levels of wealth-inequality in the US (www.youtube.com/watch?v=vttbhl_kDoo).

31 This is the central theme of Michaels, *The Trouble with Diversity*.

inescapably has effects beyond its immediate consequences to our respective selves. This is true on a modest scale for all our daily routines. At this level—symbolized by re-using shopping bags and by turning off light-switches—the link is widely recognized. What is not at all widely recognized is the disproportionate impact resulting from the practices of those who, as private owners, command immense concentrations of wealth and power. The idea that wealth and power should reside in society as a whole has inspired a long history of social struggles. But its ecological rationale—which could potentially inspire a much wider consensus—has still not been made a matter of extensive public discussion.

What is needed is indeed an ecologically grounded class-consciousness. Such a form of class-consciousness is—or ought to be—called forth not only by the ecological crisis itself, but also by the dissipation, over the past few decades, of the framework within which earlier forms of working-class consciousness arose. At the same time that industrial occupations have shifted from rich to poor countries, there has also been a rupture of the presumed link—central to traditional trade unionism—between productivity-gains and wage-increases.[32] This latter development weakens the hold of management over the policy-priorities of workers, making workers less likely to see a convergence of interest with their employers (since the bosses no longer reward higher productivity with higher wages). This in turn opens up an array of new perspectives for workers, as they must now give more attention to the wider context of their jobs.

But as the traditional spurs to organizing have withered, new provocations have arisen. The general spread of austerity policies (following the 2008 bank failures) has brought together constituencies that are not otherwise organizationally linked. With one-sixth of the US population now in poverty, with an unprecedented student loan debt crisis,[33] and with continued political attacks on the social safety net, existential uncertainty is rampant. Personal desperation fuses with a competitive and militaristic culture to ignite

---

32   Richard D. Wolff, *Capitalism Hits the Fan: The Global Economic Meltdown and What to Do About It* (Northampton, MA: Olive Branch Press, 2010).

33   Chuck Collins, "The Student Debt Time Bomb," Moyers & Co. (2015), billmoyers.com/2015/03/13/student-debt-time-bomb/

individual outbursts, often with tragic consequences.[34] While popular awareness of these dangers—as well as of the environmental
crisis—has been growing, the daunting difficulty of addressing them
renders the significance of this awareness moot. People know that
something on a large scale needs to be done, but no vehicle for an
effective global response has yet materialized. On what basis might
such a vehicle be brought into being?

PARAMETERS OF A MASS ECOLOGICAL AWARENESS

Those who deride what they call "catastrophism"[35] view mass apathy on environmental issues as the outcome of a reflexive paralysis
induced by perception of overwhelming danger. If this were correct, then one would expect progressive near-term policies on the
environment to be strongest in countries where the sense of alarm
about the ecological crisis was at its lowest. In fact, the opposite
is the case. Countries like Germany, where there is broad popular awareness of the long-term dangers (expressed, for example, in
massive demonstrations against nuclear power), are also the ones
where the most has been done *within the existing system*—as the
anti-"catastrophists" propose—to enact practical measures to protect the environment (e.g., broad diffusion of solar collectors and
wind turbines). It is the US, by contrast—where the denialist claim
that there is no environmental crisis at all has been most widely
diffused and accepted –, that has lagged behind other highly industrialized countries in taking even modest protective steps, such as
banning at least the more dangerous forms of fuel-extraction. The
role of denialism in facilitating such outcomes is obvious; blaming
weak environmental policies on the so-called catastrophism of the
ecological Left, on the other hand, is purely speculative.

The emergency represented by the environmental crisis exists
irrespective of our wishes. Any sense of complacency that might
be created about environmental trends is therefore not only counterproductive, but also, simply, false. What is disturbing about the

---

34 See Ingar Solty, "Dear Left: The NRA Is Right—The Mass Shooter as High
    Achiever," *Socialism and Democracy*, 26:3 (November 2012).
35 Lilley et al., *Catastrophism*.

approach of the anti-catastrophists is that they ignore the scientific character of projections made by environmental experts (of such developments as desertification and species-extinction), lumping the resulting forecasts together with apocalyptic religious pronouncements.[36] Whether the immediate focus is on environmental disaster or on revolutionary political transition, the anti-catastrophists routinely attribute to those whom they are criticizing a scenario imagined only by themselves. In the environmental sphere, they suggest that projections which have not yet been fully played out (e.g., depletion of the world's agricultural land) have thereby been discredited. In the political sphere, they imply that they alone recognize the importance of any form of popular activism short of a sudden and all-encompassing "tumultuous upheaval."[37]

Unlike congressional "climate skeptics" sponsored by the big oil companies, the anti-catastrophists do not deny that a species-threatening ecological crisis exists. But they do assert that our understanding of the capitalist *roots* of the crisis should not inform our political practice. Where the overt denialists weaken environmental awareness from the right, the anti-catastrophists do so from the left. Although they favor ending capitalism, they argue that this goal cannot be part of a strategy for ecological restoration.[38] They assume that advancing a socialist analysis of the ecological crisis makes it impossible to propose any constructive steps for the environment short of socialist revolution. This assumption, however, is groundless. It seems to emanate from a hegemonic (in the US) centrist ideology which denounces with self proclaimed even-handedness the "extremes" of right and left, calling instead for "moderate" measures as the only rational response. In the process, though, it overlooks the fact that the content of any drastic measures that are taken—including the degree to which they incorporate and build on measures of immediate relief—will differ radically depending on which side of the class-divide holds power.

---

36 Victor Wallis, "Ecosocialist Struggles: Reminiscences, Reflections, and Danger Signals," *Capitalism Nature Socialism*, 25:1 (March 2014), 50.

37 Lilley et al., *Catastrophism*, 124.

38 This point is made directly by Doug Henwood in his Foreword to *Catastrophism* (Lilley et al., xv). Earlier expressions of this position were discussed above, in Chapter 5.

The critique of capitalism is pertinent not only in terms of suggesting the contours of a global alternative, but also in terms of identifying near-term goals and mobilizing the social constituencies that may, whether through political agitation or direct local engagement, bring them to fruition. There is no contradiction between articulating a long-term vision and working for immediate improvements. Most specifically, ecological restoration depends on making decisions about production, transportation, construction, and consumption that run counter to what market-signals in these domains would suggest. Although the general critique of market institutions implies the need for radical social transformation, the drive to correct even very specific near-term abuses—such as toxic emissions dictated by a particular company's "bottom line"—is likely to be stronger if the link of those abuses to the wider picture is understood.[39] The wider vision serves here not only as inspiration but also as reality check; it alerts activists to the kinds of obstacles they are likely to encounter.

The obstacles in question, it will be found, relate consistently to patterns of class interest. This perception helps us to distinguish (as Judi Bari did for the timber workers) between our allies and our enemies. It enables us to pinpoint responsibility for the abuses we are attacking, and thereby to identify the targets of our organizing. Beyond this, it also alerts us to ways of transcending the stereotypically assumed clash between human needs and ecological requirements. In the caricature of a socialist approach depicted by the anti-catastrophists, the only imagined socialist agenda for confronting resource-scarcity is "a moralistic plea for austerity and discipline"[40]—an approach which they frequently characterize as

---

39 Not all purportedly pro-environmental short-term measures are compatible with long-term transformation. Such measures often involve, on the contrary, extremely dangerous technologies—e.g., emulating volcanic eruptions—designed precisely to permit the continuation of business as usual (see Clive Hamilton, *Earthmasters: The Dawn of the Age of Climate Engineering*, New Haven: Yale University Press, 2013). Among the many positive measures, by contrast, has been the outright banning, in the US, of toxic substances such as the pesticide DDT (see Barry Commoner, *Making Peace with the Planet*, New York: Pantheon Books, 1990, 41-44) and, more generally, implementation of the country's 1970s regulatory acts, as well as steps of all kinds to restore natural habitats and reduce dependence on fossil fuels.

40 Lilley et al., *Catastrophism*, 124.

Malthusian (ignoring Marx's scathing critique of Malthus for the latter's mechanistic projection of population-growth). In fact, what a Marxist critique calls into question is precisely the tacit assumption that energy-use reflects the behavior of an undifferentiated mass of humanity, with its corollary that all of "us" are complicit in the resultant assault on the ecosphere. Recognizing this assumption as purely ideological (in the sense of obscuring the real structures that shape the social consumption of energy), socialist activists can make known the *actual* loci of macro-policy decisions. By the same token, they can envisage alternative approaches based on criteria other than those of private profit. In so doing, they can advance a positive strategy which includes attention also to near-term goals. Specifically, they can distinguish—and help enable others to distinguish—between legitimate universal needs and (on the other hand) demands or structural imperatives reflecting the priorities of capital and of the capitalist class. This can draw attention to energy-wasting pursuits which might be immediately curbed, such as weapons development, prison construction, highway expansion, and the production and use of motorized sports-vehicles.

The one element of justification for the anti-catastrophists' concern is the fear that, in the words of a panel description at a recent geographers' conference, "False urgency suspends the democratic process. The management of nature is entrusted to the non-democratic techno-managerial apparatuses of state bureaucracies, the military and corporations."[41] What suspends democratic accountability, however, is not the urgency (which, with regard to the environment, is hardly "false"), but rather the class interests of those who recognize the danger but refuse to acknowledge and address its underlying causes. Foreseeing scarcity, their concern is only to assure that their own interests will be taken care of. The alternative to this stance is not to ignore or deny the urgency; rather, it is to affirm that the response must be one of universal cooperation.

To discuss how cooperation—and its requisite democracy—can be reconciled with quick and sweeping changes is to address one of the classic dilemmas of revolution. But the contours of a response

---

41 James McCarthy, "We Have Never Been 'Post-Political,'" *Capitalism Nature Socialism*, 24:1 (March 2013), 20.

have already shown themselves historically. Defying the assumption that decisive measures are incompatible with mass participation, there is an important worldwide legacy of worker-control initiatives that have been intertwined with revolutionary upheaval.[42] This accumulated experience suggests a number of observations pertinent to what we might call an effective popular ecology.

People faced with collective tasks show a level of creativity and resourcefulness that is not apparent when they are merely carrying out a boss's orders. Workers who run an enterprise feel a sense of responsibility for their workplace and also for the products that in some cases they sell directly to the public. They can address unexpected problems because they are familiar with the issues—if not individually, then collectively. Their motivation is enhanced by the sense that they are acting not only in their own interest but in the interest of the wider community as well.[43]

As far as ecologically inspired transformation is concerned, the basis for strong motivation is already evident. The tasks involved, moreover, encompass every dimension of life and can therefore engage people of all ages. Distinctions between what one does as a "job" and what one does as part of the community begin to diminish in importance. Deliberation and education become integral to the whole process. Insofar as one takes a particular social assignment or job as one's reference-point, we can say that the time then devoted—during working hours—to discussion and wider learning replaces the time previously squandered in producing surplus for the private owners of capital.

The immediate pride, identification, and sense of responsibility that accompanies such new practices is important to the time-factor in the process of transformation. Contrary to what one might imagine on the basis of mechanistic reasoning, it is not the case that thoroughgoing changes necessarily require a longer timeline than incremental ones. Quick and sweeping transitions can joltingly

---

42 Wallis, "Workers' Control and Revolution" (n. 14).

43 See the documentary films on workers' initiatives during revolutionary moments in Chile (1972-73) and Venezuela (2002), cited in Wallis, "Workers' Control and Revolution." For a general analysis, see Richard D. Wolff, *Democracy at Work: A Cure for Capitalism* (Chicago: Haymarket Books, 2012).

upend the mental horizons of the population caught up in them. Long-unquestioned roles and categories suddenly no longer make sense. This is particularly important to the reconfiguration of practices affecting the environment. One of the major requirements here is to reverse the vast displacement of human labor-power by capital- and energy-intensive processes, especially for the production of food. The shift that could then take place away from rigidly defined job-roles would make it possible to diversify the nature of everyone's work and to reintegrate quickly into useful activity people who have been stigmatized as redundant from the standpoint of capital.

The most widely diffused demand in current US political campaigns is the demand for jobs. It remains unfulfilled, however, not only in the immediate sense of getting everyone "employed" (at however miserable a wage), but far more so in the more complete sense of assuring that everyone has economic security and, above all, a role in maintaining and—where necessary—restoring the means of life.

Capitalism's failure to secure the immediate goal may open the gate, for many people, to consideration of the deeper goal.

8

Intersectionality's Binding Agent: The Political Primacy of Class

In the last few years, "intersectionality" has become a widely used term among social justice advocates, as a way of referring to the convergence of various progressive struggles. Although the convergence itself has a long history, the intersectionality rubric arose in the context of academic theorizing in the late 1980s. Evolving out of that particular setting, which itself reflected the new social movements of the 1960s, it has come to be applied also in the context of movement-organizing, but in a way that typically overlooks the key role of *class* in defining the conditions under which the common success of *all* the various struggles will be possible.

The key position occupied by class is a structural phenomenon. The crucial role of class in defining life-chances may or may not be reflected in anyone's subjective perceptions. Class-based oppression or exploitation is not inherently "worse" or more painful than other forms of oppression; nor is it necessarily what first provokes anger or discontent or social awareness in a given individual (or even in a majority of individuals). There are other ways, however, in which class does distinguish itself from oppressions such as those grounded in gender or "race."[1] My intention is to explore these and to suggest why all activist projects—including in particular the over-

---

1   The reason for my frequent use of quotation marks around this term will become clear as we proceed. In no sense do I question the reality of racist oppression. What I question is the supposed biological grounding of the concept. Notions of race—as distinct from descriptive terms pertaining to people's physical features, culture, or nationality—originated in connection with agendas of domination, which required the biologically unfounded belief that some collectivities are superior to others. Discrediting the notion of race is integral to ending racism. For a particularly illuminating account of the genesis of "race" in the US, see Bar-

arching struggle for species-survival in the face of environmental dangers—will encounter frustration for as long as their protagonists continue to ignore the distinctive strategic importance of class. The underlying class implications of the ecological struggle should be clear from our discussion up to this point. But what has prevented—or dissuaded—people from recognizing their common class-interests?

DIMENSIONS OF DOMINATION

The ecological struggle is, at its core, a struggle against the idea that the human species is entitled to dominate the natural world. Humans have not always sought such domination; that approach evolved as society became divided into classes, with an incipient class of private individuals claiming proprietary rights over natural goods and then needing to defend their control over those goods against any possible incursion by others. These others, the non-property-owners, increasingly lost access to a bounty that had previously belonged at once to everyone and to no one. Although the large-property owners were individuals, each pursuing a purely private advantage, they naturally colluded with one another to form authority-structures that would reflect and uphold their common interests. Later, as capitalism evolved, the biggest property-holders became the corporations. With increasing corporate concentration, the residual domain of unenclosed public space, or "commons," or "free goods of nature," shrank even further, to the point where—at present—even potable water and clean air are being privatized and commodified.

The control that capital exercised over people advanced in tandem with its control over nature. As public space shrank, so did any opportunity for individuals to gain a livelihood outside the capitalist labor market. Conversely, as people adapted to the new conditions of market-dependence, they became less able to affirm values and practices on which a restoration of community life would depend. Instead, they became increasingly insecure and competitive. In

bara Jeanne Fields, "Slavery, Race and Ideology in the United States of America," *New Left Review* 1st series, no. 181 (May-June 1990), 95-118.

some countries (especially in northern Europe), workers' movements arrested this process before it went too far, and instituted social-welfare measures that assured at least a minimum level of personal security and general civility. Where such measures were blocked or reversed, however, as in the United States since the 1950s, civic consciousness gave way, among most people, to a narrow, interest-oriented approach to politics—an approach susceptible to particularistic appeals (around issues of ethnicity, religion, cultural priorities, schools, social services, etc.) and resistant to the kind of broad-based, socially responsible thinking required by an ecological agenda.

It is within this general framework of perpetually tightening capitalist domination—over both society and nature—that the history of the last two centuries has unfolded. Of course, there has been resistance or blowback on both fronts. The response of the natural world has been elemental, on a scale far beyond any possibility of remediation. What good are all of humanity's technological achievements when set against the disappearance of glaciers, the drying up of rivers, the melting of the polar icecap, sea-level rise, forest-shrinkage, species-loss, polluted air and water, public-health emergencies, and catastrophic climate events?[2] Is not Nature, as Engels warned, taking dramatic revenge on man's collective attempt to tame it?[3]

Human power pales next to the forces of nature; the human response to capitalist domination has been, correspondingly, far more halting—held back by some combination of flexibility on the part of the system and adaptability or inertia on the part of its subjects. To the extent that people have resisted domination, it has been on the basis of coherent political forces that have arisen expressing the interests of the majority. What has impeded such defiance, however, is the multiplicity of channels through which the capitalist class exercises its control. Apart from the agencies of direct repression (armed forces, police, private security guards) and

---

2   For a full discussion, see Ian Angus, *Facing the Anthropocene: Fossil Capitalism and the Crisis of the Earth System* (New York: Monthly Review Press, 2016).

3   In Engels' memorable words, "Let us not, however, flatter ourselves overmuch on account of our human conquest over nature. For each such victory, nature takes its revenge on us." *Dialectics of Nature* (1883).

from the various channels that impose ideological hegemony (educational and religious institutions, mass media, etc.), the dominant class relies heavily upon politicization—partly spontaneous and partly by design—of the numerous criteria of "difference" that exist within the general population, each of which constitutes a potential arena for oppressive practices, both legal and extra-legal, ranging from discrimination to petty harassment to rape to lynching.

Intersectionality refers to how the oppression of particular "identity" groups—women, people of color, cultural or religious minorities, sexual minorities, old people, people with disabilities—partakes of the larger structure of domination within which the totality of social policy is worked out. Social policy involves measures that will sooner or later affect everyone. Environmental policy is ultimately the most all-encompassing category; it infuses—although usually without being recognized—every measure that can affect economic performance, including specific regulations regarding trade, housing, public services, agriculture, etc., as well as legislation or executive decisions regarding taxation, immigration, and matters of war and peace.[4] Like advocacy on behalf of particular constituencies, advocacy around these issues is often of a specialized or "single issue" character. Ultimately, however, all these issues, just like all the forms of oppression, are interrelated. Our common task is to understand the structure of this interrelationship—this intersectionality—and, on the basis of such understanding, to build a political force capable of dismantling the power that until now has perpetuated the oppressive practices—against the natural world as well as against the popular majority.

Approaches to Intersectionality

The phenomenon of intersectionality was recognized long before the word itself was thought of. Popular revolutions have typically challenged the old order in multiple spheres.[5] Marx and Engels,

4   For discussion of the environmental component of a wide range of issues, see Chapter 4.

5   The English revolution of the mid-seventeenth century was notable for its early expressions of feminist demands; see Sheila Rowbotham, *Women, Resistance, and Revolution: A History of Women and Revolution in the Modern World* (New

for their part, spoke not only of the exploitation of the working class as a whole, but also of the special disadvantages imposed on Irish workers in England, by virtue of their nationality.[6] Marx also spoke, in *Capital*, of the extraordinary devaluation of women workers, who were "still occasionally used instead of horses for hauling barges, because the labour required to produce horses and machines is an accurately known quantity, while that required to maintain the women of the surplus population is beneath all calculation."[7] Among the countless examples from US history, we might note Herbert Aptheker's 1949 discussion of the "triple enslavement" of "the Negro Woman" and Angela Davis's 1981 remarks on how the Seneca Falls Declaration on the rights of women (in 1848) disregarded the concerns of working-class women, white as well as black.[8] Particularly influential was the 1977 Statement of the Combahee River Collective of Black feminists, which included the assertion, "We realize that the liberation of all oppressed peoples necessitates the destruction of the political-economic systems of capitalism and imperialism as well as patriarchy."[9] The existence of multiple and often overlapping lines of oppression has thus been recognized for a long time.

Intersectionality as a concept, however, first gained prominence among feminist scholars in the 1980s, as they realized that the mainstream women's movement that arose in the '60s had failed to concern itself with the aggravated oppression experienced on the one hand by black women, on account of their "race," and on the other, by lesbians and transgender people on account of their

---

York: Pantheon, 1972). An extraordinary twentieth-century example is the revolt of "half of China," described in Chapter 16 of William Hinton, *Fanshen: Documentary of Revolution in a Chinese Village* (New York: Vintage, 1968).

6   On the Irish sub-proletariat, see especially Karl Marx, "[Ireland and the English Working Class]," in Marcello Musto, ed., *Workers Unite! The International 150 Years Later* (New York: Bloomsbury, 2014), 249.

7   Karl Marx, *Capital*, vol. 1, trans. Ben Fowkes (New York: Vintage, 1977), 517.

8   Herbert Aptheker, "The Negro Woman," reprinted in Eric Foner and Manning Marable (eds), *Herbert Aptheker on Race and Democracy: A Reader* (Urbana: University of Illinois Press, 2006), 122; Angela Y. Davis, *Women, Race & Class* (New York: Random House, 1981), 53.

9   Combahee River Collective Statement, 1977, circuitous.org/scraps/combahee.html.

sexuality.[10] Of course, these two dimensions could in turn converge with each other in particular individuals, creating a further layer of complexity. The persistent issue of the movement's "middle class" character was also widely noted, with the implication that working-class women continue, as in Marx's time, to be doubly oppressed.[11] The important additional dimensions of age and disability have also been brought into view—thanks, as with each earlier step, to defiant activism on the part of some of their subjects.[12]

All this work has helped to undermine stereotypes, generate respect for previously marginalized people, and thereby broaden the scope of individual opportunity. But the basic lines of oppression, even when publicly discredited, have not lost their impact on broad sectors of society. The language of oppression has been modified, as officials deploy politically correct verbiage and enact laws against "hate speech." But at the level of daily life, in the subliminal messages of mass-marketed cultural artifacts, and in the experience of majorities within each of the affected groups, the habitual attitudes and practices continue to impose pain on a vast scale. This has been dramatically shown in the unacknowledged racism of US police practices, from the routine harassment of whole communities to the now-notorious torrent of homicides—targeting with particular vindictiveness those people of color who in any way seek to assert their rights or their dignity.[13] Symptomatic also are the officially condoned abusive acts of prison guards (especially against people of color and sexual minorities), ranging from food-deprivation to

---

10　Kimberlé W. Crenshaw, "Demarginalising the Intersection of Race and Sex: A Black Feminist Critique of Anti-discrimination Doctrine, Feminist Theory, and Anti-racist Politics" [orig. 1989], in Helma Lutz, Maria Teresa Herrera Vivar and Linda Supik (eds), *Framing Intersectionality: Debates on a Multi-Faceted Concept in Gender Studies* (Burlington, VT: Ashgate, 2011).

11　See Johanna Brenner, *Women and the Politics of Class* (New York: Monthly Review Press, 2000).

12　Margaret Morganroth Gullette, *Aged by Culture* (Chicago: University of Chicago Press, 2004); Ravi Malhotra and Morgan Rowe, *Exploring Disability Identity and Disability Rights through Narratives: Finding a Voice of Their Own* (New York: Routledge, 2014).

13　Steve Martinot, "Probing the Epidemic of Police Murders" and "Police Impunity, Human Autonomy, and Jim Crow," *Socialism and Democracy* 27:1 (March 2013), 57-77, and 28:3 (November 2014), 64-76. The shocking frequency of US police killings (an average of more than 3 per day) is documented with links to press reports at killedbypolice.net/.

medical neglect to sometimes-fatal beatings.[14] A similar disposition manifests itself in the extraordinarily pervasive violence against women, not only in the form of domestic abuse, but also within the military, at universities, and in all varieties of social spaces.[15] And the increasing acceptance of sexual minorities in some spheres—including even elective office—has been matched if not exceeded by physical attacks against them in others.

The academic discussion of intersectionality reflects in part the influence of the "new social movements" that emerged during the 1960s. What was considered at the time to be new about these movements was that they raised demands that had not been given adequate voice by the "traditional" working-class movement or its political parties.[16] The incipient intersectionality approach, before it was so named, is detectable in the theoretical response given by exponents of the new movements to the question of how those movements could ally or combine or intersect with the working-class movement—as embodied in long-established left-wing parties and in Marxist theory—and with each other.

Since the time of that initial response (which was fully formulated by the early 1980s), the intersectionality debates have come to encompass ever more unique varieties of individual experience while at the same time significantly emphasizing the dynamic interplay of the different dimensions. But the implicit original goal of intersectionality theory—that of binding the oppressed constituencies together into a coherent political force—has not been realized. In other words, there is still no entity capable of challenging the grip on power of those who, as a class, shape every aspect of social life.

Opposition to recognizing the undergirding significance of class is often based on equating class analysis with a kind of abstract universalism which fails to acknowledge the significance of differences other than those of class. Such universalism, however, cannot with-

---

14   Kevin "Rashid" Johnson, "Revisiting the Killings of Prisoners by Texas Prison Officials" (July 25, 2014), rashidmod.com/?p=1082.

15   By 2017, partly in response to Donald Trump's provocations, this became common knowledge. But see also Linda Gordon, "Anti-Woman Terrorism," *Z Magazine* 28:4 (April 2015), and the documentary films *The Invisible War* (2012) and *The Hunting Ground* (2015).

16   There is vast testimony on this. See, for instance, Van Gosse, *Rethinking the New Left: An Interpretative History* (New York: Palgrave Macmillan, 2005).

stand serious engagement with popular struggles, as it disregards the multiplicity of individual experiences out of which any sense of a wider commonality—any authentic class consciousness—must be forged. There is no incompatibility between, on the one hand, combating any and all forms of oppression and, on the other, acknowledging that their combined imposition reflects a coherent (class-based) agenda.

The reluctance to examine classes as (actual or potential) *agents* of history—rather than purely as subjective identities—can be understood historically. In any case, it will be useful to examine the assumptions that have nourished this approach. In doing so, we shall be raising the important practical question of how all the oppressed constituencies of capitalist society—itself a sometimes forgotten rubric—might be able to unify.

Social Movements and Class Interests

The original model of intersectional theorizing—in the pre-history of the intersectionality concept—centered on the class-race-gender triad. The immediate precursor to intersectionality theory was "new social movement" (NSM) theory, which contended that the working-class and socialist movements had failed to encompass the issues of race-based and gender-based oppression, and argued that this failure reflected theoretical shortcomings ultimately traceable to Marx. To overcome this failure, according to the NSM perspective, it would be necessary to cut back the reach of Marxist analysis and to treat it as being just one among several vantage points from which to derive one's understanding of social reality.

One of the more influential efforts at synthesis, from this perspective, came from a pair of authors whose impulse was to accommodate the plurality of vantage points rather than situate all of them as components of a larger common struggle. I refer to Michael Albert and Robin Hahnel, the joint authors of *Unorthodox Marxism* (1978) and *Marxism and Socialist Theory* (1981).[17] Their polemic is

---

17 Both published in Boston by South End Press, the cooperative publishing enterprise co-founded by Albert. The approach they developed gained a wide following not only through these books but also through the popular radical—

pertinent to us because of the centrality it gives to achieving a kind of transcendence of Marxism—a goal that they suggest in the first of these books and make explicit in the second. What gives their argument a certain appeal is its claim to embody a standpoint not only more up-to-date (attentive to certain recent struggles) but, above all, more comprehensive and therefore supposedly more radical than that of Marx.

Albert & Hahnel pigeonhole Marx in the same way he had long been pigeonholed by bourgeois commentators.[18] They view the potential insights of Marxian theory as pertaining solely to "economic" matters, that is, to issues involving production. They claim to embrace a "dialectical approach,"[19] but they disregard the dialectical dimensions—the complexity—of the body of theory whose impact they seek to diminish. They do not reject Marx's critique of capitalism, but they argue that his approach fails to address any oppression other than that of class.[20] They present an elaborate schema of power-relations based on four "social moments": economic, kinship, community, and political—where "kinship" refers to the reproductive sphere and therefore to gender issues; "community" refers to ethnic/cultural collectivities and hence, in their understanding, to issues of race; and "political" refers to structures of authority.[21] Despite the claim to offer a dialectical analysis, this schema posits a tight correspondence between the demographic traits of power-holders and their capacity to represent a particular social constituency. The implication is that women in high office

and strongly feminist—monthly, *Z Magazine* (co-founded by Albert with Lydia Sargent in 1989) and its early website zmag.org.

18 For a comprehensive critique of such one-dimensional views of Marx, see Kevin B. Anderson, *Marx at the Margins: On Nationalism, Ethnicity, and Non-Western Societies* (Chicago: University of Chicago Press, 2010). Anderson offers a summary of his findings in "Karl Marx and Intersectionality," *Logos: A Journal of Modern Society & Culture* 14:1 (2015), logosjournal.com/2015/anderson-marx/.

19 Albert and Hahnel, *Unorthodox Marxism*, 94.

20 On Marx and race, see Anderson, *Marx at the Margins*, Ch. 3; on Marx and gender, ibid., 197-208, and Heather A. Brown, *Marx on Gender and the Family: A Critical Study* (Chicago: Haymarket, 2013). Marx, in a passage quoted by Simone de Beauvoir at the end of her 1949 feminist classic *The Second Sex* (trans. H.M. Parshley [New York: Bantam Books, 1961], 689), posited the quality of the relationship of man to woman as key to gauging the level of overall human development.

21 Albert and Hahnel, *Marxism and Socialist Theory*, 70-71.

will advance the interests of women; Blacks, the interests of Blacks; working-class individuals, the interests of workers; gays, the interests of gays, etc.

Like many simplistic statements, these affirmations contain an element of validity. There can be no doubt that any demographic group needs to make itself heard in its own voice. But what this literal-minded approach overlooks is a twofold truth. On the one hand, there are structural traits of any social order which either facilitate or limit the capacity of its office-holders to carry out certain agendas. Merely being from a given background does not guarantee that one will "represent" one's erstwhile peers; other pressures and considerations will intervene to shape one's priorities once in office. On the other hand, we are all whole human beings and not just a jumble of demographic traits. While a society may seek to constrain the opportunities of certain categories of person on the pretext of allegedly inferior or "deviant" traits, the human aspiration to live a full life entails more than merely inverting the way in which those particular traits are regarded (touting them positively rather than negatively). What we all ultimately want is to get away from being defined by *any* socially constructed category—or combination of such categories—and to be acknowledged instead for who we are *as complete persons*.

To be sure, it is healthier to be proud rather than ashamed of cultural or gender traits that have been stigmatized. This will remain important to many individuals for as long as such stigmatization persists. But the real desideratum is that the stigmatization itself be discredited. The urge to express pride mirrors, in effect, its negative counterpart—the unrelenting social pressures that inflict, if not a feeling of shame, at least some kind of disadvantage (including fear of physical danger). Self-affirmation grounded in some particular trait—such as Black pride or Gay pride—is a vitally necessary initial response to such a condition. But it is not enough by itself to constitute a person's complete self-definition. Just as the determinants of one's supposedly "racial" traits comprise an infinitesimal portion of one's complete genetic profile,[22] so also the socially specified

---

22 Biologist Stephen Jay Gould observes, in *The Mismeasure of Man*, revised ed. (New York: Norton, 1996), 399, that "genetic variety among Africans alone exceeds the sum total of genetic diversity for everyone else in the rest of the

traits (whether physical or cultural/linguistic) by which individuals are categorized comprise only a minimal part of what shapes the personal aspirations—at once unique and universal—of each one of them. Marx and Engels put this point in a way that has not been improved upon when they evoked, in the *Communist Manifesto* (at the end of Part II), a society in which "the free development of each is the condition for the free development of all."[23]

To move in such a direction, one must look to the ways in which individuals transcend their demographic profiles. Individuals have multiple identities, which an "intersectional" approach may help us to recognize. But the problem of discerning a focal point for political struggle remains. This is where the question of class power takes on distinctive importance, because it is the holders of class power who, through their decision-making prerogatives, set the parameters for what is allowed or expected in every specific domain of the society—from jobs to technology to mass entertainment to reproductive rights.[24] This does not mean that the parameters go unchallenged, but it does mean that for a challenge to be even partially successful, it must constitute a political force. To stress exclusively the particular (non-class) identities of oppressed constituencies is to undercut the potential for such a challenge; it is to cast the protagonists as supplicants, pleading for inclusion. In order for the demands of any constituency to be effective, they must be informed by an awareness of—and commitment to engage—the larger process whereby all the constituencies may advance.[25]

---

world combined!"—implying that popular generalizations (even favorable ones) about African-descended people, even "apart from their social perniciousness, have no meaning...."

23 This is in contrast to class-divided societies, in which the opportunity for "free development" is a consequence either of privilege or of exceptional struggle. On the expressions of collective struggle, see Victor Wallis, "Song and Vision in the U.S. Labor Movement," in Lindsay Michie and Eunice Rojas (eds), *Sounds of Resistance: The Role of Music in Multicultural Activism* (Los Angeles: ABC-CLIO/Praeger, 2013), reprinted and updated as Ch. 12 of Victor Wallis, *Socialist Practice: Histories and Theories* (London: Palgrave Macmillan, 2020).

24 That the dominant role is a function of class—and not of class/race/gender—is confirmed by continuity of basic priorities even as non-white and non-male agents are assimilated into the political elite.

25 A "larger" process is, quite simply, one that involves a bigger portion of the population and therefore—insofar as it is organized—constitutes a stronger political force.

It is in this sense that *class* has a strategic or binding function that does not pertain to any of the other lines of oppression: it brings together, potentially into a coherent force, *all* the constituencies that are held down by the single most concentrated power in contemporary society, that of capital itself.[26] If we are to invoke dialectics, it should be in the sense of understanding how the pursuit of any particular demand entails, at the same time, challenging that core configuration of power. This means seeing how the continuation of any particular line of oppression serves interests beyond those of its immediate advocates or enforcers. Contrary to what is implied by the Albert & Hahnel approach, white supremacy is not in the interest of people of European descent; nor is male supremacy in the interest of men; nor is homophobia in the interest of people whose desires are heterosexual. If any of these statements seem counter-intuitive, it is only in the context of a society in which, whether by law or through other inducements, parameters of domination have been deeply instilled, making certain people more likely than others to face harassment (or worse). But there is nothing about having European ancestry, or being male or heterosexual, that necessarily predisposes one to assert some kind of supremacy on the basis of those traits. In putting down others, one narrows one's own horizons. All such supremacist attitudes benefit only the class that has an interest in keeping the majority internally divided. As Marc Lamont Hill synthesizes a similar argument (conversing with Mumia Abu-Jamal), "No one is free until everyone is free."[27] To assume otherwise is to mistake the possession of a certain relative power, status, or social acceptance for the satisfaction of one's basic, universally human emotional needs.[28]

---

26 For a fuller argument on this point, see Ralph Miliband, *Divided Societies: Class Struggle in Contemporary Capitalism* (Oxford University Press, 1989), Ch. 4 ("New Social Movements and Class Struggle"). A path-breaking critique of efforts to de-center the role of class is Ellen Meiksins Wood, *The Retreat from Class* (London: Verso, 1986).

27 Marc Lamont Hill and Mumia Abu-Jamal, *The Classroom and the Cell: Conversations on Black Life in America* (Chicago: Third World Press, 2012), 5.

28 If anything, supremacist affirmations reflect the opposite of psychological well-being, as explained in Jean-Paul Sartre's classic essay, *Anti-Semite and Jew*, trans. George J. Becker (New York: Schocken Books, 1948).

White supremacy, male supremacy, and heteronormativity are components of a larger system of power, within which each plays a strategic role, buttressed by institutions that are kept going because, in complex and sometimes contradictory ways, they reinforce the overall constellation of class power. Each of these lines of oppression has been disrupted within recent memory—and will surely be disrupted again—by determined collective action, but to dissolve any of them entirely would require a much broader transformation. It would require a culture in which the domination of one set of human beings over others—and over the natural world—has become unacceptable. The prevailing culture, by contrast, is one whose corporate and military overlords thrive on such domination. Its aspects of extreme aggression, competitiveness, and violence—at micro as well as macro levels—are integral to the agenda of growth, expansion, and global control which the US capitalist class defines as constituting the "national interest."[29] Every sphere of human interaction is vulnerable to being invaded and violated by this culture. And every legislative or judicial victory over such domination—whether in environmental protection or in the realms of voting rights or reproductive rights—is subject, as a matter of course, to ferocious rollback.

THE SUPPOSED DILUTION OF CLASS POWER

Like the understanding of multiple oppressions, awareness of class power and class interest is nothing new. For the capitalist class, it is their modus operandi. For the working-class majority,[30] however, such awareness advances or dissipates as conditions change. These conditions are partly the outcome of direct measures taken by the capitalist class (whether by law, by force, or through ideological/cultural channels), but they are partly also the result of responses by various constituencies within the working class expressing their own particular demands (whether directly job-related or involv-

---

29 See John Bellamy Foster, *Naked Imperialism: The U.S. Pursuit of Global Dominance* (New York: Monthly Review Press, 2006).

30 See the relevant occupational figures in Michael Zweig, *The Working Class Majority, America's Best Kept Secret*, 2nd ed. (Ithaca, NY: Cornell University Press, 2012), 29-36.

ing broader issues such as healthcare, civil rights, and reproductive rights). Obviously, these two sets of conditioning factors may interact.

The post-World War II period in the United States was one of severe setbacks for working-class consciousness. As the government asserted a new level of global power, it imposed a harsh regime of domestic repression. At the same time, the country's relative remoteness from wartime devastation gave it an economic advantage that made possible an unprecedented though transitory pinnacle of prosperity for major (mostly white) sectors of the working class. The combination of material wellbeing with ideological conformity led many (including most trade union leaders) to view class struggle as being foreign to the agenda of the labor movement. Add to this the negative image acquired—with whatever degree of justification—by the Communist party (and hence to some extent by progressive stances generally), and it becomes easy to see why any new wave of protest would tend to shy away from a systemic critique (centering on class power) and consequently to remain internally divided along sectoral and demographic lines.[31]

It was under these conditions that the new social movements emerged. The NSMs on the one hand helped drive the New Left, while on the other hand they defined what would remain as the movement's positive legacy when the wave of activism subsided. Reinforcing the NSMs' splintering effect was the extraordinary barrage of state violence unleashed against organizations and popular leaders that could be seen as potentially unifying the movement's various constituencies and thereby posing the threat—real or imagined—of revolution. Major leaders were marked for elimination, but student demonstrators were also attacked. Police firepower decapitated the biggest revolutionary organization (the Black Panther Party, BPP), while the courts sentenced many of its surviving cadre to long prison-terms.[32] A degree of revolutionary optimism

---

31 Victor Wallis, "Keeping the Faith: The U.S. Left, 1968-1998," *Monthly Review* 50:4 (September 1998), reprinted and updated in Wallis, *Socialist Practice*, 139-55.

32 Key moments were the assassination of Chicago BPP leader Fred Hampton (Joshua Bloom and Waldo E. Martin, Jr., *Black against Empire: The History and Politics of the Black Panther Party* [Berkeley: University of California Press, 2014]. 237-246) and, before that, the assassination of Martin Luther King, Jr., in

persisted through the late 1970s, partly inspired by movements in the Third World, but the groups partaking of it within the US became insulated both from one another and from the wider public.

Much of the residual radical consciousness filtered into academia, where the establishment of programs such as Black Studies and Women's Studies represented important victories for progressive activism. The large constituencies supporting such programs created institutional space for research and theory that transcended identitarian interests, building on new approaches generated by the 1960s movements, such as studying history "from the bottom up." Radical analysis, within this context, enjoyed a level of general acceptance that would have seemed almost unimaginable a generation earlier. On the other hand, from the standpoint of university administrations, the possible disruptive effect of such gains had to be kept in check. This would eventually be accomplished by reconfiguring higher education in line with corporate models,[33] which had the dual effect of weakening faculty freedoms and narrowing (financially) the pool of prospective students. "Diversity" and "difference" would continue to be touted, but views challenging systemic assumptions would be increasingly marginalized.[34]

In terms of keeping a lid on discussions of class power, political constraints in academia would be reinforced by the intellectual predilections associated with postmodernism. An ideological climate purged of the idea of class-conflict—continuing and fulfilling, as Fredric Jameson puts it, "the old fifties 'end of ideology' episode"[35]— fed easily into postures emphasizing purely moral denunciations of injustice and inequity. Such postures could be accommodated

---

which government complicity was later established in court records (William F. Pepper, *An Act of State: The Execution of Martin Luther King* [London: Verso, 2003]). The threat posed by both these leaders (as well as by Malcolm X in his final year) lay precisely in their "intersectional" role—their overstepping the boundaries of a less subversive because purely race-relations-oriented set of demands.

33 See Lawrence C. Soley, *Leasing the Ivory Tower: The Corporate Takeover of Academia* (Boston: South End Press, 1995).

34 This process is perceptively described and analyzed in Walter Benn Michaels, *The Trouble with Diversity: How We Learned to Love Identity and Ignore Inequality* (New York: Henry Holt, 2006).

35 Fredric Jameson, *Postmodernism, or, The Cultural Logic of Late Capitalism* (Durham, NC: Duke University Press, 1991), 263.

within established institutions provided that they did not spill over into serious examination of the interests at stake—a line of inquiry which would of course lead back to systemic considerations. If those arguing against a systemic critique could not muster sufficient persuasive power from identity-based assertions (like the demographic determinism often put forward by NSM advocates[36]), then they could turn—in the language of postmodernism—toward discrediting, via "deconstruction," what they would tar as "grand narrative," which in practice signified any explanatory structure that sought a pattern behind immediate appearances.[37] The illusory impression of depth conveyed by verbal gymnastics became a fashionable way to evade the real depth required if one was to understand how what goes on in the realm of theory relates (or not) to struggles taking place in the larger society.

While philosophy and literary studies in the 1980s were heavily marked by that type of hip yet arcane discourse (later devastatingly satirized by Alan Sokal),[38] this same period of US history was one of intense conservative reaction at the level of state policy, expressed in the imposition of fiercely neoliberal measures—privatization and austerity—both at home and abroad. The '80s was also the takeoff decade for the "war on drugs" and mass incarceration. In the absence of class analysis, the link between neoliberalism and punitive "criminal justice" policies was not widely perceived. A class-based understanding could have recognized that set of policies (which mainly targeted poor people of color) as corollary to a draconian economic agenda. It was to advance this agenda that communities previously mobilized to resist oppression would be atomized by the drug

---

36 Demographic determinism = positing an invariable one-to-one link between identity traits and policy positions.

37 "Fragmentation, indeterminacy, and intense distrust of all universalizing or 'totalizing' discourses ... are the hallmark of postmodernist thought." David Harvey, *The Condition of Postmodernity* (Cambridge, MA: Blackwell, 1990), 9. See also chapter 7 ("The Postmodern Impasse") in Carl Boggs, *The End of Politics: Corporate Power and the Decline of the Public Sphere* (New York: Guilford Press, 2000).

38 Alan D. Sokal, "Transgressing the Boundaries: Towards a Transformative Hermeneutics of Quantum Gravity," *Social Text* #46/47 (Spring/Summer 1996), and "A Physicist Experiments with Cultural Studies," *Lingua Franca*, May/June 1996, www.physics.nyu.edu/faculty/sokal/lingua_franca_v4/lingua_franca_v4.html, and the ensuing reply by *Social Text* and rejoinder by Sokal at linguafranca.mirror.theinfo.org/9607/mst.html.

trade and subsequently stigmatized, isolated from potential allies, subjected to heavy police presence, disproportionately locked up, and—as if all this was not enough—enmeshed in various legislated or administrative techniques of disenfranchisement.[39]

The class/race dynamic of these developments shows that even if one's initial concern lies with a community that is identified by "race," one is forced to view class relations as the primary determinant in the lives of its members. First of all, it is class interests that dictate subjecting certain sectors of the working class to super-exploitation (from slave plantations to present-day sweatshops). This not only benefits the balance-sheets of particular enterprises; it also helps stabilize society to the advantage of capital by blocking working-class unity and fostering an aggressively hierarchical culture among sectors that have little in their favor except, supposedly, their European ancestry. Arrangements of this sort have been in effect from the beginnings of US history.[40] Second, although the criteria of racial identity are arbitrarily defined, individuals belonging to the subordinate "races" share the objective commonality of being disproportionately working-class. Third, the small minority of the racially oppressed populations that is *not* working-class (or that has disassociated itself from its class origins) plays a strategic role—whether in elective office, as cultural shills, or as enforcers (e.g. prison wardens)—in casting the dominant agenda as "colorblind" and thereby legitimizing it.[41] Thus, finally, there is no such thing as having a complete set of interests defined by one's "racial" designation. The core interests of individuals within any racially

---

39 See Loïc Wacquant, *Punishing the Poor: The Neoliberal Government and Social Insecurity* (Durham, N.C.: Duke University Press, 2009); Michelle Alexander, *The New Jim Crow: Mass Incarceration in the Age of Colorblindness* (New York: New Press, 2012); Greg Palast, *The Best Democracy Money Can Buy: A Tale of Billionaires and Ballot Bandits* (New York: Seven Stories Press, 2016); and Mumia Abu-Jamal and Johanna Fernández (eds), *The Roots of Mass Incarceration: Locking up Black Dissidents and Punishing the Poor*, special issue of *Socialism and Democracy* 28:3 (November 2014).

40 Fields, "Slavery, Race and Ideology" (n. 1); Theodore W. Allen, *The Invention of the White Race*, 2 vols., 2nd ed. (London: Verso, 2012).

41 See Mumia Abu-Jamal, "The Perils of Black Political Power," in *Writing on the Wall: Selected Prison Writings of Mumia Abu-Jamal*, ed. Johanna Fernández (San Francisco: City Lights Books, 2015), 237-238; Michaels, *The Trouble with Diversity*, 85-86.

or culturally defined collectivity will vary in accordance with their respective class positions or class loyalties.

Of all the non-class or cross-class identities, race is the one that comes closest to having actually been *created* in the service of class interests.[42] It is on the basis of class interest that certain populations have historically been assigned a status of collective subordination. The most common pretext for such subordination is physical traits (or the assumption that a person carries the genes for such traits), but particular national/cultural/linguistic attributes—varying by site of colonization or by immigration group and host country—may be put to use in the same way. With regard to intersectionality, while it may well be the case that subjugated populations initially view their collective interest in particularistic or national terms, the experience of seeing individuals from their community exercise official functions that were previously reserved to members of the conquering power, yet without producing any notable improvement in their own condition, eventually opens them to an awareness that class issues are the decisive ones.[43]

The remaining cross-class identities—involving gender, sexuality, age, ability, and culture (including religion)—all have an existence independent of class (as did at first the traits seized upon for purposes of "racial" assignation). But the fact that the identities have a non-class aspect does not mean that they have a political impact on a par with that of class in a society shaped by class division. What distinguishes class-difference from any type of non-class difference—including whatever differences could be taken as pretexts for colonial or "racial" subordination—is that *class-difference is inherently a matter of domination*. There is no ruling class without a subject class; the former either dominates the latter or else—as a class—goes out of existence. The category of race became partially conflated with that of class—and hence viewed as entailing a power-hierarchy—only because "race" was from the very beginning linked to claims of superiority (by Europeans over the indigenous peoples of the Americas and Africa, and later also Asia). But the

---

42 See, in addition to Fields and Allen, Aníbal Quijano, "Questioning 'Race'," trans. Victor Wallis, *Socialism and Democracy* 21:1 (March 2007), 45-54.

43 In the US, this perception is sharply expressed in the commentaries by Glen Ford, Bruce Dixon, and others, at blackagendareport.com/.

"superiority" was entirely a product of conquest. Despite the claims of racist pseudo-science, it had no biological basis. Class, on the other hand, is exclusively defined in terms of the exercise of power by one set of persons over others.

No dyad of biological or cultural traits entails, in itself, a relationship of domination. Every "natural" hierarchy is offset, at least over time, in the context of the community as whole. Infants and children are at one stage dependent; but at a later stage of life, their elders become dependent on *them*. Disability, like infancy, infirmity, and old age, entails particular kinds of dependence requiring social accommodation. But none of these attributes imply domination over their subjects. Where domination is imposed, notably in the construction of gender relations, it is not because of any inherent necessity; it is because of usurpation—typically, of historic proportions—backed by repressive practices which, in the absence of tectonic social change, will be re-imposed, through force of custom, on each new generation.[44]

In summary, class stands by itself as a relationship inherently grounded in domination. "Race" was globally absorbed into the agenda of class domination with the onset of European expansion.[45] It drew on biological or cultural traits whose "racial" aspect—i.e., whose signification of any basic difference between or among peoples—was arbitrarily constructed. In the context of our present discussion, the construction of gender differs from that of race in two main ways. On the one hand, its original grounding is in a biological (reproductive) polarity that exists throughout the animal world and which under certain conditions may dictate at least temporary—

---

44 Silvia Federici, *Caliban and the Witch* (Brooklyn, NY: Autonomedia, 2004), provides important documentation on both the greater relative power of peasant-women in late medieval Europe, and the extraordinary repressive measures (witch-hunts) that were applied to force them back into the subordinate status that would come to be regarded as "normal."

45 Quijano, "Questioning 'Race'." Assertions of the superiority of one's own people have of course been put forward since ancient times. What was new in the era of European expansion was on the one hand the scale of the subjugations (especially plantation slavery) and, on the other (beginning with the 1493 Papal Bull assigning the Western Hemisphere to Spain and Portugal), making the rankings of peoples a topic of church and state policy, and of philosophical discourse—the latter culminating in the pompous speculative anthropology of Hegel's *Philosophy of History*.

not necessarily hierarchical—divisions of labor. On the other hand, the social construction of gender, unlike that of race (and no doubt because it was linked to substantial rather than superficial biological differences), was already an aspect of all human communities long before the birth of capitalism. It is therefore in no sense peculiar to the capitalist epoch. Nonetheless, gender relations are deeply affected by capitalism, which routinely embraces and—under current conditions of war and mass displacement—even accentuates pre-existing patterns of domination.[46]

With gender no less than with race, therefore, capitalism is centrally implicated in the perpetuation of oppressive practices. And the capitalist class, whether directly or through state institutions, inserts itself into every social question—and every issue of policy—in a manner that is not conceivable for any merely demographic collectivity (such as "all men" or "all whites") that might be viewed as holding the upper hand in a dyadic relationship.

THE BASIS FOR UNITY

It might appear that in asserting the political centrality of class power—and its distinctively hierarchical essence—I am merely saying what everyone knows. Clearly, this is not the case. If it were, there would be a stronger basis than has yet developed in the US for uniting all oppressed constituencies around their common class interest. As it is, we must conclude that the fragmenting effect of the factors we have noted—from the repression of the post-World War II years to the largely separate paths taken by the NSMs, to the violent "neutralization" of incipient unifying forces, to the depoliticizing impact of postmodernist academic proclivities—has so far proved to be decisive.

Within the academy, the marginalization of Marxist analysis—with its central focus on class—has been crucial. Serious researchers have thus been able to accept, citing merely subjective

---

46 An ironic example of this is the impact that US intervention has had in Islamic countries, where, despite the US's supposedly more enlightened practices in gender relations, its presence and impact have arrested a process of secularization, leading to the imposition of more extreme forms of patriarchy.

impressions, the idea that socially constructed hierarchies of race and gender operate on the same level as class domination in setting the parameters of people's lives. In a typical formulation,

> Fundamentally, race, class, and gender are *intersecting* categories of experience that affect all aspects of human life; thus, they simultaneously structure the experiences of all people in this society. At any moment, race, class, or gender may feel more salient or meaningful in a given person's life, but they are overlapping or cumulative in their effects.[47]

The emphasis here on "simultaneity" obscures the historical process through which one mode of domination generates or conditions another (or others). The intersection of the modes of domination does not make them strategically equivalent. Although any one of them may be "felt" as primary, this does not establish its driving role in an objective sense. Racist structures, as we have seen, have evolved in conjunction with economic interests; Black Panther leader Fred Hampton put the point succinctly in a speech shortly before the FBI assassinated him in 1969: "Racism is an excuse used for capitalism."[48]

As we have also noted, the instrumentalization of gender in the service of class rule is more complex than that of "race," extending over a longer span of human history, with a trajectory predating the advent of capitalism. But the current interpenetration of gender oppression with class domination is similar to what occurred with racial oppression. In the end, male supremacy as well as white supremacy is kept alive by the ruling class—tolerated if not fostered—because it is integral to the culture that upholds capital and empire. This culture is one of domination; it imposes relationships that rule out mutual respect. A political regime that condemns vast numbers of people to poverty and/or bombardment and/or military occupation requires an institutional and cultural support-struc-

---

47 Margaret L. Andersen and Patricia Hill Collins, "Why Race, Class, and Gender Matter," reprinted from the 7th edition (2010) of their *Race, Class, and Gender* anthology, in David B. Grusky (ed.), *Social Stratification: Class, Race, and Gender in Sociological Perspective*, 4th ed. (Boulder, CO: Westview Press, 2014), 942. Emphasis in the original.

48 He can be viewed making this statement in Lee Lew-Lee's documentary film, *All Power to the People: The Black Panther Party and Beyond* (1999).

ture—epitomized in military training, in right-wing bombast, and in persistent vigilantism—that perfectly matches the sense of aggressive entitlement that has always been integral to male supremacy.[49] A full-fledged assault on male supremacy would be out of the question for a political order with such priorities.

Correspondingly, resistance to both male and white supremacy is integral to developing a culture of liberation. The arena within which such a revolutionary culture can unfold, however, must be one that does not exclude those who are misleadingly assumed to benefit from the associated hierarchies: in the one case, men; in the other: whites. Again, this proposition should be self-evident. But, if the arena in question is to have this character (of being open, in particular, to everyone who is not wedded to the capitalist agenda), it must be broader than either the gender dyad or the "race" dyad, since each of these, by itself, posits a socially assigned dominant role for one of its two poles (whites over "others"; heterosexual males over "others").

Here we must once again address the way in which class hierarchy differs from the hierarchies arising within any of the various identities. In dyads other than that of class, it makes sense to seek reconciliation, because there is nothing in the original nature of one or the other party that makes it inherently dominant or subordinate. One can retain one's biological or inherited cultural attributes while shedding the status of power or powerlessness that has been attached to them. The non-class identity-traits are thus free of inherent power-implications.[50] But this is not the case with attributes of class. Even a "middle" class exists as such only with reference to the simultaneous existence of a ruling class and a subject

---

49 See Helen Caldicott, *Missile Envy: The Arms Race and Nuclear War*, rev. ed. (New York: Bantam Books, 1986); Carl Boggs and Tom Pollard, *The Hollywood War Machine: U.S. Militarism and Popular Culture* (Boulder, CO: Paradigm, 2007). The convergence of predatory practices has reached a peak under the Trump presidency.

50 The contrary position rests on the essentialist assumption that one's behavior is rigidly determined by one's biological endowments. Biology in such matters, however, is no more than "a set of potentialities." Jeffrey Weeks "The Social Construction of Sexuality," in Kathy Peiss (ed.), *Major Problems in the History of American Sexuality* (Boston: Houghton Mifflin, 2002), 3.

class.[51] The latter polarity is what determines the very existence of the category of class.

The only way to end class domination is to dissolve the class that dominates. There is no evidence that this class will dissolve itself. Individual members may repudiate their affiliation with the class, but for the class as a whole to be dissolved, its most intransigent members must be stripped of their power. This is what the eclectic notion of multiple co-equal lines of oppression fails to recognize. A book-chapter on transgender issues expresses that perspective neatly in its conclusion, where the author tells oppressed populations,

> We must move beyond the separatist mindsets that have contributed to our marginalization, and we must wholeheartedly forgive and find compassion for our oppressors, so that our efforts are not coming from a place of pain, but of healing and restoration.... Now is the time for us to come together in a united voice, as one people calling for injustice to be eradicated from our nation today, now, and forever.[52]

The immediate problem here is that the author fails to distinguish between, on the one hand, polarities that can be resolved by removing a set of artificial overlays superimposed on natural differences—as when differences of complexion lose their supposed hierarchical ranking—and, on the other, a polarity based exclusively on an enormous concentration of power exercised over the vast majority of the human species.

White supremacy can be ended, but there will still be genetic differences in physical features, including skin color. Male supremacy can be ended, but there will still be biologically grounded male and female traits, in whatever combinations. If class domination is to end, on the other hand, the class of large-property owners will have to vanish. The owners will be separated from their capital and will live like other human beings. Reconciliation can take place

---

51 "Middle class" here refers not to the mythical norm that US politicians love, but to real intermediate strata comprising no more than about thirty-five percent of the total population. Zweig, *The Working Class Majority*, 18-29.

52 Robert Hess III, "Coalition Building with Intersectional Identities," in Nagoshi *et al.* (eds), *Gender and Sexual Identity*, 160.

between individuals but not between antagonistic classes. Unity is conceivable only when the dominant pole has been removed from the class dyad, and the dyad itself disappears.

To affirm the centrality of class is in no way to diminish the importance of all the particular lines of oppression. Nor is it to suggest that the attention historically given to those lines of oppression by left-wing parties has been sufficient. The demands made by the new social movements were amply justified. Moreover, particular groups were able to organize around those demands more effectively than the Left had done, often duly incorporating (as did the Black Panthers) a radical understanding of class power. What failed to develop, however, was a comprehensive movement bringing together all the oppressed constituencies. It is at this level that NSM discourse fell short. Intersectionality theory has sought to go beyond NSM theory by expressly focusing on the links among the various oppressions. But the influence of the NSM outlook has persisted, in the failure of intersectionality theorists to see the class-configuration of power as playing a distinctive role, operating in a dimension of its own, and affecting with its sweeping capabilities the overwhelming majority of the population—in contrast to the various more specific lines of oppression, each with its own primary constituency and without the policymaking attributes (corporate or governmental) of the dominant class.

The working class is a majority not only within the total population, but also within the populations of the various "non-class" categories. Class difference thus permeates the various identities and shapes the way individuals experience them.[53] In each case, the circumstance of being working-class adds to whatever disadvantage has otherwise been inflicted on people of that identity. At the same time, a substantial majority of the working class as a whole belongs to one or other of the oppressed groupings. And the working class as a whole, including the minority within it that is *not* subject to intersecting oppressions (i.e., white heterosexual male workers), is weakened by the disunity that those oppressions generate. As for the middle class, its economically insecure strata are increasingly subject to downward pressures (e.g., in the US, the burden of student

53 Victor Wallis, "Socialism under Siege," *Monthly Review*, 47:8 (January 1996), 39.

loans), and have less and less reason all the time for viewing their own interests as being different from those of the working class.

None of these structural factors appear to be on the radar of intersectionality theory. Instead, an individual's social class is treated essentially as a personal cultural trait, in the manner of an identity-affiliation. Belonging to the capitalist class, however, means more than just possessing a certain cultural trait; it means being implicated—whether actively or not—in the exercise of power over the rest of society.[54]

Meanwhile, the convergence of popular interests is accelerated by the environmental crisis. The assault of capital on the ecosphere feeds on the same culture of domination that drives the multiple oppressions we have discussed. Looming ecological collapse underlines the urgency of uniting the overwhelming majority of people to reshape their interactions both among themselves and with the natural world. But this cannot be done without, in the process, addressing the formidable obstacle to such steps posed by the power of capital.

---

54 Ange-Marie Hancock, in her flagship book for the "Politics of Intersectionality" series that she edits (*Solidarity Politics for Millennials: A Guide to Ending the Oppression Olympics*, New York: Palgrave Macmillan, 2011), never mentions the capitalist class, thereby disregarding the agency exercised by capital (not exclusively through white males) over society as a whole. Although she calls for "wide-scale social change in the direction of social justice" (183), her book does not explore the structural barriers to that goal.

9

ECONOMIC / ENVIRONMENTAL CRISIS AND CONVERSION

I recall that in the first classroom lecture I gave, in September 1968, I referred to capitalism as being in crisis. I have never stopped saying this, year after year. But doesn't such repetition vitiate the meaning of "crisis"? How can a crisis be more than a transitory episode? If the condition is chronic, are we not then speaking an enduring structure, rather than a historically specific moment?

My answer is that there is no incompatibility between these two assertions. The crisis is indeed historically specific, but it is also enduring. The routine short-term crises of capitalism have a cumulative impact, arising from the various steps that are taken—via private transactions (corporate mergers etc.) or via legislation or administrative decree—to restore capitalism's "natural" expansive thrust. The most notable outcome of such steps, in their totality, is a steady increase in the concentration of wealth, both nationally and globally.[1] Related measures include government stabilization policies and the search for new and more favorable terms of business in other countries. Given the limits to markets and resources, however, expansionist agendas run into opposition both from rival imperial powers and from anti-colonial resistance movements, creating a scenario of permanent war. With the consequent bolstering of military establishments (and the instilling of fear in the general population), capital tends to shed its earlier flexibility, becoming

---

1   This dynamic is memorably described in Section I of the *Communist Manifesto*. On current levels of concentration, see Institute for Policy Studies, *Billionaire Bonanza 2017*, summarized at www.commondreams.org/news/2017/11/08/ three-richest-americans-now-own-more-wealth-bottom-half-us-combined-report

more overtly hostile to progressive forces and adopting a more intransigent stance against any challenge to its power.[2]

The environmental crisis is even more obviously chronic than the capitalist crisis, given the cumulative effects of successive collapses such as the sudden release of previously sequestered methane, the melting of the polar icecap, the spread of deserts, and extinctions of species. Each of these turning points signals a speed-up in the larger dynamic of devastation. Both the release of methane and the disappearance of the heat-reflecting icecap serve to accelerate the process of global warming that had already been launched by the ubiquitous burning of fossil fuels. Desertification destroys vegetation that would otherwise restore carbon to the soil, while drought-conditions combine with fierce winds to stoke forest fires on a scale unprecedented in human history.[3]

The environmental crisis and the capitalist crisis are not only structurally comparable (with discrete events along each dimension combining to produce a cumulative acceleration effect), they are also intertwined. Capitalism reaches its most extreme embodiment—in the form of a rapacious global empire governed directly by the super-rich, and with military outposts on every continent[4]—in a process that both propels and is propelled by the sudden escalation of environmental dangers, of tipping points, and of local or regional catastrophes. Significantly, the arc of US military interventions from northern Nigeria to Afghanistan—a vast region whose peoples happen to be mostly Muslim—is also an arc not only of petroleum deposits, but also of drought, desertification, food shortages, civil strife, and massive emigration.[5]

---

2   On the US case, see Jane Mayer, *Dark Money: The Hidden History of the Billionaires Behind the Rise of the Radical Right* (New York: Penguin Random House, 2017).

3   The fires were those of December 2017 in California. On the general acceleration of ecological tipping points, see Ian Angus, *Facing the Anthropocene: Fossil Capitalism and the Crisis of the Earth System* (New York: Monthly Review Press, 2016), esp. Ch. 4; for an overview of the "planetary emergency," Fred Magdoff and Chris Williams, *Creating an Ecological Society: Toward a Revolutionary Transformation* (New York: Monthly Review Press, 2017), Ch. 1.

4   See David Vine, *Base Nation: How U.S. Bases Abroad Harm America and the World* (New York: Henry Holt, 2015.

5   A study published by the US National Academy of Sciences (www.pnas.org/content/112/11/3241) found a direct link between an extreme drought in Syria

The immediate response of capital to the environmental emergency proceeds along two complementary paths. On the one hand, reacting to looming shortages of cropland, fresh water, and energy resources, capitalist forces intensify their expansionist and militarist thrust in a desperate scramble to concentrate in their own hands—by privatization and/or by regime-change—control over as much as possible of the earth's riches.[6] On the other hand, so far as the "home" population is concerned, capital increasingly resorts to the most aggressive, retrograde, racist, and misogynistic ideologies, securing for itself a perverse base of popular support[7] while continuing its habitual pursuit of unrestrained economic growth and perpetual technological innovation, and treating environmental impact as a secondary concern or—with Trump and his team—as a nuisance to be systematically trampled on.

Like the crises of capital and of the environment, the progression of capitalist technological upheaval is at once historical and structural. It takes shape as an uninterrupted succession of inventions and "upgrades," but is also marked, in the course of this relentless advance, by specific new phases, reflecting multi-dimensional qualitative leaps that are manifested both in production relations and in social, political, and cultural developments. One such phase was marked by the introduction of the automobile. On the production side, this brought with it the deafening discipline of the assembly line; on the consumption side, it brought a drastic reconfiguration of social space and the whole way of life associated with suburbanization.[8] Another key moment was the rise, after 1945, of the petrochemical industry. Production zones became carcinogenic wastelands, while the output of plastics led to the industry-imposed fad of disposability, whose emblematic outcome is huge floating

---

(2007-2010) and the outbreak of that country's civil war (report in *New York Times*, March 2, 2015).

6   Michael T. Klare, *The Race for What's Left: The Global Scramble for the World's Last Resources* (New York: Henry Holt & Co., 2012).

7   Such trends are evident throughout the advanced capitalist world, but appear with particular force in the US. See John Bellamy Foster, *Trump in the White House: Tragedy and Farce* (New York: Monthly Review Press, 2017).

8   Paul A. Baran and Paul M. Sweezy, *Monopoly Capital: An Essay on the American Economic and Social Order* (New York: Monthly Review Press, 1966), 219f, 302ff.

islands of plastic bags polluting the world's oceans.[9] Cutting across all these specific impacts, of course, was the epochal surge in the burning of fossil fuels and emission of greenhouse gases.

The new technological phase that frames the current crisis (the one set in motion by the 2008 financial meltdown) is characterized most generally by pervasive computerization.[10] The associated innovations aggravate and amplify the overall crisis, in that they make it easier for the capitalist class to continue, with minimal opposition, the pursuit of its expansionist and ecologically devastating agenda:

• They replace human labor-power in many occupations (skilled as well as unskilled), thereby exacerbating unemployment and creating downward pressure on wages.

• They facilitate the coordination of work at widely dispersed sites around the globe, thus making enterprises less dependent on the domestic labor-force of any given country while weakening the labor movement everywhere.

• They displace routine tasks onto uncompensated users or consumers, who must then invest individually in the necessary instruments (expensive items like computers, smart-phones, etc.) and acquire the skills to use them.[11]

• They make possible a new form of military aggression, epitomized by drone warfare, in which targets are attacked from great distances with no risk of casualties to the aggressor (whose leaders subsequently respond with hypocritical denunciation when its own citizens are subjected to terrorist attacks).

• They introduce a new source of untraceable corruption into the electoral process, as electronic voting machines are subject to surreptitious programming by their corporate owners.[12]

---

9   Barry Commoner, *Making Peace with the Planet* (New York: Pantheon Books, 1990), 53f.

10   For general discussion, see Christian Fuchs, *Internet and Society: Social theory in the Information Age* (New York: Routledge, 2008), Eran Fisher, *Media and New Capitalism in the Digital Age* (New York: Palgrave Macmillan, 2010), and Wolfgang Fritz Haug, *Hightech Kapitalismus in der grossen Krise* (Hamburg: Argument Verlag, 2012).

11   To the extent that such skills are now acquired at a very early age, other problems arise. On adverse health effects, see Chapter 4, note 29; on other issues, see the sources cited below, note 15.

12   See Mark Crispin Miller's study of the 2004 US presidential election, *Fooled Again: The Real Case for Electoral Reform* (New York: Basic Books, 2007).

- They provide a new medium for a constant flow of instantaneous one-way messaging from those in power to the general population (e.g. Trump's tweets).
- The imbalance between a steady barrage of messages from a centralized source and the disparate responses from diverse oppositional sources reinforces the power of the state to shape public opinion.
- The same dynamic obstructs any attempts to refute deliberate misinformation. Thus, in the last months of the 2016 US election campaign, Facebook carried a higher number of invented stories (e.g., one which asserted that the Pope had endorsed Trump) than it did of reports of actual events.[13]
- Search engines such as Google divert research away from dissident sources of news and analysis; Facebook, Google, and Twitter, all of which operate globally, collaborate directly with the US government to impose wide-ranging political censorship (on the pretext of combating terrorism).[14]
- The shift of all transactions to digitized formatting—whether we're speaking of credit-card purchases, internet-searches, social networking, or interactions with police or other authorities—facilitates total surveillance.
- The mass addiction to social networking and to the use of hand-held electronic devices that are always within immediate reach has effects which, although not yet fully understood, are surely conditioned by profit-calculations on the part of their designers, and have tended to reinforce pre-existing proclivities—some of them dangerous—among their users.[15]

The most advanced technology, typified by such developments, does not necessarily indicate the greatest efficiency. In fact, the opposite is more commonly the case, as one sees that what spurs

---

13 www.buzzfeed.com/craigsilverman/viral-fake-election-news-outperformed-real-news-on-facebook?utm_term=.tcaBrl32l#.yw5EGBKJB

14 theintercept.com/2017/12/30/facebook-says-it-is-deleting-accounts-at-the-direction-of-the-u-s-and-israeli-governments/;   www.wsws.org/en/articles/2018/01/18/cens-j18.html

15 Adam Greenfield, *Radical Technologies: The Design of Everyday Life* (London: Verso, 2017), 24. See also John Lanchester, "You Are the Product," *London Review of Books*, 39:16 (August 17, 2017), and Henry A. Giroux, *America's Addiction to Terrorism* (New York: Monthly Review Press, 2016), Ch. 2.

the incessant pursuit of the underlying "breakthroughs," apart from the perpetual drive to create new things to sell, is precisely the institutional irrationalities—ranging from traffic-congestion to war, to massive population movements, to speculative financial transactions, to stratagems for criminal activity, to the unanticipated ill effects of previous breakthroughs—that the apparatus as a whole is expected to address.

All these phenomena put an unnecessary and avoidable strain on the Earth's resource-base. Their chaotic interplay, on top of the already galloping deterioration of the natural environment, is a source of constant danger to communities and individuals—in rough proportion to the precariousness of their physical or social existence—but is at the same time, by contrast, a source of reinforcement to the power of capital. In effect, the very disorganization of the social whole serves to keep people from recognizing any intentionality in the structures of domination, as the locus of power is obscured by the surface appearance of a seemingly random set of barriers to any effective popular challenge.

WHAT KIND OF RESPONSE?

The obstacles to a popular counter-thrust only magnify its urgency. Because of the complexity of the power arrangements—and of all the social factors that reinforce them—we should not expect a coherent challenge to them to emerge all at once. The evolution of any such challenge will reflect the particular conditions of each region or country in which it is undertaken.

Looking at the US case, which, with the know-nothing arrogance of its ruling class,[16] is surely the most recalcitrant of all, we can nonetheless see a number of encouraging signs. These include: 1) numerous surveys since 2012 showing an openness to socialism (without precedent since the 1930s), especially among young people and among African Americans; 2) the unexpected resonance of

---

16 "Know-nothing" refers emblematically to the denial of scientific findings on climate change, but is expressed more generally in refusing to recognize the illegality of such things as (1) civilian settlements sponsored by a military occupying power, (2) imposing "regime-change" on other countries, and (3) issuing military threats and ultimatums (as in Trump's UN speech on North Korea).

a political campaign—that of Bernie Sanders in 2016—that located the blame for people's hardships squarely in the extreme concentration of wealth;[17] 3) the successes of Socialist or independent Left municipal councilors in Seattle and in Richmond, California;[18] 4) the sudden growth in membership of socialist organizations following Trump's 2016 victory; 5) the proliferation of radical sources of information and analysis on current affairs, thanks partly to new dimensions of "citizen journalism" made possible by social media (e.g., documenting killings by police); and 6) the massive popular mobilizations that have arisen in response to those killings and to Trump's investiture, his Muslim travel-ban, and the August 2017 explosion of white-supremacist violence in Charlottesville, Virginia.

What is lacking, of course, is the revolutionary political force that can build on these developments and carry them to the next level. The term revolution has itself been abused in the rush by politicians of every stripe to tap the depths of mass anger.[19] The question is how to channel this anger into an informed and sweeping response—the authentic revolution that, as Marx put it, will become possible when theory grips the masses. The relevant theory will have to speak at once to people's immediate concerns and to their long-range hopes. Ecosocialist theory does this, in ways we have explored but have yet to be widely implemented. We have seen that there are organic links between an ecological agenda and a working-class agenda; these links need to be highlighted at every opportunity. This can be done partly through the production of quality educational materials, but it also requires organizational outreach—in the spirit of intersectionality—across lines of "specialization."

Environmental disasters amplify the impact of already existing oppressive structures. A dramatic example was the impact of Hurri-

---

17   See Jan Rehmann, "Bernie Sanders and the Hegemonic Crisis of Neoliberal Capitalism," *Socialism and Democracy*, 30:3 (November 2016).

18   On the Richmond case, see Steve Early, *Refinery Town: Big Oil, Big Money, and the Remaking of an American City* (Boston: Beacon Press, 2017).

19   Examples: the right-wing "Reagan revolution" of the 1980s; the "Our Revolution" project initiated by Bernie Sanders in 2016 to elect progressive Democrats; use of *Révolution* as the title for Emmanuel Macron's neoliberal credo in his 2016 campaign for the French presidency.

cane Katrina's flooding of New Orleans in 2005.[20] Not only did the waters themselves obliterate a whole low-income African American district, but the authorities failed to evacuate the victims, in some cases even blocking their escape-attempts with deadly force. Especially revealing is the authorities' subsequent use of the disaster to push through an agenda of privatization and gentrification which made it impossible for some 200,000 evacuees to return to their hometown. A similar example was Hurricane Sandy's flooding of shoreline communities in New York City in 2012. Again, the authorities failed to provide adequate assistance to those rendered homeless. Significantly, the most effective help was given by radical activists from the Occupy Wall Street movement, mobilized for the purpose as "Occupy Sandy."[21]

On a global scale, the pattern is that the most severely affected zones are the ones that have done least to bring about the environmental crisis. Their inhabitants are then displaced either internally or internationally. War and environmental disaster, often in combination, drive swelling numbers of would-be migrants toward more prosperous regions, where their presence—actual or prospective— is then targeted to political advantage by the very forces whose economic policies aggravate even further the dangers that prompted them to flee in the first place.

How can recognition of this whole dynamic become a part of mass awareness? The initial step is most likely to be negative: a visceral rejection of the established order. At present in the US, the grounds for such rejection are felt—albeit to varying degrees and often incoherently—in multiple constituencies. At a mass level, the sentiment is perhaps strongest and most sharply focused among prisoners, both because of the treatment to which they are routinely subjected[22] and because of the opportunities they have for collective reinforcement of their perceptions. While each constituency

---

20 See Naomi Klein, *The Shock Doctrine: The Rise of Disaster Capitalism* (New York: Henry Holt, 2007), 406-421; Eric Mann, *Katrina's Legacy* (Los Angeles: Frontlines Press, 2015), 132-150.

21 Benjamin Shepard, "From Flooded Neighborhoods to Sustainable Urbanism: A New York Diary," *Socialism and Democracy*, 27:2 (July 2013).

22 See Victor Wallis, "*13th* and the Culture of Surplus Punishment," *San Francisco Bay View*, August 2017, reprinted in Victor Wallis, *Socialist Practice: Histories and Theories* (London: Palgrave Macmillan, 2020), 177-83.

must come to consciousness on its own terms, all must be ready to see how their own struggles are bound up with those of other oppressed groups—and with the wider struggle for human survival in face of the devastating continuation of capitalist plunder.[23]

Ecological struggles, as we have seen, are vital not only for the sake of our collective long-term survival but also, more immediately, as offering a unifying theme around which movements representing various specific oppressed constituencies can come together. We have explored this scenario from the standpoint of some of these groups, noting especially their common interest in resisting capital's perpetual drive toward domination and expansion. We have seen that in order to build an alternative framework, we must above all replace market and profit-driven decisions with decisions grounded in basic human needs and valorizing the interactions of water, air, and living organisms on which we all depend.

This principle has many interrelated practical implications. In order for a needs-based economy to emerge, everyone must participate in the formulation of specific goals and methods. This is not a matter of external compulsion. Rather, it's the only possible approach for assuring that everyone's needs are taken into account. For people to see this link between process and outcome, they must be persuaded that their voices can be heard. This means that there can be no great social cleavages, and that everyone is equipped with at least a minimum level of competence in handling the concepts and technologies pertinent to running a community and to deliberating on wider issues.

Linked to this is the need for a culture of cooperation. No matter how competent one is, one must also be guided by the perception that one cannot advance one's own interest at the expense of others. Again, this is not an imposed requirement; it is a simple recognition of the reality that trying to outdo or outbid others leads to outcomes in which everyone loses. The "winners" lose in the sense that they destroy the feelings of trust and comradeship which, beyond their intrinsic value, are essential to success in the common undertaking.

---

23 The ongoing plunder was most recently embodied, in the US, in the opening of public lands in Alaska and Utah to extractive operations, as well as in the continuation of fracking at multiple sites.

Apart from these principles guiding human interaction, there are certain insights that we can recognize as having emerged from the achievements and the shortfalls of environmental policy up to now. While the costs and dangers of fossil fuels are widely acknowledged, as are those of nuclear power (at least among most environmentalists), there are other equally important insights—touched on to varying degrees throughout this book—that are less often noted. We need to keep them in mind:

1. The single most calamitous human impact on the environment is modern warfare—characterized not only by its heavy weaponry and frightful human casualties, but also by extravagant fuel consumption, emission of toxins (intended as well as well as unintended), deliberate interference with weather patterns, collateral damage to marine life, and a stupendous diversion of time, resources, and ingenuity away from possible constructive measures that could address the hardships and systemic breakdowns bequeathed by capitalist development.[24] Militarism, expansionism, and environmental plunder are all of a piece, and find their fullest expression in US policies. An essential task both for environmentalists and for peace activists is to join forces, as the demands of each group reinforce those of the other.

2. The human environmental footprint consists of far more than just greenhouse gases from fuel-burning. The question of whether non-toxic, non-polluting, and non-carbon-emitting energy sources can be tapped, transmitted, and stored on a sufficient scale to satisfy current or increased levels of utilization is not settled among ecosocialists. There are varying levels of confidence in the future potential of solar, wind, and other alternative technologies.[25] What is certain, however, is that there are *limits to available raw materials* for high-tech products;[26] that all these products, with each advance

---

24 Gar Smith has gathered documents of destruction on many fronts in his edited collection, *The War and Environment Reader* (Charlottesville, VA: Just World Books, 2017).

25 For an optimistic view, see David Schwartzman, "How Much and What Kind of Energy Does Humanity Need?" *Socialism and Democracy*, 30:2 (July 2016).

26 Klare, *The Race for What's Left*, Ch. 6.

in their capabilities, compound the levels of energy-consumption; and that there are also *space-limitations* in terms of how much land can be removed from its life-sustaining functions for the sake of accommodating expansion of the built environment. No matter how abundant the supply of clean energy might be, therefore, it will be necessary to reconsider and redefine what has to be produced and in what quantities, and how the built environment is to be configured. In the interim, however, solar and wind technology are rapidly becoming economically competitive with the technology of fossil fuels, while on the other hand, the big energy corporations use their political muscle to obstruct any conversion process, so that they can continue reaping profit from their existing investments.[27]

3. International attention, if not action, has been focused primarily on global warming, with its direct consequences in the form of sea-level rise and catastrophic climate events. But all these effects intersect with other destructive trends such as the more general loss of habitat as well as direct human "harvesting" of many species, particularly in the oceans. Imbalances are created that have unintended consequences. For example, the disappearance of sea turtles leads to a proliferation of jellyfish, which feed on fish eggs, depleting fish populations.[28] Meanwhile, the shrinkage of forest areas has well known effects not only on the supply of oxygen but also on the water cycle, which in turn relates to the vitality and quality of the soil. Remedying such effects requires, at a minimum, developing policies that are grounded in a holistic view of the environment rather than in the market for agribusiness-related supplies and products. This calls into question the concentration of land ownership and the whole private/corporate framework within which decisions affecting soil-health and natural cycles are made.

4. Mostly at the margins of mainstream environmentalism, a lot of on-the-ground work has been done toward reversing the pro-

---

27 According to the World Economic Forum, "the cost of solar energy generation in 2015 has decreased to as low as one sixth the cost in 2005" (www.weforum.org/agenda/2017/09/next-energy-revolution-already-here/). This does not stop the expansion of drilling and fracking operations.

28 Magdoff and Williams, *Creating an Ecological Society*, 31f.

cess whereby carbon is steadily emitted into the atmosphere. This project, known as *regenerative agriculture*,[29] is especially valuable as an alternative to the various science-fiction-type schemes that corporate researchers and military planners have dreamed up, such as shooting reflective devices or other foreign substances into the upper atmosphere, with the inevitable unintended consequences.[30] Unlike such high-tech approaches, regenerative agriculture is based on taking into account all the conditions that affect the life and health of the soil. It is the direct opposite of the manipulative and toxic approach taken by the agro-chemical complex, whose flagship corporation Monsanto cornered the market for its herbicide by genetically engineering cash-crop seeds that would be resistant to it.[31] Regenerative agriculture is based on practices that include mixing crops, shifting areas of grazing, and in general taking steps to keep the soil covered with carbon-absorbing vegetation, which would at the same time maximize its water retention. Such measures have the combined effect of counteracting climate extremes, stabilizing agricultural production, and, by preserving the soil's minerals, improving the nutritional value of the foods that grow in it.[32]

5. Despite the damage and extinctions that have already occurred, we should keep in mind that an ecologically sound agenda is not just a defensive reaction against threats to survival; it is also a proactive plan for recovery and restoration—of humanity as well as nature. To the extent that it can repair the destruction wrought by capital, it will open the possibility of a good life for everyone—a

---

29 See Paul Hawken's voluminous compendium, *Drawdown: The Most Comprehensive Plan Ever Proposed to Reverse Global Warming* (New York: Penguin, 2017), esp. the section on "Regenerative Agriculture," 54f. See also the project "Biodiversity for a Livable Climate," bio4climate.org/

30 The range of consequences is discussed in a 2014 report by Nicola Jones at e360. yale.edu/features/solar_geoengineering_weighing_costs_of_blocking_the_suns_rays For a comprehensive critique of the geo-engineering approach, see John Bellamy Foster, "The Long Ecological Revolution," *Monthly Review*, 69:6 (November 2017), 5-11.

31 Wenonah Hauter, *Foodopoly: The Battle Over the Future of Food and Farming in America* (New York: New Press, 2012), Ch. 12.

32 Magdoff and Williams, *Creating an Ecological Society*, 213-258; Judith D. Schwartz, *Cows Save the Planet, and other improbable ways of restoring soil to heal the Earth* (White River Junction, VT: Chelsea Green Publishing, 2013), Chs. 4, 6.

modest yet revolutionary improvement over the current condition and prospects faced by a majority of the world's people.

CONVERSION

The question of how we get from here to there has been the framing question of all serious revolutionary thought for the last two centuries. It certainly permeates the various chapters of this book. Clearly, there are many dimensions to the process. We need to keep in mind the interdependence between the different levels at which the necessary steps must be taken. Polemics between local and global orientations, between those who favor directly establishing ecological communities and those who advocate building political movements to challenge ruling-class power, are pointless and counterproductive. Both types of activity will continue to be indispensable; each will moreover strengthen the other. Local alternative communities will provide necessary models, not only of economic and agricultural practices, but also of cooperative human relations. In so doing, they will provide valuable support for struggles that are fought on the wider stage. From the opposite direction, gains made on the wider stage—initially, curbing the extraction of fossil fuels and protecting freedom of communication; eventually, contesting for state power—will always be integral to universalizing ecologically sound structures and practices.

Insofar as this whole process involves steps to be taken at the national level, it is useful to draw upon the tradition of thinking in terms of economic conversion.[33] This notion has typically arisen in reference to situations requiring emergency planning—notably in a context of war—and has not necessarily been linked to the reconfiguration of power relations. It has the twin advantages, though, from our present standpoint, of being practical-minded and of being comprehensive, entailing responsibilities—e.g., for an ethic of service and for the avoidance of waste—that extend from the

---

33 Cf. Victor Wallis, "Socialism, Ecology, and Democracy: Toward a Strategy of Conversion," *Monthly Review*, 44:2 (June 1992).

national down to the household level.[34] It certainly implies a scenario in which the crisis itself stands at the forefront of everyone's daily preoccupations.

Ecological conversion challenges the entire agenda of capitalist rule. It therefore cannot expect to command universal support. But it can nonetheless be put forward with the universalistic framing that is customary for scientific exposition. It clearly situates those who advocate "business as usual" in a besieged position. But this is where they belong, as the weight of scientific opinion is against them. We, on the other hand, can be confident that the call to end capitalist rule is the implicit cry of the vast majority, whose demand is that they/we be able to continue to live.

---

34 For a sketch of corresponding priorities for US federal executive departments, see Victor Wallis, "Economic/Ecological Crisis and Conversion," *Socialism and Democracy*, 23:2 (July 2009), 98ff. A current example of comprehensive emergency planning is Cuba's response to rising sea levels: www.sciencemag.org/news/2018/01/cuba-embarks-100-year-plan-protect-itself-climate-change

EPILOGUE

Although only four years have elapsed since the original publication of this book, it seems that we have already crossed certain thresholds that define a new historical moment.

The awareness of planetary emergency is not new; that has been present at least since 1988/89 (the years of James Hansen's NASA climate report and Bill McKibben's bestselling *The End of Nature*), if not since the first Earth Day (1970) or even earlier. By 2018, it was impossible, except for those with political blinders, not to be alarmed by the accumulating environmental disasters – and the associated scourges of military conflict, widespread misery, and displacement of peoples.

But consider what has happened between early 2018 and the onset of 2022. In relation to the themes of this book, four dramatic new developments, partly interrelated, come to mind: (1) the COVID-19 pandemic; (2) the most severe economic downturn since the 1930s; (3) acute polarization in US society, with massive protests against racism confronting a burgeoning fascist movement, and with a revival of militant labor struggles; and (4) a further giant step from direct to virtual modes of interaction, with hardly any physical space (including the deep oceans) now left untouched by cyber-technology.

All this has occurred *within* the framework of ecological collapse – a scenario of impending doom whose scope already far outstrips even the most pessimistic projections that focus purely on the ravages of a particular pandemic.[1] The dangers of this moment are

---

1   Andreas Malm, *Corona, Climate, Chronic Emergency: War Communism in the Twenty-First Century* (London: Verso, 2020), 14ff.

meanwhile amplified in the United States by its aggressively capitalist governance, which, in stifling a popular economic program, only strengthens the fascist response. The ensuing conflicts – along with the usual distractions perpetrated by corporate media – have regrettably drawn attention *away from* the underlying framework of environmental breakdown.

As a result, at the very moment when the ecological danger has reached a level of unimaginable urgency,[2] it remains at the margins of US public debate. This was already the case before the Russian invasion of Ukraine, and has become even more so since. Politicians and media neglect to give environmental issues the attention they cry out for, limiting themselves at best to talking about reform-proposals such as the Green New Deal which fail to question capital's underlying expansionist drive or its preference for high-tech approaches over respect for natural processes. Meanwhile, the profit-driven political elite has seized the occasion to undo whatever limited safeguards it had previously accepted against the invasive practices of, especially, the fossil-fuel industry (oil drilling, fracking, pipeline construction, private takeover of public lands, etc.), and is instead pushing forward with projects that include saturating the oceans with sonar devices – including underwater drones – that wreak havoc on marine life.[3]

The sidelining of the environmental emergency is not merely regrettable; it also reflects blindness to biological reality, inasmuch as the new trends in question, far from being unrelated to ecological breakdown, are all conditioned by it and/or have implications for addressing it. The post-2018 developments reflect a broader evolution that already precluded any return to some previous state

---

2   The 12-year time-span for decisive action proclaimed in 2018 by the UN's Intergovernmental Panel on Climate Change is felt with particular force among the youngest; see Greta Thunberg & family, *Our House Is on Fire: Scenes of a Family and a Planet in Crisis* (New York: Penguin Books, 2020). For continuing coverage of the breakdown, see Ian Angus et al. at climateandcapitalism.com

3   Arthur Firstenberg, "Cell Towers on the Ocean Floor," https://www.cellphonetaskforce.org/wp-content/uploads/2022/01/Cell-towers-on-the-ocean-floor.pdf; Lindy Weilgart, *The Impact of Ocean Noise Pollution on Fish and Invertebrates*, https://www.oceancare.org/wp-content/uploads/2017/10/OceanNoise_FishInvertebrates_May2018.pdf

of normality. The "normal" routines of capitalism – the constant striving for expansion and domination; the draconian wage-regime; indifference to environmental "externalities"; scorn for the public sector – are what generated the current turmoil. War only further exacerbates it. The resulting crisis has alerted more and more people to the need for systemic change. Creating the necessary movement for such change, however, is a task that the human species has barely begun to address. It requires, as a first step, a continuing collective effort of the kind I have undertaken in this book: to comprehend the interconnections – whether destructive or potentially healthy – among *all* the domains (populations or issues) affected by capitalist practice.

Cumulative and converging disruptions have produced a potentially revolutionary setting, but there is not yet a matching revolutionary political force. Billions of people have urgent needs that are not being met, and tens of millions of them have protested against oppressive practices ranging from environmental plunder to military aggression to racist terror to super-exploitation. But the protests have been fragmented, and power remains concentrated in the hands of a privileged elite – the global capitalist class – whose priorities have not changed and which, in its extreme expression (Trumpism), insulates itself more than ever from recognizing the scope of the shared calamity and consequently, far from seeking real solutions, prefers to weaponize mass constituencies under the classic fascist battle-cry for moments when the working class begins to awaken: "fighting socialism."

The COVID-19 pandemic has laid bare core traits of the oppressive structures. Most broadly, the conditions favoring outbreaks of new infectious diseases flow from the breakdown of biodiversity, i.e., the destruction of wildlife habitats (through deforestation, desertification, etc.), the resulting displacement of their accustomed denizens, and the consequent increased exposure of humans to zoonotic viruses.[4] All this underscores the catastrophic impact of urban sprawl and also of capitalist agriculture, whose applications

---

4   See Malm, *Corona, Climate, Chronic Emergency*, 42ff; also Rob Wallace, *Dead Epidemiologists: On the Origins of COVID-19* (New York: Monthly Review Press, 2020), and Vandana Shiva, *Oneness vs. the 1%* (White River Junction, VT: Chelsea Green, 2020).

of synthetic fertilizers, pesticides, herbicides, and GMOs have at the same time *directly* decimated the populations of pollinator-species such as bees which are crucial to the reproduction of plants and whose decline, if not reversed, threatens land-based life in its entirety.[5] Industrial agriculture and the capitalist processed-food and beverage industries, premised upon overconsumption and cheapness, also help generate the "pre-existing health conditions" such as diabetes and obesity that make the virus more deadly.[6]

More specifically, however, COVID-19 differs from earlier coronaviruses in that, although developed from animal sources, it appears not to exist in nature in the form in which it began to infect humans.[7] We should therefore recognize that it may have been synthesized in the course of a type of experimentation – called "gain-of-function" – designed to make pathogens more transmissible and/or more virulent. Gain-of-function studies are a common practice related to the development of new drugs; they are defended as being pertinent to understanding how pathogens may spread. While the full history of COVID-19 is not yet known, the location of an internationally funded virology lab in the city where it first came to public attention (Wuhan, China) – surely not the only Chinese city that has "wet markets" – cannot be overlooked.[8]

Contrary, however, to Donald Trump's persistent refrain, even if the hypothesis of lab manipulation were to be confirmed, this would still not justify calling COVID-19 "the China virus." For one thing, there is evidence that the virus was present in Europe before

5   As for marine life, it is threatened not only by pollution, overfishing, offshore oil drilling, and underwater cellphone towers, but also by acidification, overheating, and deoxygenation. See Ian Angus, https://climateandcapitalism.com/2020/10/24/triple-crisis-in-the-anthropocene-ocean-part-three-the-heat-of-3-6-billion-atom-bombs/

6   See Mark Bittman, *Animal, Vegetable, Junk: A History of Food, from Sustainable to Suicidal* (Boston: Houghton Mifflin Harcourt, 2021).

7   Birger Sørensen et al., "The evidence which suggests that this is no naturally evolved virus" (July 2020), a scientific paper summarized (and linked to) by Aksel Fridstrøm at https://www.minervanett.no/angus-dalgleish-birger-sorensen-coronavirus/the-evidence-which-suggests-that-this-is-no-naturally-evolved-virus/362529.

8   Rowan Jacobsen, "Could COVID-19 Have Escaped from a Lab?" https://www.bostonmagazine.com/news/2020/09/09/alina-chan-broad-institute-coronavirus/; Alex de Waal, "Lab Leaks," *London Review of Books*, 2 Dec. 2021.

the Chinese outbreak.[9] For another, US agencies were heavily involved in the relevant lab studies. Specifically, after the US government in 2014 formally suspended gain-of-function research (a ban that remained in effect until December 2017), that research was outsourced to Wuhan, with funding from the US National Institutes of Health, by the director of the National Institute of Allergy and Infectious Diseases, Dr. Anthony Fauci.[10] The virology research was thus under joint US/Chinese direction, making precise accountability uncertain, although the potential military applications of such research are obvious.[11] Significantly, Wuhan was also the site, in October 2019 (shortly before the COVID outbreak), of Military World Games attended by 300 members of the US armed forces.[12] This muddies the question of where the infection originated, raising the possibility that the US army's Medical Research Institute of Infectious Diseases (at Fort Detrick, MD) could have had a role in it.

We should not be surprised to find a militaristic hand in research related to the spread of pathogens, which is inherently dangerous.[13] As we have seen at a number of points in this book, the military is heavily implicated in the environmental crisis as a whole, not only through the direct destruction it inflicts, but also through its depletion of resources and its enforcement of the capitalist order

---

9   See Dean Baker's 12/30/2020 report, https://cepr.net/new-york-times-joins-trumps-anti-china-crusade/

10 See https://www.newsweek.com/dr-fauci-backed-controversial-wuhan-lab-millions-us-dollars-risky-coronavirus-research-1500741 and Christina Lin, "Why US Outsourced Bat Virus Research to Wuhan," https://asiatimes.com/2020/04/why-us-outsourced-bat-virus-research-to-wuhan/. On Fauci's 50-year career at the center of federal health policy, see Robert F. Kennedy Jr., *The Real Anthony Fauci: Bill Gates, Big Pharma, and the Global War on Democracy and Public Health* (New York: Skyhorse, 2021).

11 This is not to suggest that the military interests of the US and China are equivalent. Research can be for defensive as well as offensive purposes. Although no government will admit to having an "offensive" agenda, it is clear that forward military projection has for years been directed by the US against China, and not vice versa. On past US deployment, see Thomas Powell, "Biological Warfare in Korea: A Review of the Literature," *Socialism and Democracy*, 33:2 (July 2019).

12 See Tom Squitieri's report in *American Prospect* (10/19/2020), https://prospect.org/coronavirus/did-the-military-world-games-spread-covid-19/

13 See the reporting generated by the 2007 campaign to block a bio-weapons research lab at Boston University, http://fairfoods.org/stopthebiolab/stopthebiolab/

(by indoctrination as well as by force of arms). Biological warfare has a long history, grounded in its distinctive attributes of not destroying physical property and of being difficult to trace. Along with drone-attacks and cyber-warfare, it accelerates the trend on the part of imperialist military strategists – in the wake of US fiascos in Vietnam, Afghanistan, and Iraq – away from reliance on ground forces. As with all forms of modern warfare, its impact extends far beyond purely military targets. COVID-19 would simply be an extreme example of this, the only irony being that if it was indeed synthesized in a lab, its release would most probably have been inadvertent, not linked to a particular military campaign.

Whatever the final verdict as to whether or not COVID-19 was lab-created,[14] the overarching point is that the pandemic is in either case a manifestation of capitalist crisis. On one hand, the lab-creation scenario reflects some combination of (1) the business interests of drug companies in their constant push to develop new products and (2) the all-encompassing militarization driven by perpetual economic expansion and the scramble to assure "energy security" and raw materials in the face of a shrinking resource-base. On the other hand, the "spontaneous" scenario, based on the collapse of biodiversity, represents an advanced stage of the metabolic rift imposed by capitalism on the natural world.[15] Or, in Vandana Shiva's words, "The health emergency of the coronavirus is inseparable from the health emergency of extinction, the health emergency of biodiversity loss, and the health emergency of the climate crisis."[16] The two scenarios thus have common roots and – as suggested by the role of industrialized food production in creating the health-disorders that aggravate COVID infections – are mutually reinforcing.

The capitalist economy, except where buffered by previously instituted social services (mainly the fruit of 20th-century working-class movements), is ill-equipped to respond to the virus. The US ruling class, reflecting capitalism in its most undiluted form, let the pandemic precipitate an economic collapse. Instead of supplying the necessary healthcare and financial security, it left working people at the mercy of the job market. Companies shut down, tens

---

14 On this uncertainty, see Wallace, *Dead Epidemiologists*, 88-95.
15 See the present book's Introduction, p. 4.
16 Shiva, *Oneness vs. the 1%*, 177.

of millions of workers lost not only their wages but also their health insurance, and the government did little to rescue them, leaving a population which by January 2021 had the highest infection rate of any advanced country,[17] compounded by spikes in hunger and homelessness. Instead of implementing comprehensive measures to limit the spread of the virus (as was done successfully not only in China Cuba and Vietnam, but also in South Korea Taiwan Iceland and New Zealand), it acquiesced in the characteristic capitalist impulse to tout a magic-bullet-type response – with mixed effects but with a vast potential market – in the form of globally administered vaccines.[18]

Within the US working class, those who have had the highest proportion of their numbers laid off and/or exposed to the contagion – whether because of their widely heralded yet poorly paid "essential jobs" (e.g., in food, transport, and healthcare services) or because of conditions of poverty or incarceration – have been African Americans and Latinos, disproportionately the undocumented immigrants among them. These same populations have also been the principal scapegoats for a political leadership which, depending on which party holds top office, may be more or less openly racist, and more or less disposed to offer the working class small-scale relief, but in either case is blind to the calamitous impact of the economic system it so unreservedly embraces.

The culture of the US police, inherited from the days of slavery and turbo-charged by decades of militarization, inserts itself with deadly effect into this miasma, targeting particularly those of African descent. With so much illness and hardship imposed on black people during COVID's first three months, it is unsurprising that George Floyd, who on 25 May 2020 became the emblematic vic-

---

17 It would subsequently be overtaken by several European countries. For regular updates, see https://www.worldometers.info/coronavirus/

18 The search for a vaccine that could be globally imposed has been the longstanding project of multi-billionaire entrepreneur Bill Gates, whose outsized role in shaping world health policy was documented in a 2-hour filmed report by James Corbett posted in June 2020 but subsequently taken down by YouTube for "violating [its] Community Guidelines." See also Kennedy, *The Real Anthony Fauci*, 298-315. For details of the campaign to stigmatize medical responses other than hospitalization or vaccination, see Meryl Nass, MD, "How a False Hydroxychloroquine Narrative Was Created" (2021), https://merylnassmd.com/how-false-hydroxychloroquine-narrative/

tim of police murder – his face a worldwide symbol – was himself living at the margins and infected with the virus. Viewing the entire historical conjuncture in which Floyd's murder took place, we find a toxic continuum between, on one hand, officially sanctioned indifference to the extinctions of species and, on the other, the callous mindset that can enable an agent of the state, acting in full public view and with an assumption of entitlement, to exert the lethal pressure of his bodyweight for more than nine frightful minutes on the neck of a defenseless individual.

Mass uprisings are often sparked by such a singular outrage. But the viral display of this police killing came at a moment when awareness of system-failure was already widespread. Although the pandemic and the sudden rise in unemployment were more recent, the very entry into the US presidency (in 2017) of so cynical and dangerous a figure as Trump – capping the disaffection instilled by decades of anti-working-class neoliberal policies that provoked the 2011 Occupy movement – reflected the complicity of *both* capitalist parties in failing to give more than a token nod to the material needs of the majority.[19]

The demonstrations that took place throughout the United States were thus responding to more than just police brutality. They called into question the *institution* of the police and therefore, implicitly, the social order of racialized capitalism that the police are assigned to uphold. Awareness of this link has not yet solidified at a mass level, but arguments for defunding or even abolishing the police point ultimately to capitalist class interest as the decisive factor behind police power.[20] Meanwhile, the crowds of anti-racist protesters, many of whom – because of official indifference to their economic vulnerability – were at risk of eviction from their homes, could hardly fail to see that the forces directing the police are the very ones that make the day-to-day conditions of their lives increasingly unbearable.

---

19 Particularly striking has been the marginalization by top Democrats of the insurgent movements represented by the Sanders campaigns of 2016 and 2020. See Victor Wallis, *Democracy Denied: Five Lectures on U.S. Politics* (Trenton, NJ: Africa World Press, 2019), Ch. 5.

20 See Kristian Williams, *Our Enemies in Blue: Police and Power in America*, 3rd ed. (Oakland, CA: AK Press, 2015), Ch. 5: "The Natural Enemy of the Working Class." Cf. the arguments around prison abolition, e.g., Angela Y. Davis, *Freedom Is a Constant Struggle* (Chicago: Haymarket, 2016), 25f.

It has been widely noted that the recent protests differ from the urban rebellions of the 1960s in that they are no longer limited to black neighborhoods but instead target core institutions (as well as symbols of racial oppression) while involving people of all ethnicities. This converges with the multi-ethnic response now elicited by environmental struggles, as the localities that are most severely threatened – e.g., by coastal flooding or by pipeline construction – draw into the movement poor and heavily nonwhite communities that were under-represented in the early years of green protest.

At the same time, likewise cutting across racial lines, the recent period has seen a sharp resurgence of labor organizing and strikes.[21] Like the anti-racist steps, these do not necessarily address environmental policy issues, but they nonetheless signal an increased sense of urgency, which in turn leads growing numbers of people to take initiatives and risks that they would not previously have contemplated. It remains to be seen to what extent alarm sparked by the Ukraine crisis and the consequent escalation of nuclear brinksmanship will add further to collective consciousness-raising.

The conditions of pandemic impinge on these struggles in ways that have yet to be fully comprehended. On the one hand, they obviously magnify the discontent; on the other, the virus poses obstacles in terms of health-risk to those who would become active, whether in mass protests or in face-to-face organizing. The threat of infection from bus or train travel discourages the planning of massive gatherings in the centers of power. This has advantages as well as drawbacks, however, as it may widen each locality's direct public exposure to the protests, thereby reducing the reliance on media coverage and giving more scope to face-to-face communication between activists and their neighbors.

But the pandemic also raises issues of its own which may add to the already considerable disarray within the working class. On one hand there is a demand for full protection from contagion in the workplace; on the other, there is uneasiness about one-size-fits-all vaccine mandates. Right-wing forces have channeled some of this uneasiness into libertarian-type protest against public health guidelines of any kind. Top US public health officials, on the other hand,

---

21 See Kim Moody, "Upticks, Waves, and Social Upsurge: The Strikes of 2021 in Context," *Labor Notes* online (11/15/2021).

have close ties with the pharmaceutical industry, which leads them to promote patented remedies – and especially vaccines – over the building of natural immunities and the use of unpatented, generic, and low-cost treatments. They therefore curb the distribution of such treatments, sanction doctors who prescribe them, and censor – both directly and through mass media and social networks – informed public discussion of them.[22]

But along with these short-run effects, the pandemic also raises, more sharply than ever before, the urgent need for steps associated with socialism. These include, most immediately, (1) free universal healthcare, (2) secure income and housing for everyone, and (3) a drastic reduction of prison populations. More fundamentally, it reminds us of the need to improve the general conditions for public health, which would call into question, among other things, the capitalist food-industrial complex[23] and the multiple sources of air and water pollution. Overcoming these ills would specifically entail socializing health services and building a vast sector of public works, which could guarantee full employment while establishing projects ranging from housing construction to energy production to biodiversity restoration to the creation of public art.

Into this mix of responses comes the one widely noted *positive* offshoot from the pandemic, namely, the initial sudden reduction in air and noise pollution brought on by the disappearance of much car and plane traffic during the early weeks of the lockdown. This is a potentially powerful spur to reconsidering the real costs of, and the actual need for, all the travel that relies on those particular types of conveyance. Yet another jolt to business as usual came in the response to Russia's February 2022 invasion of Ukraine. Although it is too early, as of mid-March, to assess the full impact of the massive sanctions against Russia (let alone of the war itself), what is already clear is that the sudden spike in petroleum prices will give rise – as did the oil crisis of the 1970s – to deliberation at multiple levels on how to overcome current patterns of oil-dependence.

The covid-related slowdown generated plans that could be quite ambitious, as in the case of Milan (Italy), which foresaw banning

---

22 On this censorship, see Kennedy, *The Real Anthony Fauci*, 218-220, 358-360, and Nass, "How a False Hydroxychloroquine Narrative Was Created" (note 18).

23 See Bittman, *Animal, Vegetable, Junk*, esp. 184-200.

auto traffic from the city center.[24] The war-related oil crisis could provide further stimulus along these lines. Even with a shift from cars and planes to buses and trains, however, the question remains of how to reduce *the total level of demand* for mechanized travel. More specifically, to what extent may the new technologies and applications that have emerged under conditions of lockdown be deployed – along with urban redesign and the general reallocation of space – to permanently reduce travel-related energy consumption? This is where we address the fourth on our list of post-2018 developments: the massive replacement of in-person encounters – from family reunions to college classes to party conventions to high-level global conferences – with "virtual" interaction.

Deliberation on this prospect raises the whole theme of conversion discussed in this book. We need to keep in mind that appropriate decisions cannot be arrived at on the basis of market forces, and that the necessary overall transformation would have to call into question the entire culture associated with capitalism – particularly in the virulent form it now takes in the US. Using less energy means living on the basis of a different set of values. While reducing long-distance travel via teleconferencing may be a useful step, we should not forget the resource- and energy-costs or the potential health risks entailed by its associated technological infrastructure.[25] Nor should we ignore the political censorship applied to the corresponding platforms, whether by governments or by corporations such as Facebook, Google, and Zoom.[26] What is ultimately needed, both for maximizing popular control and for adapting to Earth's carrying capacity, is less reliance on global networks (except

---

24 See Jessica Corbett's April 2020 report, https://www.commondreams.org/news/2020/04/21/milans-plan-limit-cars-after-covid-19-lockdown-lauded-excellent-example/ and also the pioneering collection, *Free Public Transit*, eds. Judith Dellheim and Jason Prince (Montreal: Black Rose Books, 2018).

25 A notable example is the environmental impact of mining lithium (a crucial component of high-tech communications devices). See Kate Aronoff et al., *A Planet to Win* (London: Verso, 2019), 147-53. For an update to my treatment of communications technology in Chapter 4 of this book, including references on the dangers of 5G (5th generation) wireless technology, see Victor Wallis, "Technology and Ecosocialism," *Perspectives on Global Technology and Development*, 20:1 & 2 (2021).

26 See https://academeblog.org/2020/09/23/zoom-youtube-and-facebook-censor-event-at-sf-state/; also YouTube's video announcement of its censorship policy regarding covid vaccines: https://support.google.com/youtube/answer/11161123?hl=en&ref_topic=10833358

for exchanges of information and ideas), based on creating greater diversity and self-sufficiency *within* each geographically defined unit, of whatever size.[27]

This type of shift is a direct manifestation of the broader requirement to go beyond a mere switch in sources of energy and to envision an actual cutback of total global production. Obviously, the cutback would not apply or have the same proportions everywhere; it would have to be guided by a democratically informed assessment of basic needs, both in each locality and on the global canvas. At the broadest level, there would have to be cutbacks in the Global North but not in the Global South. More specifically, however, what would have to be cut would be production that serves every country's ruling class, whether for its lavish personal consumption or – even more importantly (as discussed in Chapter 1) – for the products, infrastructures, and services on which ruling classes depend for the accumulation and protection of their wealth.

While the ruling class itself will resist such an agenda, the rest of the society can be won over to it in ways corresponding to the lives and needs of each particular sector. At the most general level and in terms of long-term plans, the goal of local biodiversity will remain crucial. But the related allocation of resources to the various localities is itself a process that requires (as we noted in Chapter 3) national or regional coordination. This is particularly evident with regard to rail networks and electric power grids. Moreover, success at this wider level will be necessary in order to assure immediate material improvements for the working-class majority.[28]

Awareness of the long-term vision was advanced in 2020 with the free-access Internet release of the documentary film *Planet of the Humans*,[29] which casts a critical eye on the corporate "green

---

27 In a polemic, "On Leftism and Leftists, Reds and Greens" (*Green Horizon* 41 [2020]), Steve Welzer argues that ecosocialists, including myself, fail to see the importance of the local dimension. The latter is central, however, to my critique of capitalist agriculture and of long-distance travel and trade, and also to the implementation of workers' self-management, as touched on in this book and discussed at greater length in my *Socialist Practice: Histories and Theories* (London: Palgrave Macmillan, 2020), Ch. 7.

28 This point is emphasized in Matthew T. Huber, *Climate Change as Class War: Building Solidarity on a Warming Planet* (London: Verso, 2022).

29 Produced by Michael Moore and directed by Jeff Gibbs, the film has reached, through various venues, over 12 million viewers.

energy" scenario in terms of (1) limitations or adverse side-effects of its particular technologies,[30] (2) its heavy reliance on the mining of toxic ingredients such as lithium and cobalt, (3) its continuing partial resort to fossil fuels, and (4) its integration, under capitalist sponsorship, into a wider agenda of perpetual economic expansion. The film provoked a storm of angry responses, culminating in a drive to suppress it.[31] Although it ultimately stayed in circulation, certain justified criticisms of its treatment of solar and wind technology (and of its "overpopulation" slant) obscured its larger message of the need to reduce total human impact on the environment – and undertake the planning that will have to go into this.[32]

But "reduced human impact," although indispensable as a long-term goal, does not address the requirement of attracting political support from the working class. As Matthew T. Huber points out, the "less is more" approach "will not attract the masses of working-class people in an increasingly unequal economy."[33] As we noted in Chapter 7, many labor unions propagate the capitalist assumption that there is a clash between workers' interests and environmental protection. The only persuasive challenge to this assumption is a political agenda that highlights improving conditions for the working class as central to any ecological transition. Although the project will ultimately entail a reconfiguration of social space and a new set of values,[34] in the short run it must offer working people tangible material benefits. These benefits, however, need not consist in a proliferation of privately acquired goods; what is crucial is that there be secure access to basic necessities.

Through what kind of process will the necessary ecologically inspired planning emerge? The recent experience of the pandemic offers one example of how the initial condition of society-wide debate may be provoked. A similar impetus may come from the sudden rise in fuel prices and the resultant strain on geographical

---

30 For background, see above, 119-122.
31 On the interests driving the campaign against *Planet*, see Max Blumenthal's investigative report, https://thegrayzone.com/2020/09/07/green-billionaires-planet-of-the-humans/.
32 See David Cobb's critical review of the film in *Green Horizon* 41 (2020).
33 Huber, *Climate Change as Class War*, 167.
34 See Wallis, "Technology and Ecosocialism" (note 25).

mobility. Although any such jolt is unwelcome, its damaging effects also prompt reconsideration of established routines. When our daily practices can no longer be undertaken reflexively but instead become the subject of conscious and often collective deliberation – driven by some combination of dread, anger, and hope – then we're in a moment conducive to wide public discussion of radically new approaches to life.

This is the type of setting that can accelerate red/green revolution. Whatever political obstacles such a revolution faces in any given country, society-wide questioning and organizing will be a necessary feature everywhere. This should be facilitated not only by anxiety arising from the pandemic and from the even vaster danger of environmental collapse (hastened of course by war), but also by the obscene spectacle of class polarization that is now on display, especially in the US, as workers suffer a disastrous loss of well-paying jobs while the biggest capitalists further augment their already astronomical fortunes through digitization, government subsidies, and stock transactions.[35]

Capitalist hegemony over media and electoral politics means that such developments do not get the degree of public scrutiny they merit. Nonetheless, a growing popular awareness has sharpened ideological conflict, particularly in the United States, in whose 2020 presidential election the incumbent, a quintessential capitalist, brazenly sought to limit the franchise of certain constituencies so as to assure himself of a "victory" that would be out of reach if all were enabled to cast ballots (and have them counted). This agenda, implemented in part via sabotage of the Postal Service (whose expanded role in gathering votes was made necessary by the risk of contagion at polling places), amounted to planning a coup d'état. In even contemplating so extreme a step, the incumbent (Donald Trump) was in effect recognizing that *majority* opinion was resolutely opposed to his priorities. Unable to sway a sufficient portion

---

35 *Guardian* report: https://www.theguardian.com/business/2020/oct/07/covid-19-crisis-boosts-the-fortunes-of-worlds-billionaires/. For continuing analysis, see Richard Wolff's program *Economic Update* (democracyatwork.info).

of this majority, he instead resorted to assaulting the citizenship rights of its most vulnerable (and most oppositional) sectors.[36]

Even without Trump as its official figurehead, however, the ruling class as a whole is becoming increasingly intransigent. The voter suppression agenda is supported by the entire Republican establishment, but *neither* of the dominant-party elites can properly address the society's problems – least of all fending off environmental catastrophe. While the Republicans are overtly self-serving, the Democrat leadership makes a show of supporting at least a few of the necessary changes, but then blocks most of them in practice (e.g., universal healthcare, demilitarization, and radical environmental measures), for fear of the threat they pose both in the short run to profits and in the long run to capitalist hegemony.[37] Within this setting, authentically democratic drives are kept in check as their street-level expression runs up against an increasingly militarized enforcement apparatus, joined at times by fascist vigilantes. Meanwhile, with the global outsourcing of industry and the preeminence of finance capital, inequality continues to intensify.

In this context, the introduction of ever more sophisticated digital applications serves, among other things, to reinforce social stratification, as poor communities lack access to the instruments they would need in order to be fully connected. The odd blend, especially in the US, of ultramodern technology with antiquated social and institutional structures[38] thus continues to stifle move-

---

36 See Greg Palast's pre-election cautionary report, *How Trump Won 2020* (New York: Seven Stories Press, 2020). The Democrats engage in comparable repression against potential Green Party voters when they litigate in various states to strip that party of its ballot-line. On the fascist drive behind the Trump campaign, see William I. Robinson's trenchant analysis (10/25/2020), https://truthout.org/articles/to-defeat-fascism-we-must-recognize-its-a-failed-response-to-capitalist-crisis/; also Jason Stanley, "America Is Now in Fascism's Legal Phase," *Guardian*, 12/22/2021.

37 On the overall Democrat/Republican dynamic, see Wallis, *Socialist Practice*, 3.

38 The antiquated constitutional structure allows for a president to take office without winning the popular vote and to potentially hold onto power via state legislatures tinkering with the Electoral College, with the final outcome of the election possibly depending either on a 1-state 1-vote showdown (ignoring differences in state populations) in the House of Representatives or on the verdict of highly partisan Justices holding lifetime appointments to the Supreme Court. See Wallis, *Democracy Denied*, Ch. 1.

ment toward the now desperately needed transformation of the prevailing value-system.

In opposition to this condition, the new wave of social protest presents a ray of hope. As we've noted, it embraces a wider range of communities and – compared to its immediate predecessors (the 1960s protests) – embodies a more thorough awareness on the part of the masses, especially among younger people (who've grown up in the midst of climate disasters, the 2008 financial meltdown, and the prospect of lifelong personal indebtedness), that capitalism itself can no longer meet the needs of the majority. This awareness has been expressed most directly in the Youth Climate Strike and in efforts by young people to challenge in court the prospect of a stolen future (as well as in widespread youth support for Bernie Sanders' 2016 and 2020 presidential campaigns, which gave distinctive emphasis to the climate crisis). It reflects a visceral sense that the environmental threat overshadows all other prospects. Children not only perceive the danger; they also are fated to live the greatest portion of their lives under the more severe conditions. To the extent that they find a path to survival, it will approach, in varying ways, the vision of red/green revolution.

This vision, however, must be constantly elaborated and updated. While the underlying principles are clear – overcoming class division, reversing the expansive dynamic inherent in capitalism, and restoring biodiversity –, the processes involved are complex and will remain so. On the political side, it will be necessary to continuously reconcile the requirements of decisive leadership with truly democratic agenda-setting – a prospect enhanced in the US by the recent resurgence of working-class militance in the form of extended strikes.[39] On the side of environmental policy, it will be necessary – starting with the question "What can we do without?" (Chapter 1, above) – to engage in a thoroughgoing critique of the whole way of life that has escalated into a nightmare of plunder, waste, violence, hyper-concentration of wealth, and indifference to the rest of humanity and the natural world.

---

39   For current reports, see the monthly bulletin, *Labor Notes*; for historical examples of working-class action in times of crisis, see Wallis, *Socialist Practice*, 31-35, 116-19.

Only in the context of such a critique, *shaped continuously by a wide public*, will it be possible to terminate the relentless assaults on the ecosystem and to launch the transformations of land-use and of economic activity that are indispensable to liberating the potential restorative powers of Nature. As I discussed in Chapter 9, a promising start in this direction has been made in the realm of regenerative agriculture. But there is more. It has now become apparent that an equally important arena of restoration is the oceans, whose life-giving role is being undermined not only by acidification, rising sea-temperatures and consequent de-oxygenation, but also by high-tech military activities, which are directly destroying marine life.[40] As has only recently come to be understood, whales play a vital role in capturing carbon and in fertilizing the phytoplankton that account for a huge portion of the photosynthesis by which oxygen replaces CO_2 in the Earth's atmosphere. In the words of a report published by the International Monetary Fund, "When it comes to saving the planet, one whale is worth thousands of trees."[41] Here once again we see that natural restorative potential is threatened with destruction while capital builds, in this case, costly "direct air carbon capture" plants which can have only a fraction of the impact of undisturbed natural processes in reversing climate-change.

The COVID-19 pandemic, by amplifying the nightmare scenario, has created an enlarged opening for the necessary discussion, even as such a process confronts a new obstacle in the form of Internet- and social-media censorship. But the need to advance the debate is absolute, given the scope and pace of environmental breakdown and given also the desperate measures that the ruling class is willing

---

40   See, in addition to the sources cited above (note 3), Koohan Paik-Mander, "Whales Could Save the World's Climate, Unless the Military Destroys Them First," *Counterpunch* online, 12/16/2021.

41   "[E]ach great whale sequesters 33 tons of CO_2 on average, taking that carbon out of the atmosphere for centuries. A tree, meanwhile, absorbs only up to 48 pounds of CO_2 a year." Ralph Chami et al., "Nature's Solution to Climate Change: A Strategy to Protect Whales Can Limit Greenhouse Gases and Global Warming," *Finance & Development*, December 2019, https://www.imf.org/external/pubs/ft/fandd/2019/12/pdf/natures-solution-to-climate-change-chami.pdf, 35. On the potential of restoration projects, see Ed Yong, "The Enormous Hole That Whaling Left Behind," https://www.theatlantic.com/science/archive/2021/11/whaling-whales-food-krill-iron/620604

to take – egged on by a strident fascist sector – in order to block anything even approaching an ecosocialist political agenda.

An early in-depth response from a Left perspective to the COVID moment is Andreas Malm's above-cited *Corona, Climate, Chronic Emergency*. Malm explains well how loss of biodiversity creates the conditions for such pandemics, and he also notes the need for "draconian" measures to strip away the power of "fossil capital." But the methods he proposes for drawing CO2 out of the atmosphere do not include regenerative agriculture or species-preservation, relying instead on high-tech and energy-intensive approaches.[42] As his exposition makes clear, this approach stays within a capitalist logic; indeed, it resembles the dangerous geo-engineering scenarios promoted by those whose embrace of fossil fuels he condemns. He concludes by asserting, "all we have to work with is the dreary bourgeois state."[43]

While it is obvious that in the near term we must accomplish what we can through pressure on the bourgeois state, it is equally clear that a complete set of counter-institutions and behaviors must evolve – capable ultimately of exercising power – if the capitalist growth-imperative is to be overcome. Part of what is needed to motivate this project is adequate mass awareness of how deeply resistant the bourgeois state is to the full scope of the requisite changes. In the case of the world's preeminent military power, the US, while its party structure can accommodate debates about environmental reform, the state will maintain its overall destructive agenda as long as its "national security" structures remain aloof from the general population. These structures, staffed by unelected personnel, operate overwhelmingly behind closed doors; their priorities prevail regardless of which party holds top office.

Full exposure of the practices these structures engage in – ranging from weapons research to surveillance operations to contingency planning to systematic torture, up to and including

---

42 Malm, *Corona, Climate, Chronic Emergency*, 138-47; an alternative vision is expressed by Shiva in *Oneness vs. the 1%*, Ch. 1.

43 Malm, *Corona, Climate, Chronic Emergency*, 151. The geo-engineering schemes and their proponents are discussed in Naomi Klein, *This Changes Everything: Capitalism vs. the Climate* (New York: Simon & Schuster, 2014), Ch. 8.

assassination – is part of the broader task of political education that must be taken up if we are to attain the level and quality of popular participation necessary to the revolutionary process of ecological conversion. Without such exposure, people all too easily remain stuck in the notion that their leaders would be "above" the kind of nefarious scheming that those practices reflect.[44] It is urgent that the popular majority be disabused of such an assumption. Environmentalists learned in 2015 of the conscious deception about greenhouse gases perpetrated by the petroleum industry since the 1970s and still reflected in present-day media and politics. With the official response to COVID-19 – Trump learning in early February 2020 of its gravity yet for six crucial weeks pretending the opposite – we faced a similar deception, costing tens of thousands of lives. While the global impact of the COVID deception may be less far-reaching than that of climate denialism, its effects were more immediate and disclosure of the lie came with less of a time-lapse after its initial propagation. This should have made it easier to respond with the necessary level of thoroughness and mass involvement.

But such a response has yet to develop, at least in the US, where objections to corporate-driven health policy have been amplified more by the Right than by the Left. This is ironic, because although particular impositions by public health officials may be ill-advised, that does not mean that health policy overall can be entrusted – following the right-wing agenda – to private operators. For matters of universal concern, we cannot dispense with certain common norms of behavior, which must be authoritatively enacted. What we can legitimately insist upon is not a supposed "right" to defy such norms, but rather the right to have a role, as informed citizens, in their formulation. An emergency such as a pandemic gives new immediacy to this age-old democratic principle, which is exactly the basis on which a response to the broader environmental crisis must be grounded.

Whatever the future trajectory of COVID-19 or any other virus, the environmental danger will remain, and the capitalist class will

---

44 Hence the US government's vindictive pursuit of whistleblowers and of journalists who, like Wikileaks founder Julian Assange, would make public their revelations. Among research sites that explore the nefarious practices, see https://covertactionmagazine.com/ and https://www.corbettreport.com/

not give up trying to block responses that threaten its bottom line. There will thus be a permanent need for a political force that can burst through that barrier, both with immediate measures and with a long-term vision. The red/green revolution cannot come all at once, but it must nonetheless be both rapid and sweeping.

Acknowledgments

Original places of publication of chapters (or parts of chapters) are indicated below. All the chapters have been augmented by new references and/or new illustrative examples, and have been revised where necessary for greater readability; Chapters 8 and 9 include entirely new sections. I am grateful to Routledge Journals for permission to use articles originally published in *Capitalism Nature Socialism* (CNS), *International Critical Thought* (ICT), *New Political Science* (NPS), and *Socialism and Democracy* (S&D). I thank the editor of *Monthly Review* (MR), John Bellamy Foster, for permission to use articles originally published in MR. I thank the founding editor of *Das Argument*, Wolfgang Fritz Haug, for permission to use articles originally published in that journal. Thanks to other listed individuals are for their comments on prior drafts of the respective chapters; none of them should be held accountable for my final formulations.

Chapter 1. From CNS, 12:1 (March, 2001). A short selection from this article appeared previously in CNS 8:4 (December 1997) followed by an exchange with James O'Connor. Thanks to Daniel Faber, Joel Kovel, and James O'Connor.

Chapter 2. From S&D, 14:1 (Spring 2000). Based on presentation at May 1999 conference on Progress organized by the Institute for Critical Theory of Berlin (InkriT); originally published (in German) in *Das Argument*, No. 230 (1999).

Chapter 3. From CNS,15:2 (June 2004). Based on presentation at June 2000 symposium in honor of Richard Levins, at the Harvard School of Public Health.

Chapter 4. From CNS,17:2 (June 2006); originally a chapter in Anatole Anton and Richard Schmitt, eds., *Toward a New Socialism* (Lanham, MD: Lexington Books, 2007). Thanks to Karen Charman, Milton Fisk, Joel Kovel, Ronald Price, Richard Schmitt, and David Schwartzman.

Chapter 5. From MR, 60:6 (November 2008). Thanks to Brett Clark, John Bellamy Foster, Fred Magdoff, and Greg Meyerson.

Chapter 6. From MR, 61:9 (February 2010). Originally presented at the 6th International Marx & Engels Colloquium, Centro de Estudos Marxistas, University of Campinas (São Paulo), Brazil, November 2009, and published (in Portuguese) in Andréia Galvão et al., eds., *Capitalismo: Crises e Resistências* (São Paulo: Outras Expressões, 2012).

Chapter 7. From ICT, 3:4 (2013). Thanks to Frank Ackerman, David Gilbert, Ben Manski, and Richard Rosen.

Chapter 8. Extensively revised from article in NPS, 37:4 (December 2015). Thanks to Jocelyn Boryczka, Jennifer Leigh Disney, Johanna Fernández, David Gilbert, Rebecca Hollender, and Roberta Salper.

Chapter 9. Includes passages from article "Capitalism Unhinged: Crisis of Legitimacy in the United States," S&D, 31:3 (November 2017). Thanks to members of the S&D editorial board and to Wolfgang Fritz Haug. An earlier version of the S&D article was presented at the June 2017 InkriT conference on "Crisis of the Political" and published (in German) in *Das Argument*, No, 323 (2017).

Epilogue. Thanks to Johanna Fernández, Carl Grey Martin, Joseph G. Ramsey, and Alan Wallis.

INDEX